IMAGES
of America

MANISTEE COUNTY

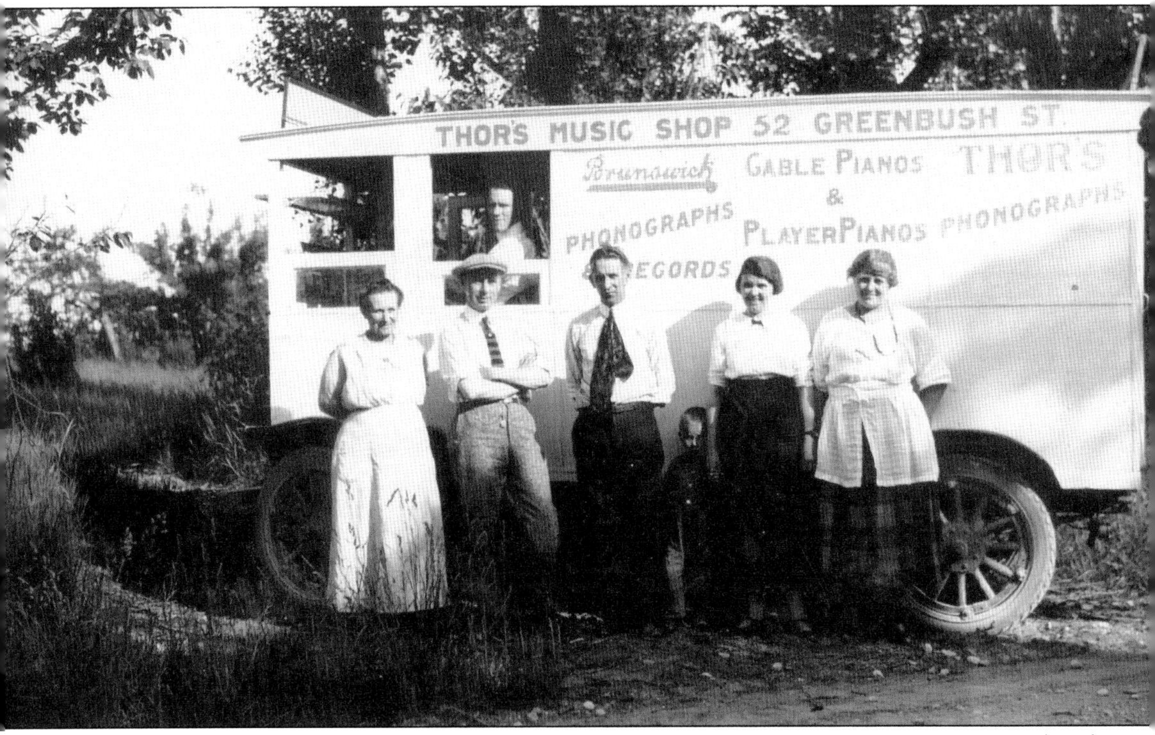

Among his other business enterprises, Thor Andresen, son of Danish immigrants, owned and operated a music store on 52 Greenbush Street, where he sold the latest phonographs, pianos, player pianos, and other musical instruments. This photograph of the Thor's Music Store delivery truck, taken sometime in the 1920s, represents the spirit of community and family enterprise that built Manistee into a thriving region out of the wilderness. Thor's mother, Hansine Andresen, stands on the far left. Thor is in the center, with his wife, Jennie, on his left. The other people are unidentified.

On the cover: Please see above. (Courtesy of Sandee Jones.)

IMAGES
of America

MANISTEE COUNTY

Shannon McRae

ARCADIA
PUBLISHING

ISBN 978-0-7385-4124-2

Published by Arcadia Publishing
Charleston, South Carolina

Printed in the United States of America

Library of Congress Catalog Card Number: 2006930971

For all general information contact Arcadia Publishing at:
Telephone 843-853-2070
Fax 843-853-0044
E-mail sales@arcadiapublishing.com
For customer service and orders:
Toll-Free 1-888-313-2665

Visit us on the Internet at www.arcadiapublishing.com

This book is dedicated to the Doyle family: my mother, Maureen; my aunts Katie, Ellen, Terrie, and Molly; my uncle Mike; my other uncles and aunts; and my innumerable and much-beloved cousins for simply, pleasantly, being family on all occasions. It is also written for the entire Doyle clan—the descendants of Thomas Kenny and Ellen Lynch—many of whom I met for the first time at the Manistee reunion in 2004. Without that occasion, this book would never have been. Finally, it is for all the families of Manistee County—those represented here and all the others with equally essential stories, in hope that all will find ways to tell them.

Contents

ACKNOWLEDGMENTS

Local history belongs to the people who lived it. Credit for this book can be given to the many individuals who generously contributed their images, stories, and time to its making. All errors are my own.

I am indebted to Steve Harold of the Manistee Historical Society. His encyclopedic knowledge of Michigan history exceeds even the vast museum archives to which he graciously provided access. His weekly historical columns for the *Manistee News Advocate* served as my model for exemplary social history. Most of the historical information in this work comes from those and from discussions with him.

Carol Schimke proved an essential contributor, patiently volunteering a great deal of time and assistance. I am grateful to Don and Janet Stroup of the Brethren Historical Association, Lyle Matteson of the Arcadia Area Historical Society, and Brian Smith of the Kaleva Historical Museum. Also helpful were Monsignor Gerard Guzikowski of Guardian Angels Parish and parishioners Clarence Nowak, Mary Ann Kaczmarek, and Janet Newman-Graham. Jane Cole, Celine Burke, and Doug Jensen all generously provided rare photographs and information about their churches' histories. Thanks to the Wallace family: Dave, Matt, and Ann, along with John Dexter for shared images and personal memories of Camp Tosebo. Jon Rose of the city of Manistee and Timm Smith of the Manistee Fire Hall were both more than generous. Also helpful were Pamela Spoor of the Manistee County Library, Ron Steinberg of the Ramsdell Theater, Jeff Sternberger of the Portage Point Inn, and Linda Spencer of the SS *City of Milwaukee*. Nedra Evans provided valuable background information. Bob Kenny's tour of the Kenny farm put family history into greater context, as was Jim Krolczyk's tour of the Kenney house and family plot.

Special thanks go to Anna Wilson and John Pearson of Arcadia Publishing for their clear guidance, and patient assistance.

My mother, Maureen McRae, and my aunt Katie Kennicott provided essential instruction on Zen and the art of walking up to complete strangers. Aunt Katie and Cindy Dempsey also told me most of what I know about Doyle and Kenny family history. I never understood before now why authors commend the patience and generosity of their partners. Final sincere thanks, therefore, go to Stephen Brandon for getting me to write this book in the first place, listening to me obsess, ferrying me around, making strawberry preserves, and remaining endlessly patient with a writer's process.

INTRODUCTION

The story of Manistee County is in most ways a typical American story. The county's phenomenal growth, decline, and subsequent revival as an attractive tourist destination are local manifestations of larger forces that shaped American history between the mid-19th and early 20th centuries. But Manistee is also unique, with tales of its own that would take a dozen books to tell properly. This book of images aims only to offer an array of small windows into Manistee's fascinating past.

Several circumstances combined to cause Manistee's emergence, along with the Great Lakes region, as a major economic and industrial power by the mid-19th century. As Americans began to migrate west in search of land and opportunity, they settled first in the new frontier east of the Mississippi and between the Ohio River and the Great Lakes that was then called the Northwest Territory. Upheavals in Europe and Canada caused mass immigration to the United States. For all who could muster the basic resources and endure the inevitable hardships, the vast pine forests of the northern territories offered opportunities for a better life.

The American industrial revolution of the early 19th century set the stage for phenomenal economic and industrial expansion. When the Erie Canal opened in 1825, grain and lumber could finally be transported easily and cheaply through the lakes and the canal. Settlers from the east could conveniently travel west by riverboat and schooner. Those settlers needed supplies with which to build homes and towns. The white pine forests of northern Michigan served that purpose.

Michigan's population soon grew to the 60,000 free citizens required for application to statehood under the rules of the Northwest Ordinance, and thus it became a state in 1837. Abundant natural resources—miles of white pine forest and a long, branching river emptying into Lake Michigan—all ensured Manistee's position as a vital node in this growing industrial network.

The stage was set, the first actors quickly entered, and the play began. In the fall of 1840, around the time that the Government Land Office survey was nearly completed and the state was divided into the counties that exist today, two brothers from southern Michigan, John and Joseph Stronach, sailed a small boat up the Lake Michigan coast. They came to the mouth of the Manistee River, searching for some suitable place to build a mill. They found one, but frustrated by an intractable log jam, they returned home until spring. In mid-April, John Stronach, this time with his son Adam, chartered the schooner *Thorton* out of St. Joseph, Michigan, and returned to Manistee. They arrived on April 16, 1841, a time of year when, in northern Michigan, snow and ice often have not yet melted.

No available record tells us what kind of men the Stronachs were. But they had the cash to hire a schooner, to buy machinery and supplies, and the wherewithal to make a life in the wilderness. Besides the occasional abandoned mission and local American Indians, mostly Ottawas, who by this time were probably too accustomed to sporadic encounters with missionaries and traders to find the presence of white people noteworthy, the Stronachs saw nothing familiar: few if any other white people, no buildings, no machines, no water supply but the river and the lakes, and certainly no towns. Nevertheless, they set up their mill, began logging, brought the rest of their family up the coast, and after several frustrations eventually established themselves on the Little Manistee River at what is now called Old Stronach.

Other white settlers soon followed, apparently with minimal resistance from the Native communities, John Canfield among them. They bought land cheaply, or else simply set up operations on federal land. Then, immigrants began to arrive from Canada, England, Germany, Ireland, and Scandinavia, fleeing unbearable circumstances in their home countries and willing to work long hours under harsh conditions in exchange for steady wages and the promise of land and freedom from oppression. These men were hired by mill owners, or later, contractors who represented the owners, and thus began the transformation of the forests into a valuable commodity, and the making of Manistee.

The facts regarding 19th-century labor history are not always pleasant. The American dream of enormous wealth and success was only realized by a few—typically those who, like the Filer family and the Canfields, had sufficient capital to begin with. Most struggled just to survive. Early immigrant groups such as the Irish that arrived America in the early 1800s often suffered a worse fate than the one they had left behind—working hard labor on the Erie Canal and the canals of New Orleans or in the Pennsylvania coal mines, or living by their wits in the slums of New York. Irish who arrived a decade or so later in the 1860s might, after forced conscription into the Civil War on both sides, find work building the Transcontinental Railroad. Those who came to Manistee, however, found genuine opportunity, and many thrived. For the most part, anybody who could tolerate the long hours and rough living conditions, who managed to save his initially meager wages, and who had the social wherewithal to form associations with other individuals that could assist their advancement enjoyed historically unprecedented social mobility.

The iconic self-made man so fundamental to the American mythos existed as actual fact in Manistee—Louis Sands, T. J. Ramsdell, and Thomas Kenny, to name a few. Their homes, their buildings, and their indelible marks on the landscape itself stand even today as testament to their individual accomplishments. But success in any major endeavor requires community support as much as individual effort. Manistee's newly burgeoning ethnic communities of German, Scandinavian, and Irish provided that support for each other, as evidenced by the multiple ethnic societies and churches that were established, built, and paid for by member subscription. Most of these beautiful monuments remain in use, lovingly preserved and tended by the descendants of the original builders.

Manistee's growing sense of itself as a civilized community after the Civil War is attested in histories written at the time. Citizens celebrated the arrival of the young lawyer T. J. Ramsdell, the man who would settle the many legal issues that had begun to arise in this frontier town. They established congregations, benevolent societies, and the banks and office buildings required to aid the rapidly growing region. By this time, women were an established presence, and they engaged themselves energetically—sometimes fervently— in the ethical debates of the time—particularly the highly controversial topics of temperance and suffrage.

By 1869, Michigan was producing more logs than any other state. The development of narrow-gauge logging railroads and other steam-driven logging technologies in the 1870s increased the efficiency with which trees could be transported from previously inaccessible regions, down the rivers to Manistee for processing, and across the lake to the rapidly exploding markets of Chicago and Milwaukee. Manistee was assured another viable industry with the drilling of the first successful salt well in 1881. At this time, another wave of immigrants arrived—more

Germans and Scandinavians, but also thousands of Polish people, all displaced by political upheavals in their own countries, avoiding forced servitude in the armies of conquering regimes or facing starvation. These new arrivals supplied the now booming Manistee economy with a fresh and plentiful labor force. They opened groceries, small businesses, churches, and parochial schools, went to work in the salt factories, the mills, and the railroads, and cleaned the houses and tended the children of the wealthy. These arrivals became the town's new middle and working classes. Many of these Polish settlers lived initially in shanties they built on company land: on Lake Michigan near Canfield's Mill and on the Manistee Lake's shore in the planned community of Filer City.

The Homestead Act of 1863 drew another type of settler to northern Michigan. Any person over 21 or who headed a household—man, woman, newly arrived immigrant, or former slave who could successfully build a dwelling, clear, and farm at least five acres on a 160-acre parcel of land for five years—could claim the property. After creating homesteads in the woods with minimal funds or equipment and with children and animals to feed, these extraordinary individuals set up as farmers, shopkeepers, or sometimes as small industrial contractors in the villages and townships outside the city. Manistee Township, Brown Township, Onekama, Arcadia, Marilla, and Maple Grove were all founded this way. Many descendants of those original families remain, on productive farms or in comfortable homes that their great-grandparents built from nothing.

These outlying villages play another essential role in Manistee history. By the end of the 19th century, Manistee had become one of the largest shipping ports on the Great Lakes, and by some accounts had more millionaires per capita than any other American city. But the vast forest the Stronachs came to was now reduced to mile after mile of burnt-over stumps. Faced with economic collapse, speculators looked outside the city for solutions.

Beyond Manistee, land associations had formed specifically to find profitable uses for the cut-over and ruined property all across the northern regions. In 1900, local representatives from two of these organizations contacted two groups of people whose circumstances rendered them eager for land, and whose cultural values ensured that they would be ethically bound to work for what they got and improve their lot even under the most adverse conditions: the Finns, who settled in Kaleva, and the German Baptist Brethren religious sect of Indiana and Ohio, who founded the village of Brethren. Both of these communities remain, still retaining the same values with which they accomplished their successes and the same pride in their unique heritage that gave them the wherewithal to do so. The village of Wellstone was similarly formed when a land association bought several thousand Central European immigrants by train from Chicago.

In Arcadia, some 20 miles up the coast from Manistee, things were a little easier. In 1880, Henry Starke built a mill of his own. By 1895, Arcadia had several mills, prosperous farms, a pier, ships, and a railroad of its own and economically interdependent railroad villages such as Henry, Springdale, and Copemish. Locals say that Arcadia's industries rivaled Manistee's. In 1906, when Starke's mill burned and the lumber industry had finally collapsed for good, Arcadians simply built a furniture factory, thus retaining the town's economic vitality well into the 1950s.

The economic boom of the late 1800s gave rise all over America to a new class of people who, perhaps for the first time in history, had sufficient time and money for recreation. This leisure class offered an entirely new market for the struggling region. In the early 1900s, fashionable tourists from Milwaukee and Chicago came across Lake Michigan on steamers to stroll along the grand streets of Manistee, Onekama, and Arcadia to buy postcards, eat ice cream, partake of a healthful mineral bath at the Briny Inn, or attend theatrical performances at the Ramsdell Theater. Outside the city, they might stroll around the grounds and the beaches of Onekama's luxurious Portage Point Inn or send their boys to Camp Tosebo. Newly constructed streetcar lines in Manistee allowed city residents to relax at Orchard Beach or wealthier families to retreat to their new cottages at Red Park

After World War I, Manistee County lost much of the massive population of the previous century. Many young men who had enlisted in the war settled elsewhere once they returned, in search of greater opportunity. But those who remained continued to strive and modernize, replacing sawmills and lumberyards with hydroelectric dams and power plants, drawing a steady stream of tourists across the lake in steamers or along the fresh novelty of paved roads in their automobiles.

When Century Boat set up on Manistee Lake in 1927, company advertisements associated the sleek, stylish wooden boats with Manistee scenery and fashionable modernity. The new firm supplied the region yet again with another vital economic lifeline during the Depression, as did the Hardy Salt and Morton Salt Companies. While neither of these more recent industries is represented here due to limitations of scope, their presence is as essential to Manistee history and its recent economy as any of those that do appear here. Also insufficiently represented here is Manistee's Native American community. Credit for the present-day economic vitality of Manistee belongs to the Little River Band of Ottawa Indians and their newly built and thriving Little River Casino. Like the other communities of Manistee who tell their stories in this book, their persistence, their adaptability, and their success under adversity testify to their vision and strength.

This book offers a partial history in photographs. On their own, historical images are quaint at best, offering a nostalgic vision of a bygone age, to be traded on eBay or in antique shops as charming collectibles. When they are accompanied by stories—the names and the accomplishments of the people in them as told by those who remember them—these images become extraordinarily valuable. They link us to the time, the place, and the people whose 19th-century dreams and deeds brought our 21st-century world into being. The past is not lost. Rather, it forms the actual substrate of our present. In one sense, Manistee is a typical semi-rural American county with a regionally typical history. But the stories its citizens tell are unique tales told by people with clear and singular memories, who know exactly who they are and where they came from, and are justifiably proud of it. These stories need to be told so that we can all remember who we are.

One

Loggers and Pioneers

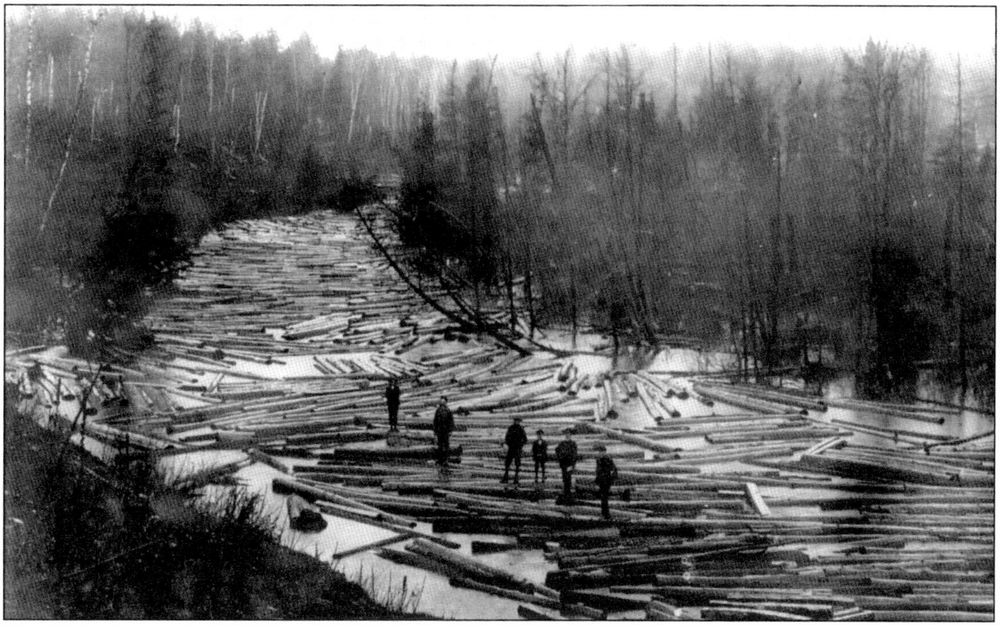

Few images exist of Manistee before 1880. Both photography and settlement were too new, and getting photographic equipment onto the frontier proved difficult. Frequent fire destroyed what once existed. The photographs in this chapter, from the late 19th or early 20th centuries, approximate the earliest days of logging and settlement in Manistee County, and chronicle its growth into an economic and industrial center. This image of the Big Manistee River choked with thousands of logs, and of the men responsible for clearing them, offers one such glimpse. At first, all transportation of cut timber from the forests happened by river. Until 1868, when the Manistee River Improvement Company was formed to keep the rivers clear and the logs moving, logjams made such transport impossible. As shown here, logs accumulated so densely that the men had to stand on them to work. Before bridges were constructed, logjams also offered the only available river crossing; some were so solid that draft animals could easily cross. All images in this chapter and the next are courtesy of the Manistee Historical Museum, unless otherwise noted.

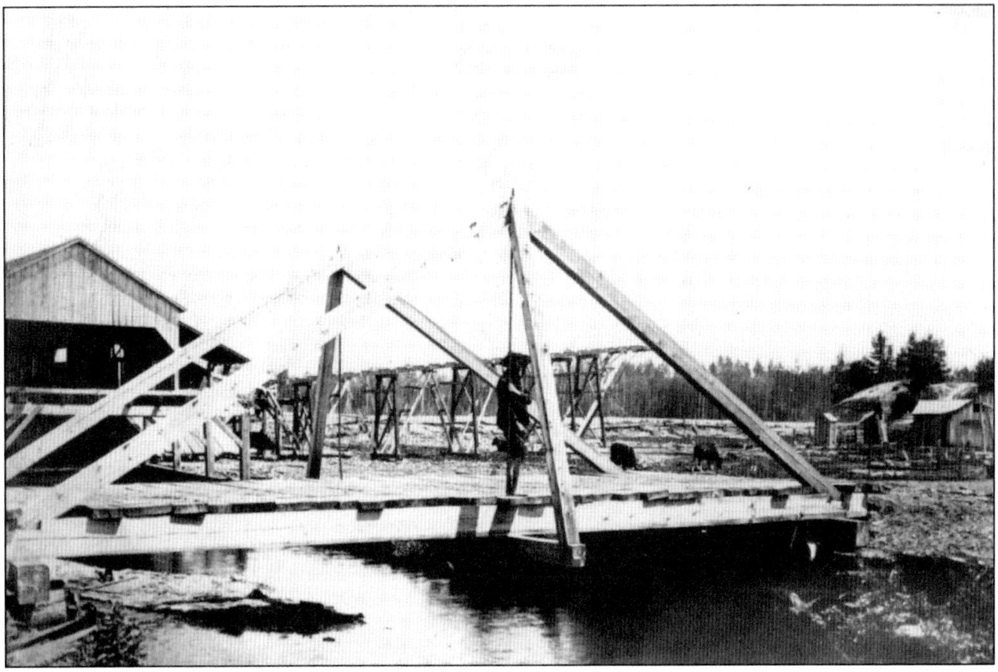

Although the Stronachs founded the Manistee lumber industry, relatively little is known about them. They had purchased a waterpower mill site on the Little Manistee River, but also temporarily set up a mill in a set of abandoned government buildings in the area around the present junction of Michigan 110 and U.S. 31. Later, perhaps as late as 1845, the family moved to the property on the Little Manistee and set up permanent operations there. A small village grew up around the mill. The photograph above, of the bridge built across the Old Stronach Mill spillway, is one of the few images of that settlement. After James Stronach died in 1858, Adam Stronach took over the business. The mills at Old Stronach were eventually abandoned in favor of a new site on Manistee Lake, shown below, where cargo schooners could load and unload directly at the mill.

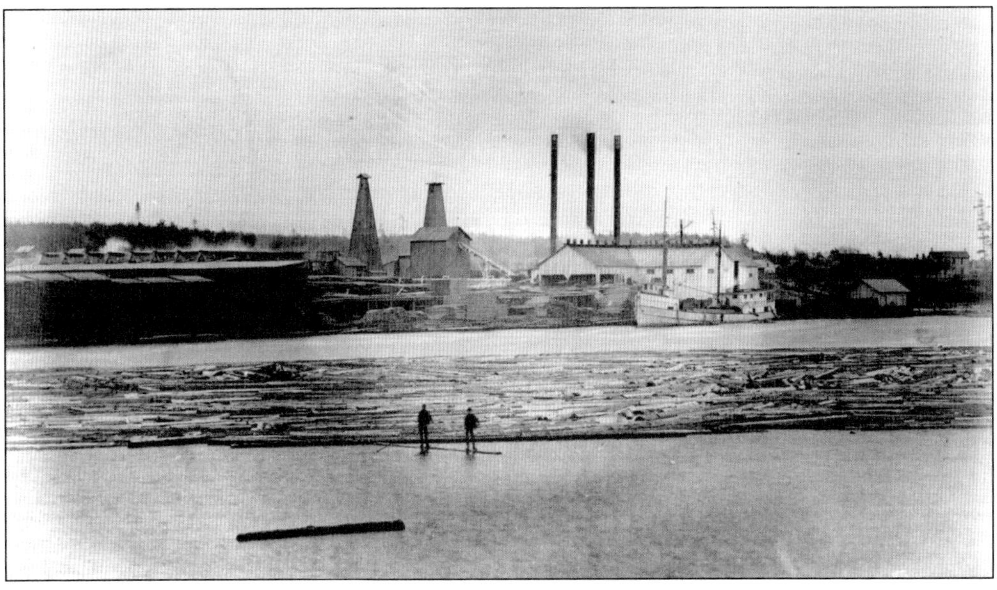

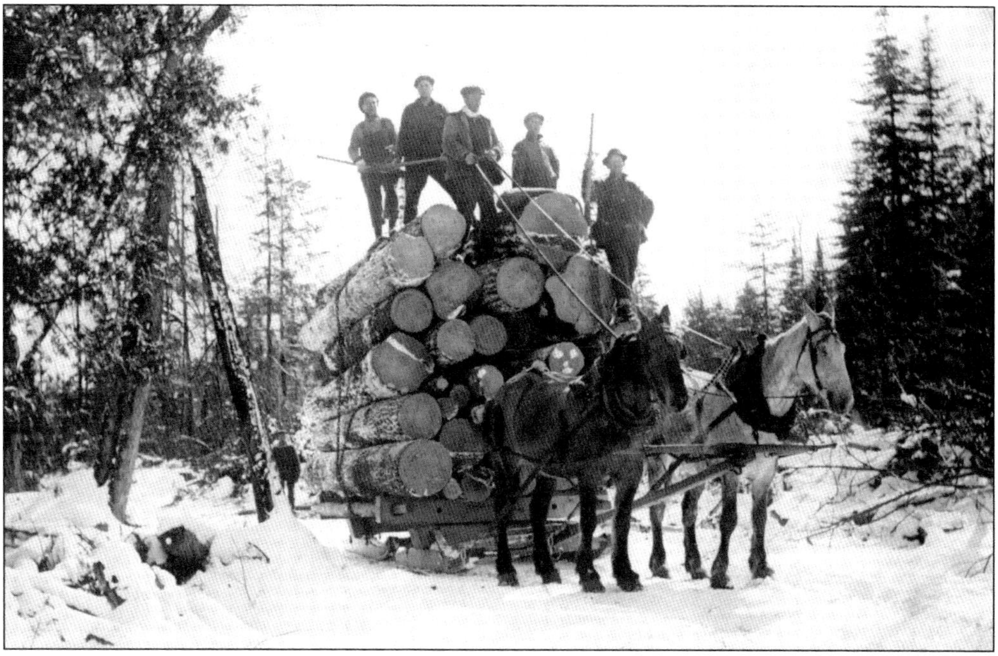

Before railroads, logging only occurred in winter. Logs were transported from the woods to the nearest stream by horse-drawn sleds such as this one. This photograph, taken near Lemon Lake in 1905, indicates that the practice remained practical for transporting logs short distances through the woods even after the railroads came.

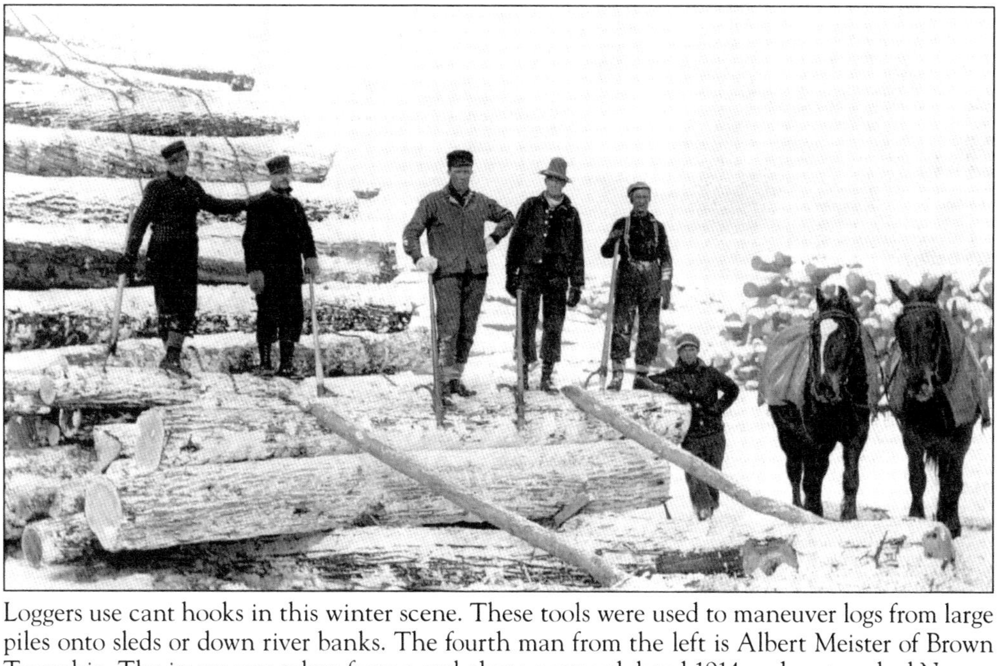

Loggers use cant hooks in this winter scene. These tools were used to maneuver logs from large piles onto sleds or down river banks. The fourth man from the left is Albert Meister of Brown Township. The image was taken from a real-photo postcard dated 1914 and postmarked Nessen City. Albert probably had it taken of himself while away from home to send to his sister Anna, the card's addressee. (Courtesy of Carol Schimke.)

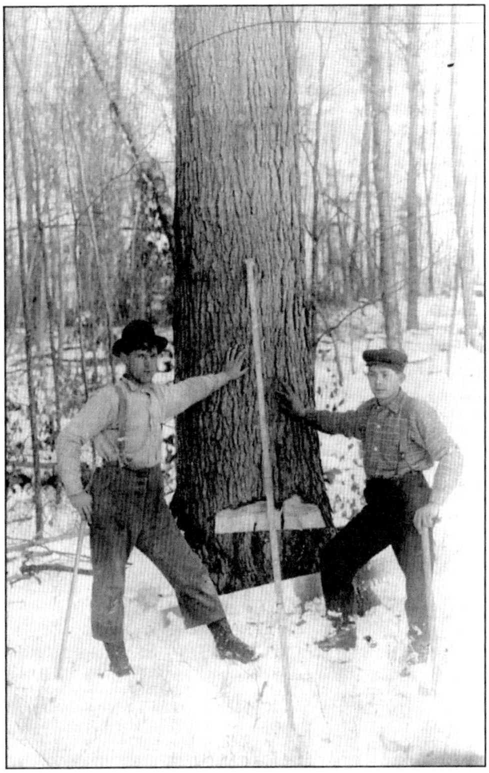

Early loggers felled massive trees with axes—work that required strength, stamina, and skill. Men chopped in pairs, as seen in the photograph to the left, taken in a Hoxeyville camp at the beginning of the 20th century. Working opposite, they would chop to the center until the tree toppled. The invention of the crosscut saw sometime in the 1880s added efficiency. Below, Ross Williams (left) and Clyde Morris (right) pose with axes at Ward Camp near Lemon Lake in 1905. A crosscut saw leans on the tree. Working in teams of four, two men would chop a notch and then two sawyers would fell it by sawing opposite the notch. As seen here, the crosscut saw could also be used to make the notch. These workers are quite young; some started as early as age 13. (Left, courtesy of Clarence Nowak.)

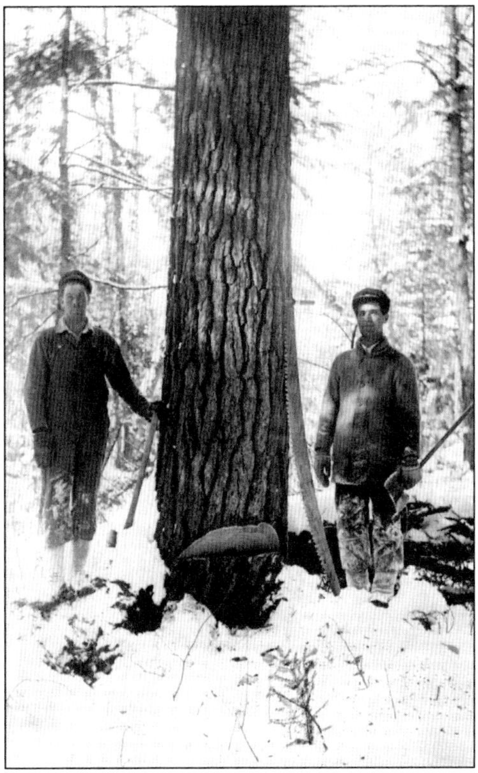

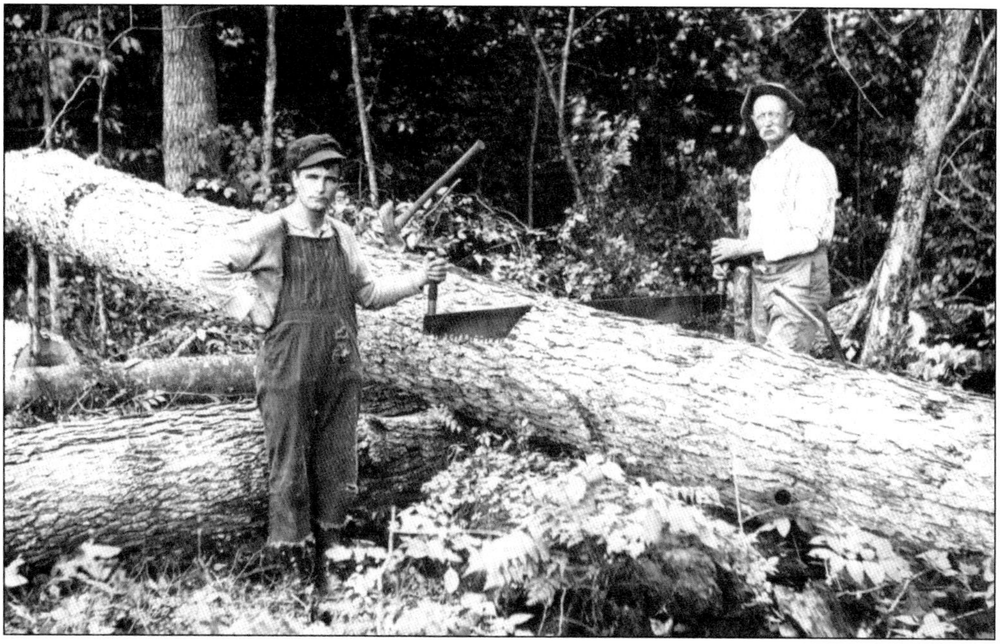

Once the trees were felled, another team of sawyers would cut them into logs. These logs would then be "scaled," or graded and stamped with the name of the specific lumber company, to be identified at the other end of the river.

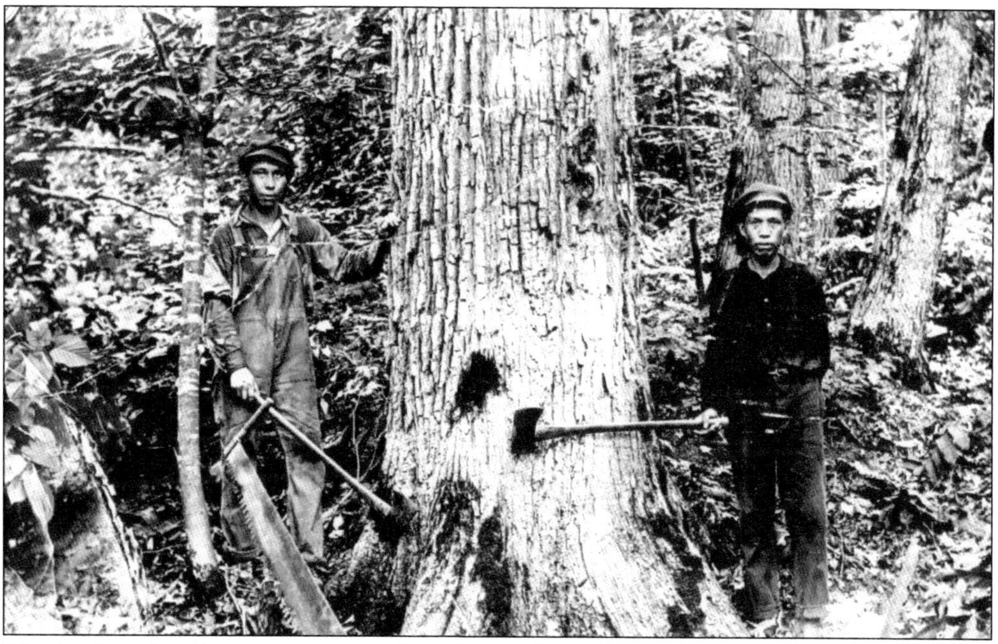

The hard work of logging was typically taken up by recent immigrants hoping to get a start in America. First to arrive were French Canadians, next Irish, then Germans and some Scandinavians. As this photograph shows, however, young locals from the Ottawa community also sought work in the woods, hoping to improve their own conditions. Although Native American culture and history were quite separate from those of the early white settlers, the two populations influenced each other more than is commonly realized.

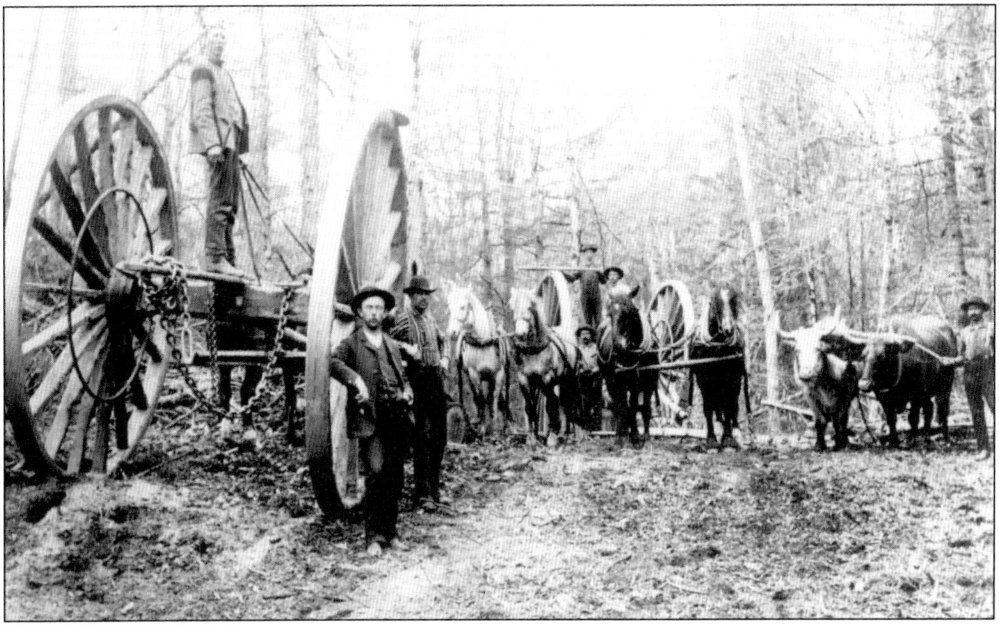

Logging sleighs could only move a few miles and required snow to operate. Mild winters were disastrous, and mills were expensive to run. Lumbermen needing returns on their investments thus sought technological solutions. In the 1870s, Silas Overpack perfected big logging wheels such as the ones seen here. This innovation extended the harvest season into springtime. Oxen were used, as shown above, but many camps preferred horses. The man standing on the wheel is identified as "the boss." Another innovation to speed the process was the "jammer," depicted below. Horse-powered like the big wheels, yet small enough to be maneuverable through the woods, they were set up at the cross-haul. The wheel or sled was placed beside it, and workers hoisted logs quickly up onto it for transport to camp.

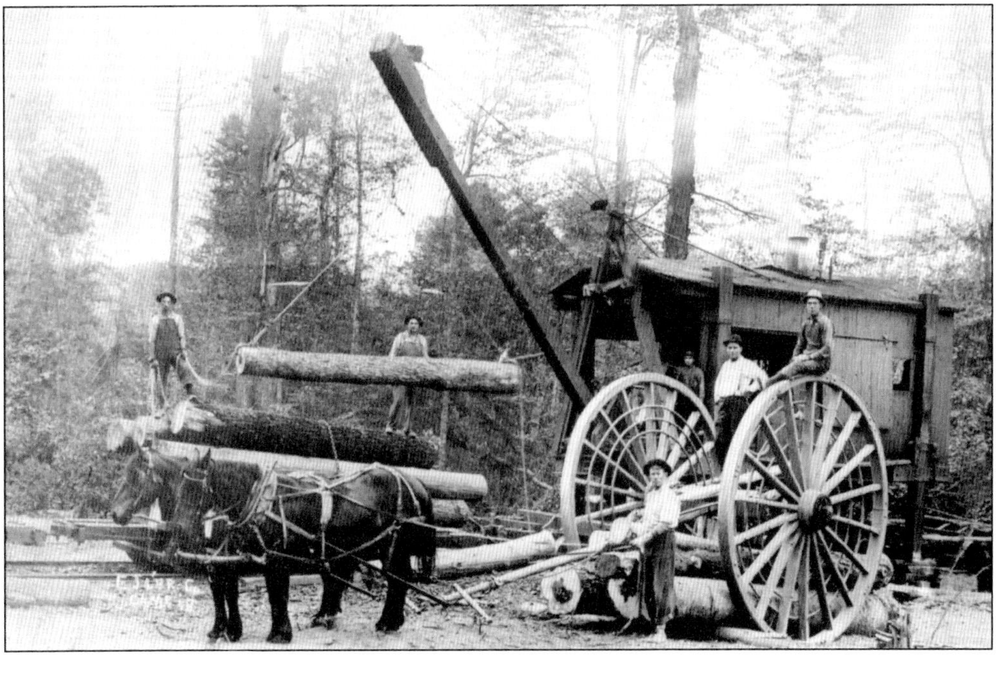

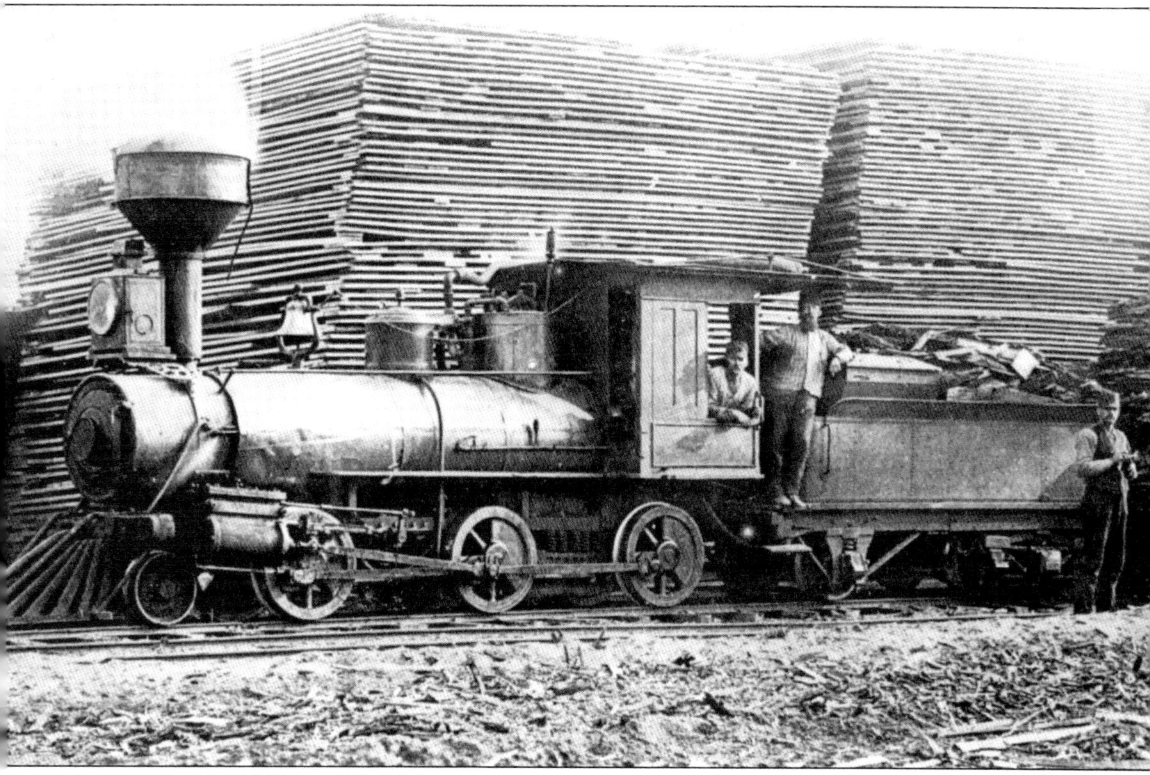

The Bear Lake and Eastern 2-6-0 No. 1 locomotive is pictured at the Hopkins Manufacturing Company sawmill at Bear Lake about 1890. The introduction of the three-foot, or narrow-gauge, railroad track to northern Michigan in 1877 enabled a revolution in the lumber industry. It allowed for the year-round, day-and-night rapid transportation of lumber. Winfield Scott Gerrish, a lumberman from Clare County who had admired a small wood-burning steam engine called the Baldwin locomotive at the Great Centennial Exhibition of Philadelphia in 1876, was the first in the area to build and use such a railroad in Clare in 1877. Manistee lumbermen soon followed suit. The Bear Lake and Eastern Railroad opened its narrow-gauge line in 1882. It ran between Pierport via Bear Lake to Springdale and Maple Grove, until ceasing operations in 1902. (Courtesy of Clarence Nowak.)

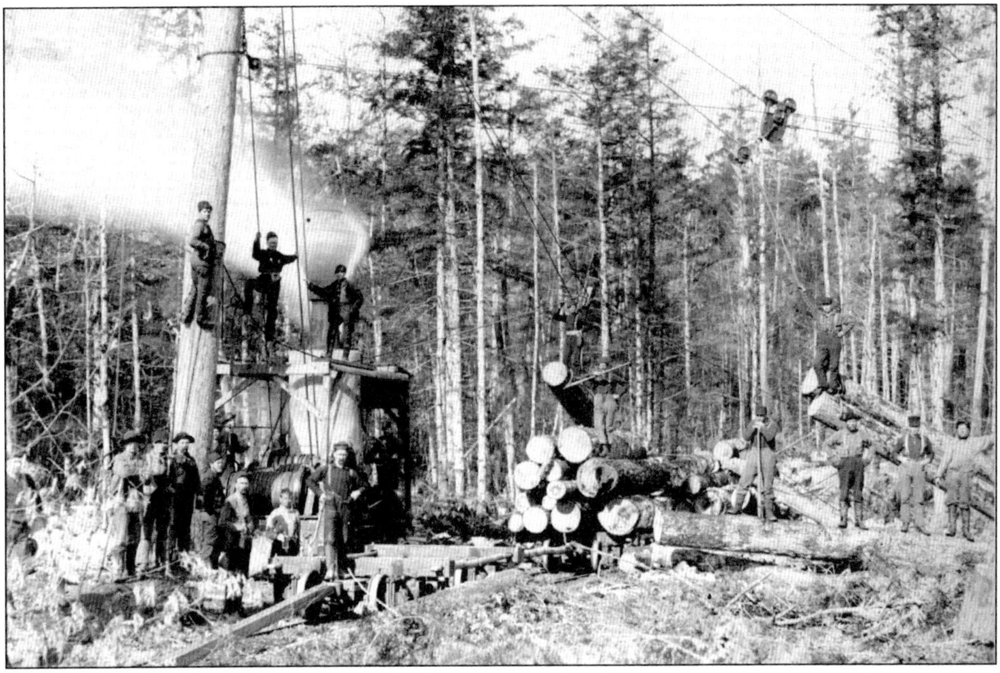

Steam technology improved speed and efficiency in other logging operations as well, such as the steam log loader pictured above. It could be brought in along the railroad tracks and placed on a siding, where logs could be loaded directly onto waiting flatcars. The floating log lifter shown below improved operations at the other end of the river. It enabled mill workers to remove logs from the water much more efficiently. At the height of the logging industry in the 1880s, logs were sometimes loaded unprocessed directly onto trains and ships, in order to reach their markets more quickly. While steam power made their work easier to some extent, loggers were now expected to work faster and to put in longer hours to keep up with rapidly increasing demand.

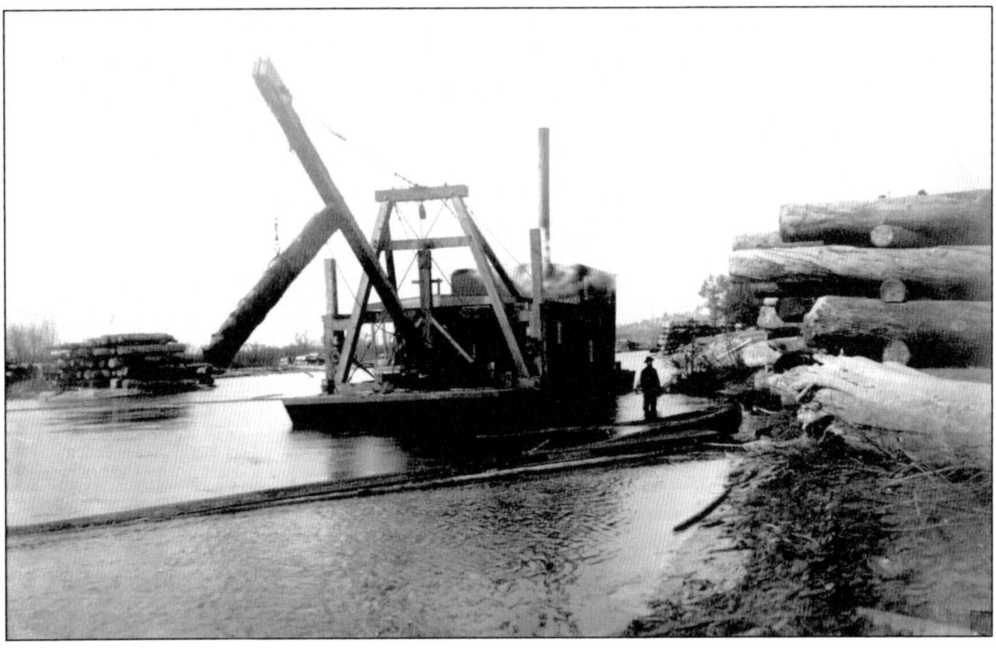

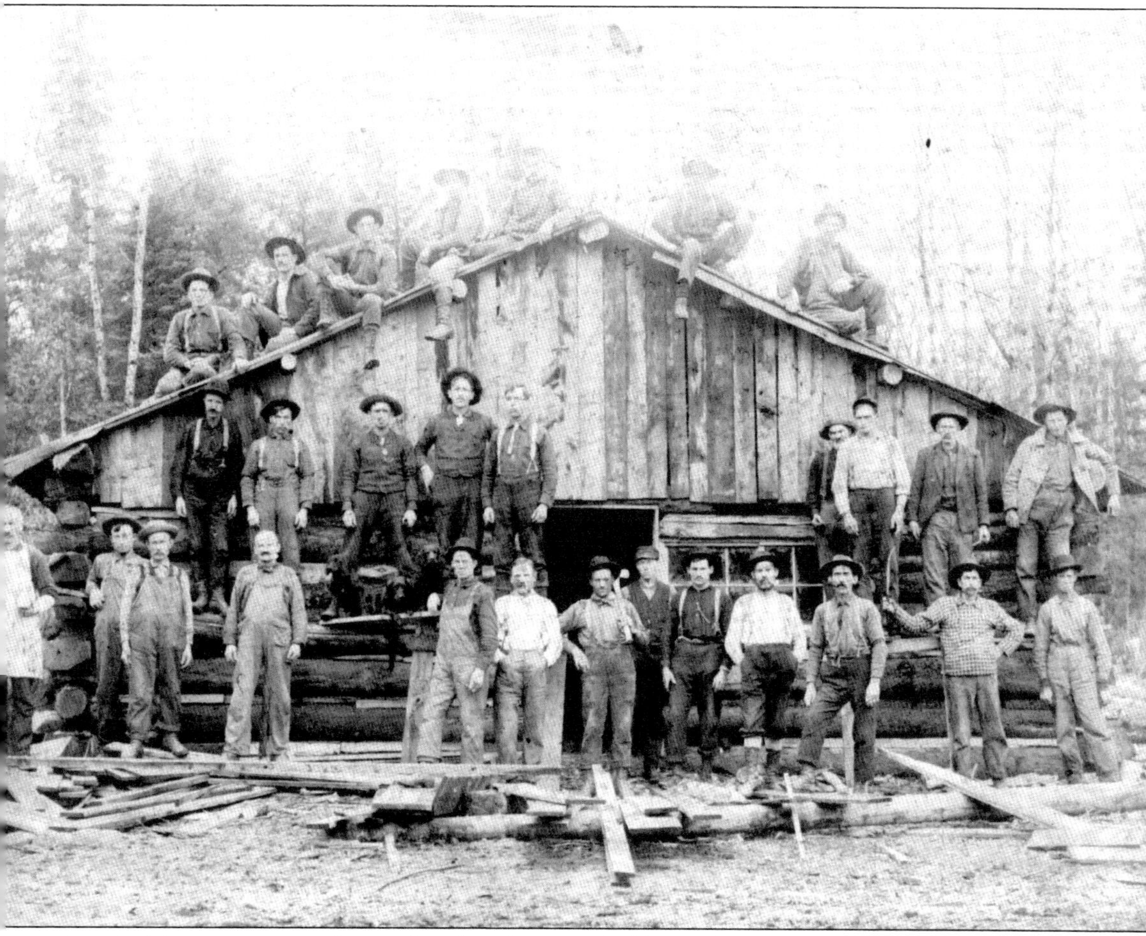

A typical logging camp is depicted in this photograph, likely taken in the 1880s. Camps usually consisted of five or six buildings of log-cabin-type construction. Their appearance was unrefined; they were not intended as permanent structures. The best construction was reserved for the log scaler, the camp foreman, and the company office and store. Largest was the crew's bunk house, with adjacent dining hall and kitchen. Other buildings housed animals and the blacksmith. Men worked dawn to dusk six days a week, with housekeeping and tool repair on Sundays.

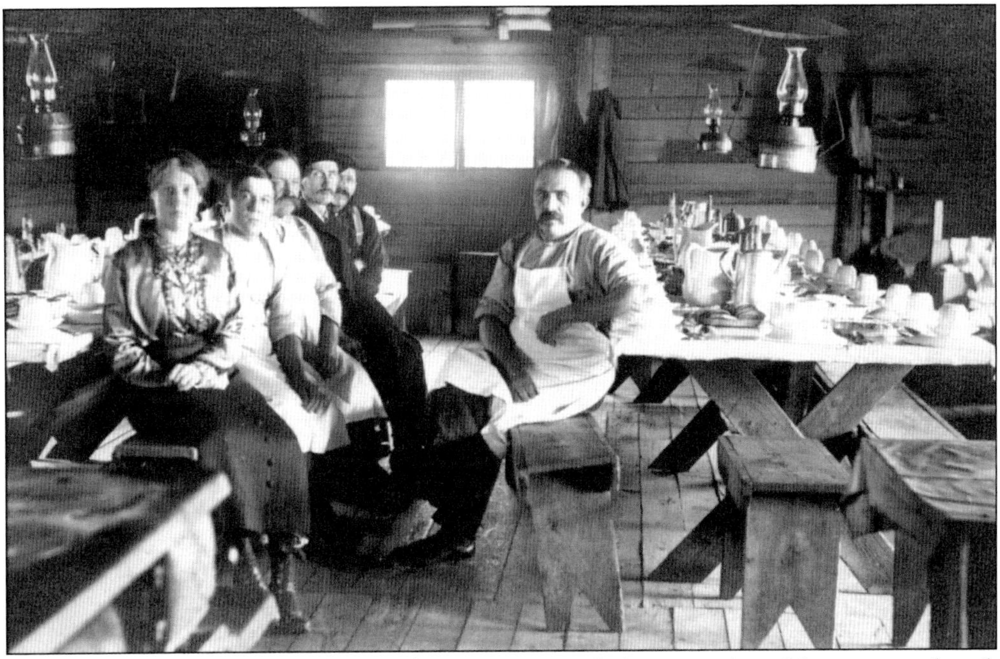

Camp meals were plain but substantial. Loggers ate such fare as pork and beans, corn bread, molasses cake, and tea or coffee. The above photograph, taken at the start of the 20th century, depicts a typical camp kitchen. The kitchen staff, on the left, consists of recent immigrants. The cook, seated on the right, is identified only as Vancolen. The well-dressed woman is atypical; lumber camps were strictly male environments, and her clothes are finer than those of a kitchen worker. Vancolen also appears outside his dining hall in the center of the image below. The man to the left with the dogs is unidentified. To the right is the "cookee," whose responsibilities included calling the men in for meals with the long tin Gabriel Horn he holds. (Courtesy of Clarence Nowak.)

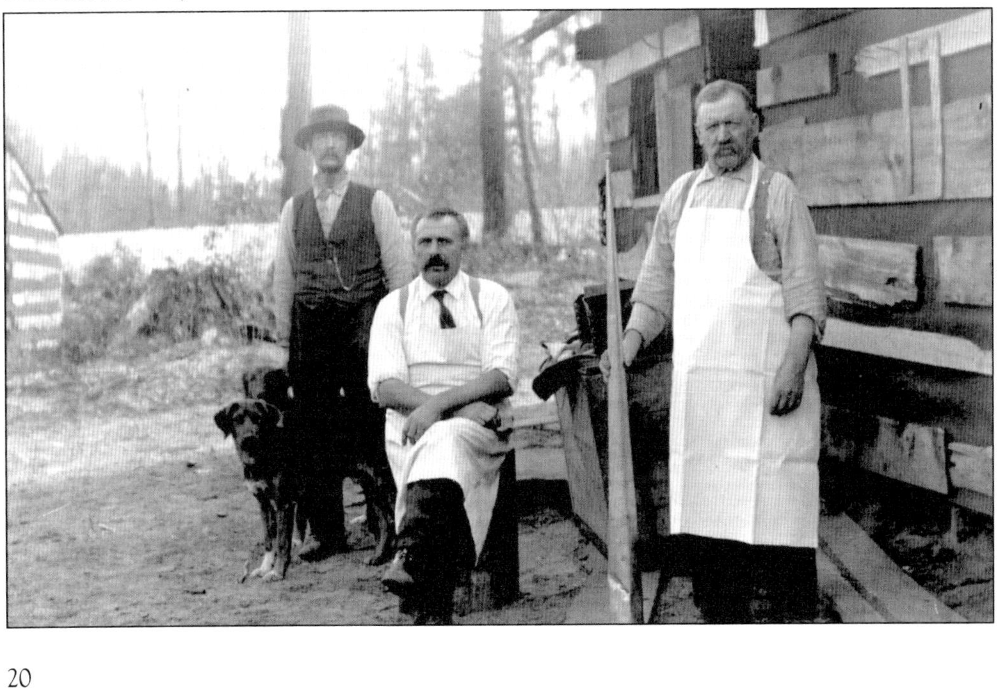

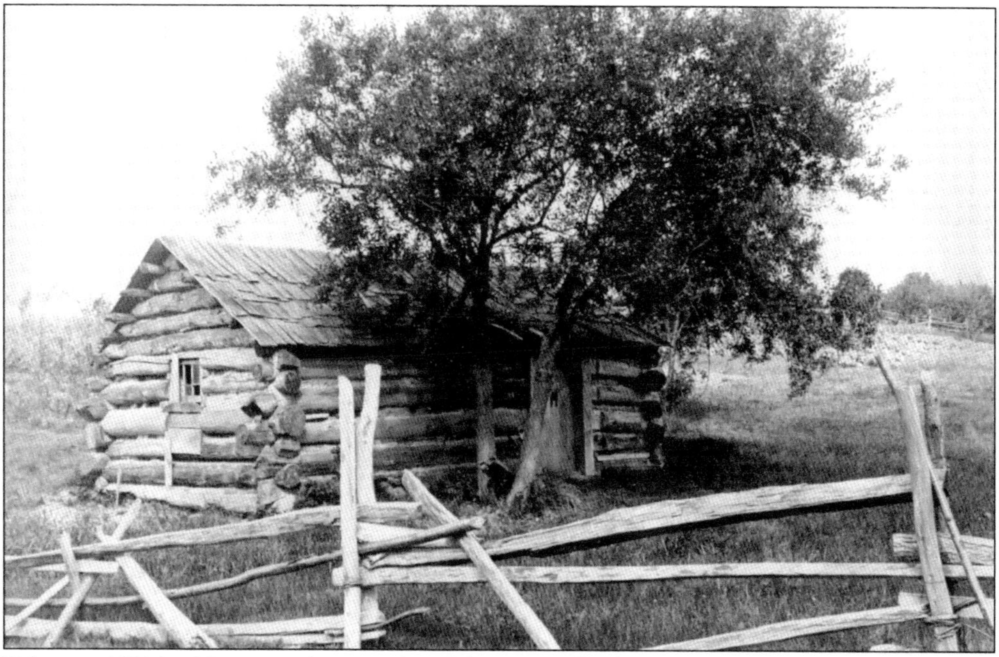

Taken in 1889 by Manistee photographer Edwin Russell, these views depict two different types of the homesteader's cabin. The one above shows an early homesteader's cabin built in Manistee County in the 1860s. It was located near the Big Manistee River, about eight miles from Manistee on the old river road. Solidly constructed, it appears to have been built for permanent use by established settlers. The cabin below has been hastily constructed of scrap lumber, presumably used only until the family acquired the resources to build something better. Homesteaders were faced with the challenge of building permanent structures, clearing land, and raising sufficient crops to feed themselves, their children, and their animals—generally with no money to start and no resources but helpful neighbors.

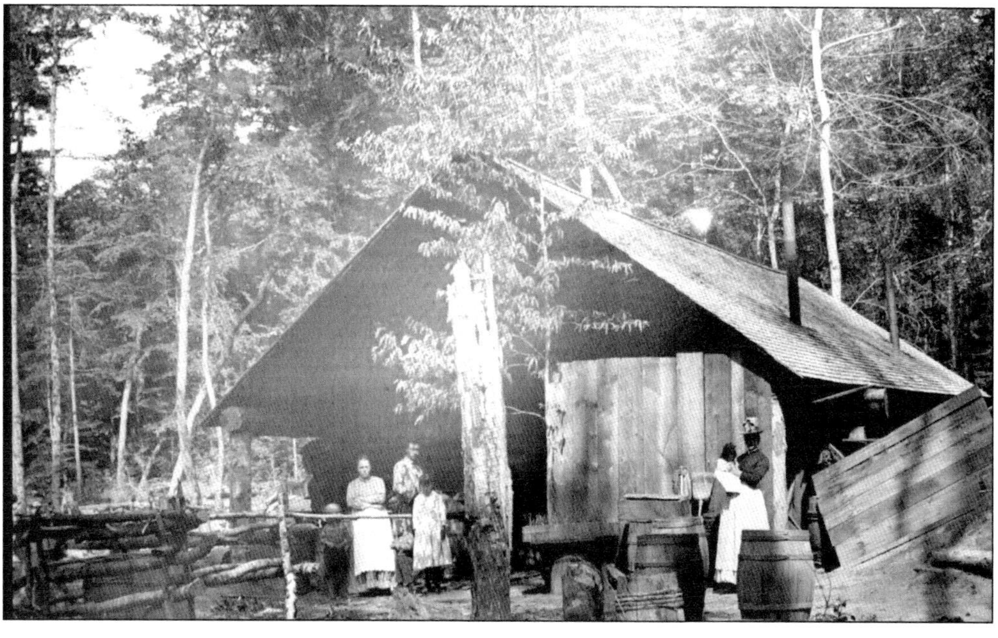

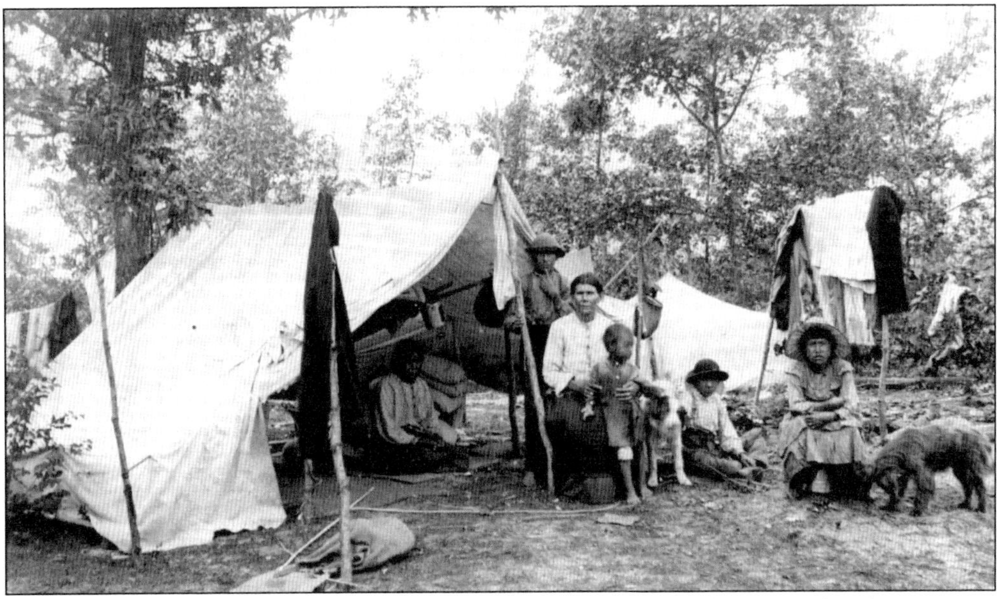

Most historical accounts of Manistee mention Native Americans only as part of the bygone past. Increasingly marginalized by development of lands that often still belonged to them, American Indians nonetheless retained a constant presence. The photograph above shows an Ottawa family at its summer camp. Farmers and hunters, Ottawas traveled with the seasons. In summer, families would tend their farms and gather food until their winter trip south. Depicted below are two families posed outside of a cabin. Note especially the corset on the girl seated fourth from the left. The late 1800s saw a nationwide drive to "civilize" Native tribes through religious conversion, discouraging traditional customs, and enrolling children in boarding school, where they were dressed in garb that 19th-century school founders considered proper attire. Whether this girl attended such a school or was dressed for the photograph is unknown.

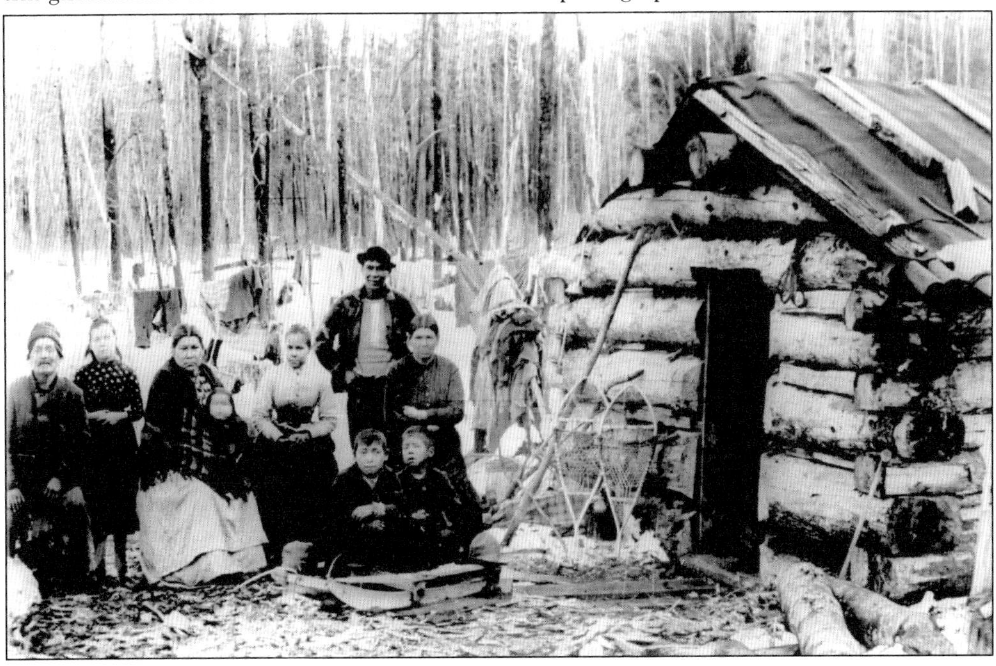

Two

THE ONES WHO MADE IT HAPPEN

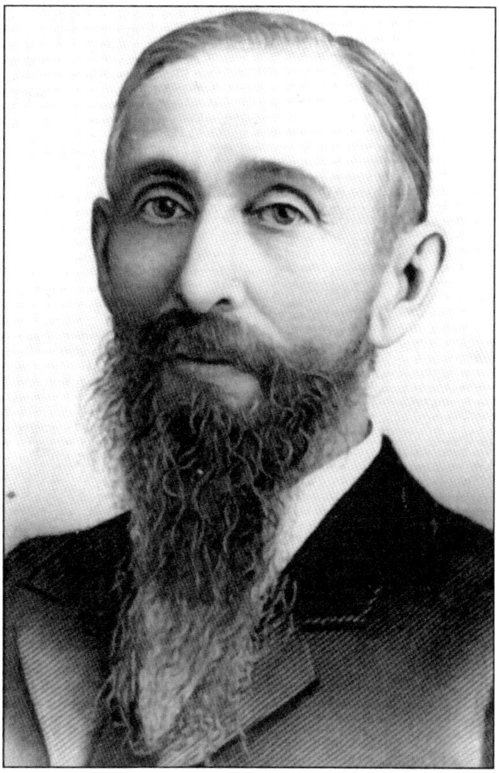

The lumber era left Manistee with a 19th-century legacy of elegance and wealth that is still very evident in the city today. One of the most prominent figures of that era was John Canfield. He came with his father to Manistee about 1848, shortly after the Stronachs arrived. The Candfields' sawmill operations soon far outstripped the Stronachs'. One of the first and most successful of Manistee's legendary lumbermen, John became sole owner of the original mill site in 1868. Although this site was destroyed for the fourth time by the "Great Fire of 1871," he persistently rebuilt and then expanded his holdings. He gained his wealth by several means. One was by maintaining financial interest in several other mills. Another was by owning the transportation lines required to move lumber from his mills. He owned an extensive tug fleet and built his own railroad line in 1888. Finally, John Canfield set up a subcontracting network, whereby he would establish a contract with a mill or camp operator, who would in turn hire workers who contracted directly with the operator.

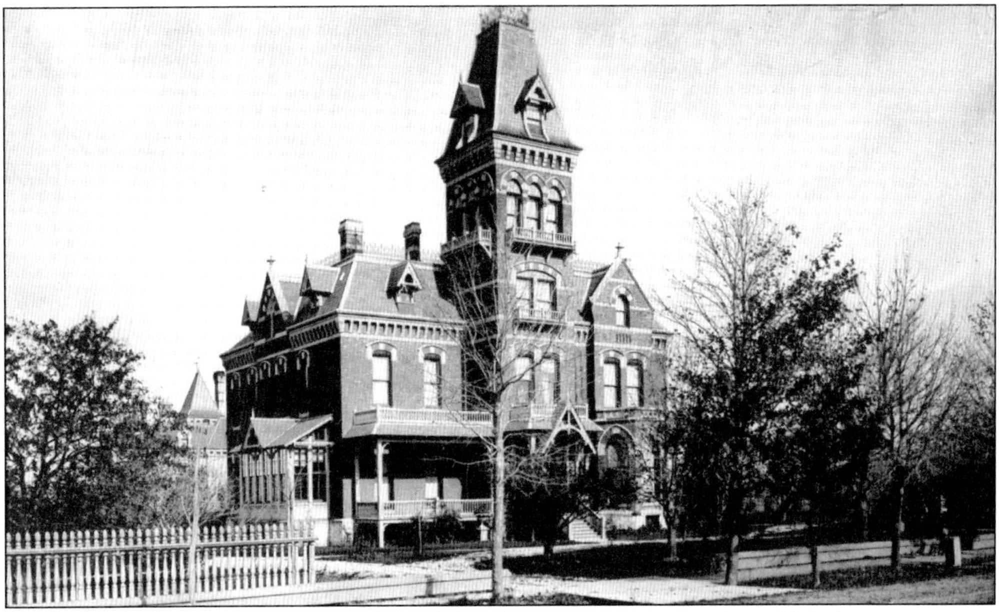

John Canfield's residence was as spectacular as his career. Completed in 1877, the site covered an entire city block and was bounded by Fourth, Third, Cedar, and Elm Streets. The top of the tower was 82 feet from the ground, with a panoramic view of the lake and its traffic, various other Manistee industries, and the thousands of acres of timbered land that still remained.

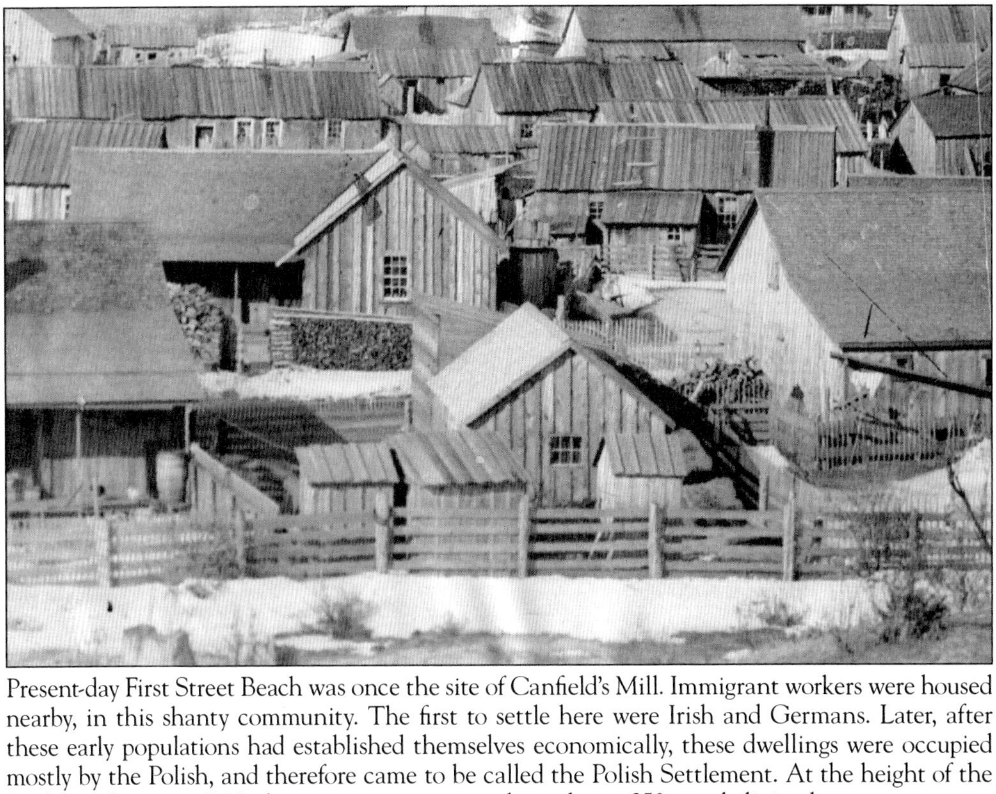

Present-day First Street Beach was once the site of Canfield's Mill. Immigrant workers were housed nearby, in this shanty community. The first to settle here were Irish and Germans. Later, after these early populations had established themselves economically, these dwellings were occupied mostly by the Polish, and therefore came to be called the Polish Settlement. At the height of the lumber industry in 1890, the government census showed over 350 people living here.

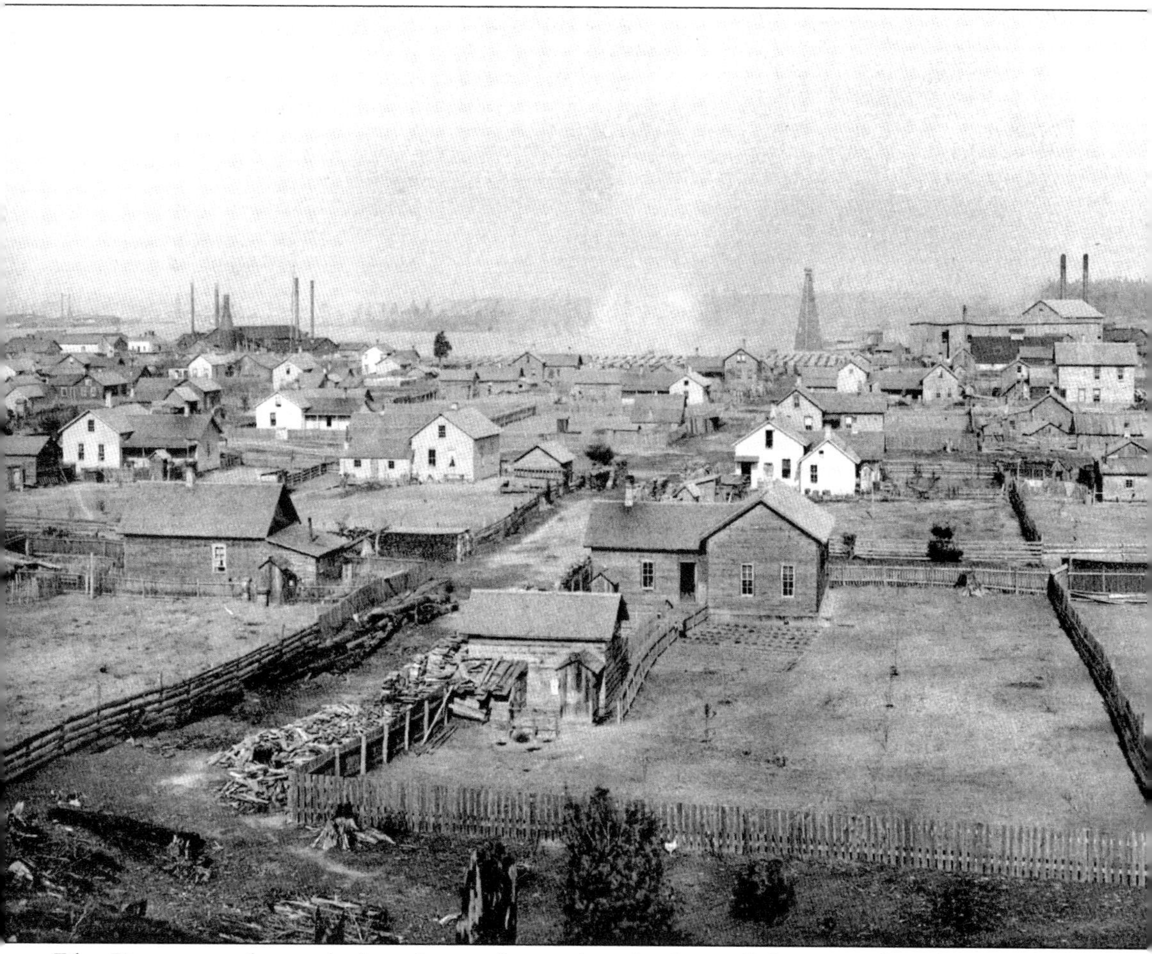

Filer City was another worker's settlement. Located on the shore of Manistee Lake, where it still remains, it was built as a company town in 1868 by the firm of D. L. Filer and Sons. Apparently, the socially minded Filers intended it to stand as a model community and an alternative to tenements such as the Canfield shantytown. It was advertised as a village with clean, well-lighted homes priced between $50 and $100 so that workers could afford them. As this image shows, Filer City was indeed much less crowded than its counterpart near Canfield's Mill. In 1883, the population was at a reasonable 350. That year, the city directory editors described the community as containing "a good school house and a large number of handsome dwellings." In 1900, however, the new influx of Polish immigrants caused the population to burgeon to 1,000, leading to cramped living conditions.

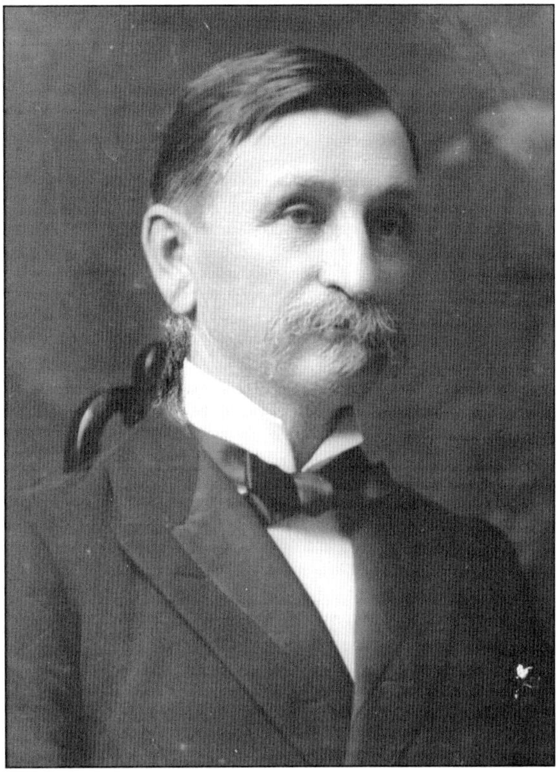

Elihu Golden Filer (left) and Delos Warren Filer (below) made up the firm of Filer and Sons. Like many men of the Victorian age who strived for progress through industry, these brothers planned Filer City from the beginning as an essential component of a state-of-the-art mill operation. E. Golden, who had trained as a lawyer and had been taken as a prisoner during the Civil War, expanded and modernized from his father's day. Filer and Sons was the first in the area to use a steam feed and a steam log turner and to install the efficient band saw. His brother D. Warren was primarily known for his retiring nature and for his many contributions to various charities.

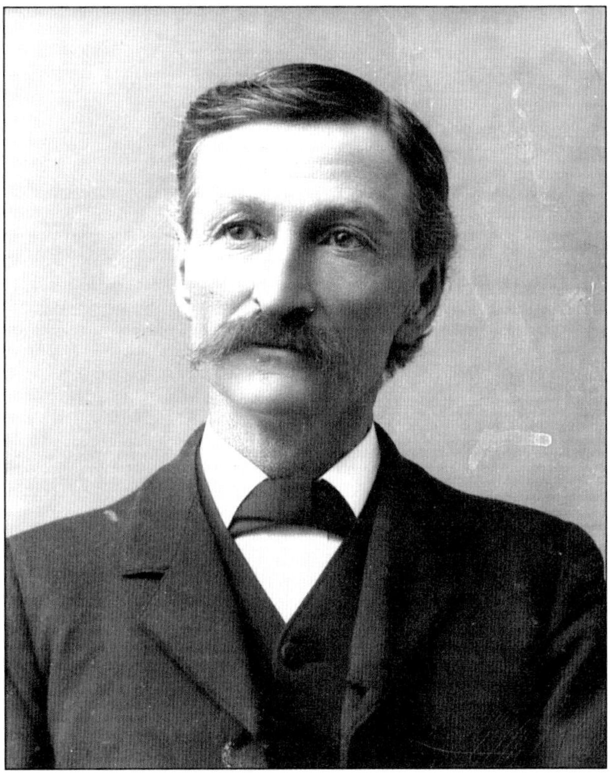

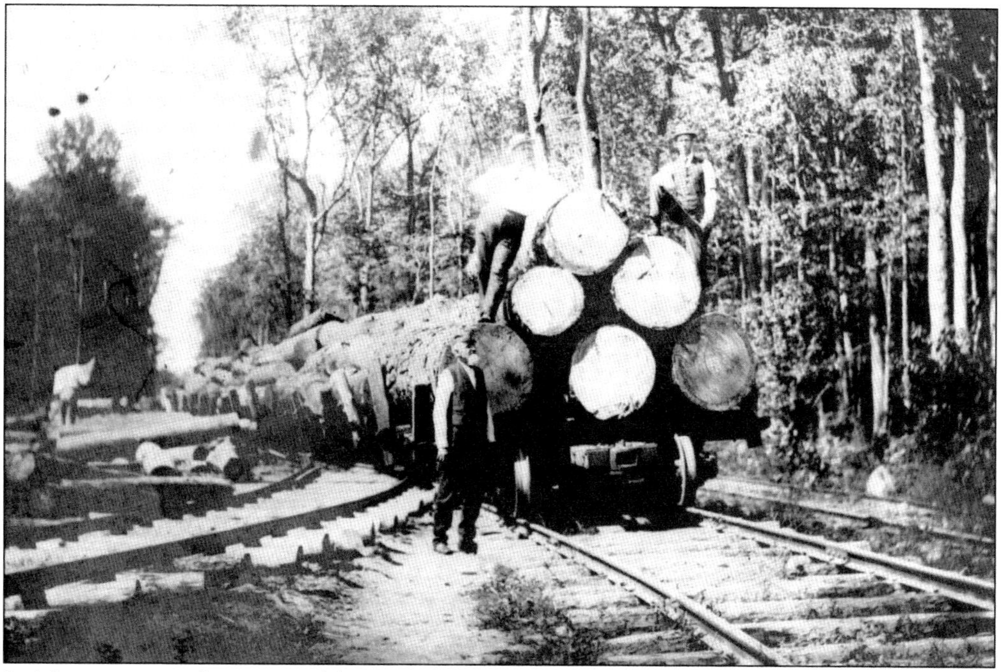

In Manistee, it truly was possible to start with nothing, work hard, and earn a fortune, as did Louis Sands. In the photograph above, he stands beside a loaded car of his railroad. The men on the logs are unidentified. The lower middle log is inscribed, "This tree scaled 4222 feet." Born on a Swedish farm in 1826, Sands immigrated to the United States on an ore freighter. Upon arrival in Manistee, he was hired by a Canfield contractor. He went unpaid that year, but persisted for several more years and made his own contract with Canfield. In 1868, he began developing 40 acres of property on what is now Eastlake. This became Sands Mill, seen below. Fortunate to arrive during a booming economy, because he refused to accumulate debt, Sands succeeded when others failed during subsequent financial panics.

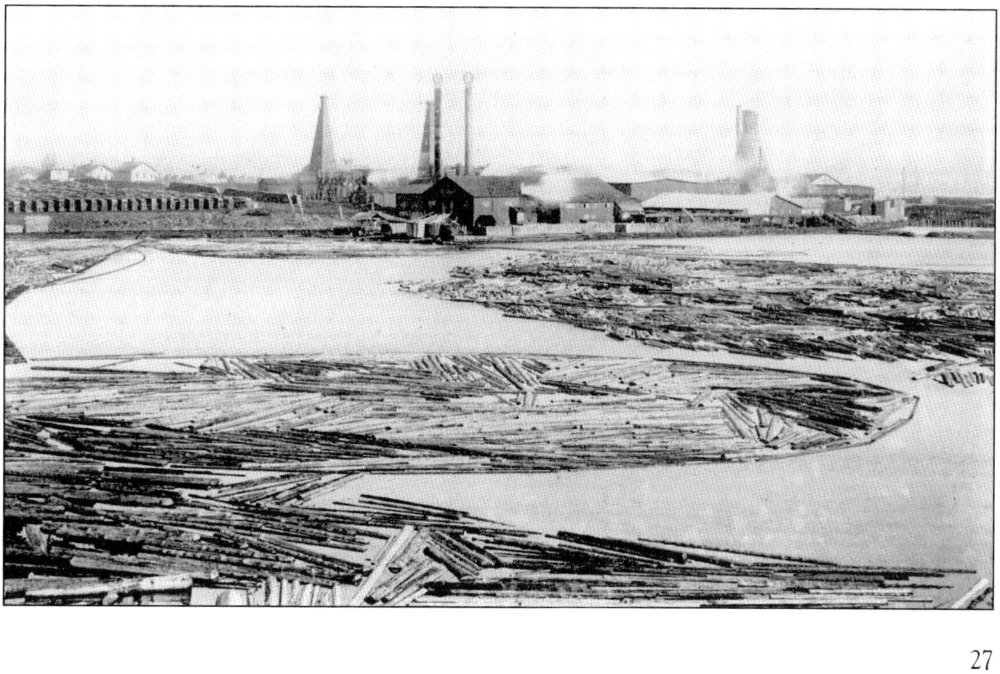

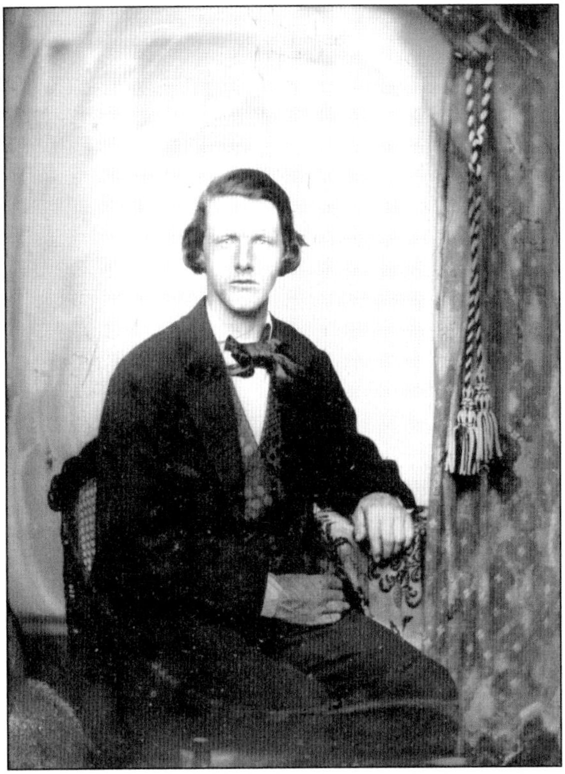

Thomas Kenny's story is a similar realization of the American Dream. Born in Ireland in 1842, he was orphaned at age seven when his parents died of the fever that decimated the population during the Potato Famine. His older brother Edward left for America, working for 10 years until he could return to Ireland for Thomas and the five other siblings. At 13, Thomas found work contracting for another Irish lumberman and was eventually promoted to camp foreman. The tintype photograph to the left shows a very young Thomas Kenny, probably shortly after he arrived in the 1850s. In the image below, he sits with his wife, Ellen Lynch Kenny, likely around the time of their marriage in 1868. Tintypes were immensely popular in the 1860s because they made photographic portraits accessible to the working class. (Courtesy of Cindy Dempsey.)

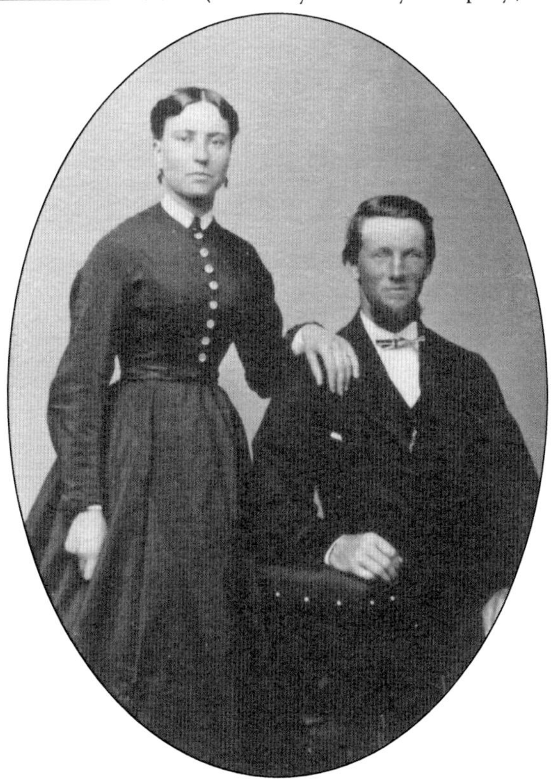

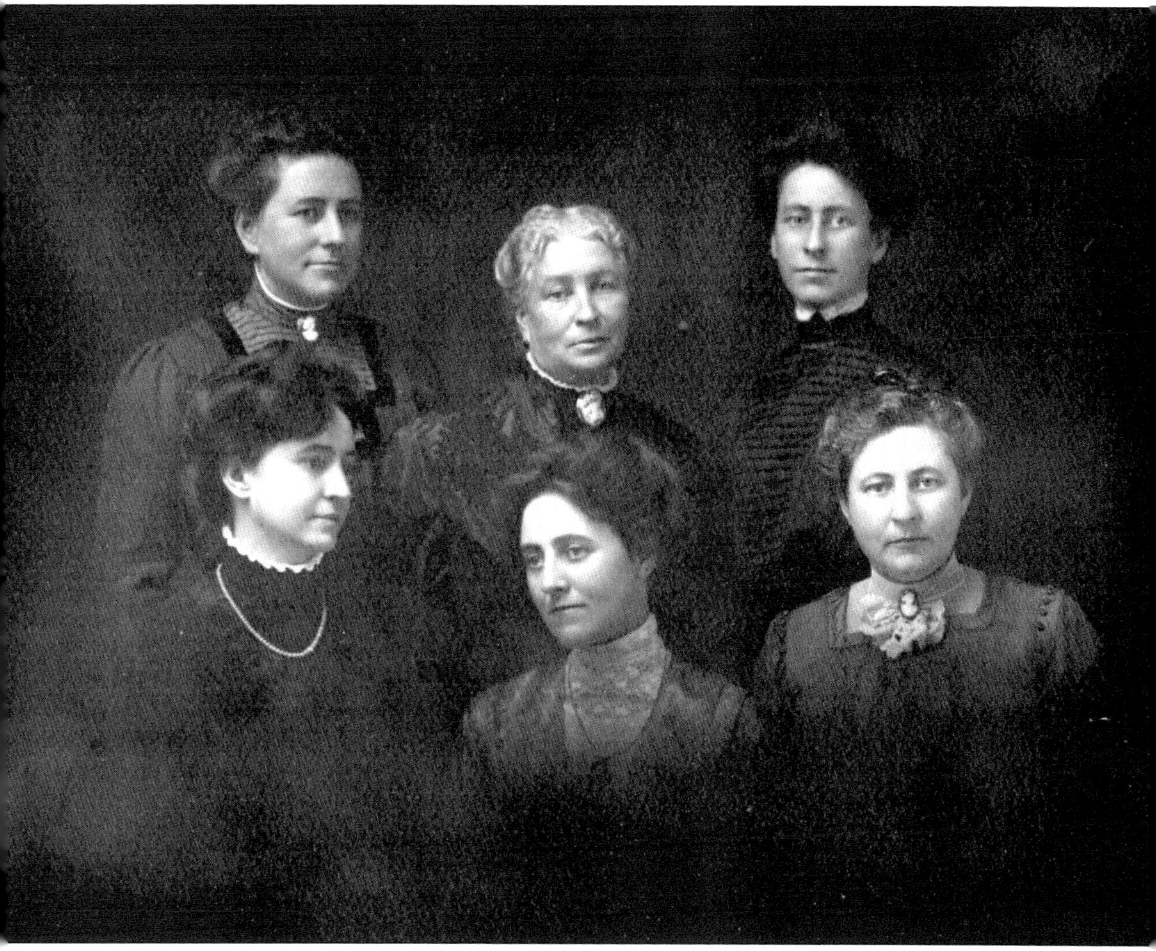

Once Thomas Kenny married, he changed his career to one more suitable for family life. He opened a grocery store on the corner of First and Sibben Streets, which at that time was a thriving business district, and the couple began raising their children. They had six girls who lived and two boys who died young. In 1879, Thomas returned to the lumber industry, this time in management as partner to Patrick Noud, sorting logs under contract to the Manistee Boom Company. This formal portrait of Thomas Kenny's well-dressed wife and daughters, made in the prestigious Hanselmann Studios of Manistee, reflects the elegant lifestyle his family enjoyed as a result of his slow, steady rise from an orphaned immigrant to a community leader. Pictured here, from left to right, are the following: (first row) Clare, Cicile, and Kate; (second row) Mary, Ellen, and Agnes. All of the girls married into prominent local families except Agnes, who became a businesswoman in her own right. (Courtesy of Cindy Dempsey.)

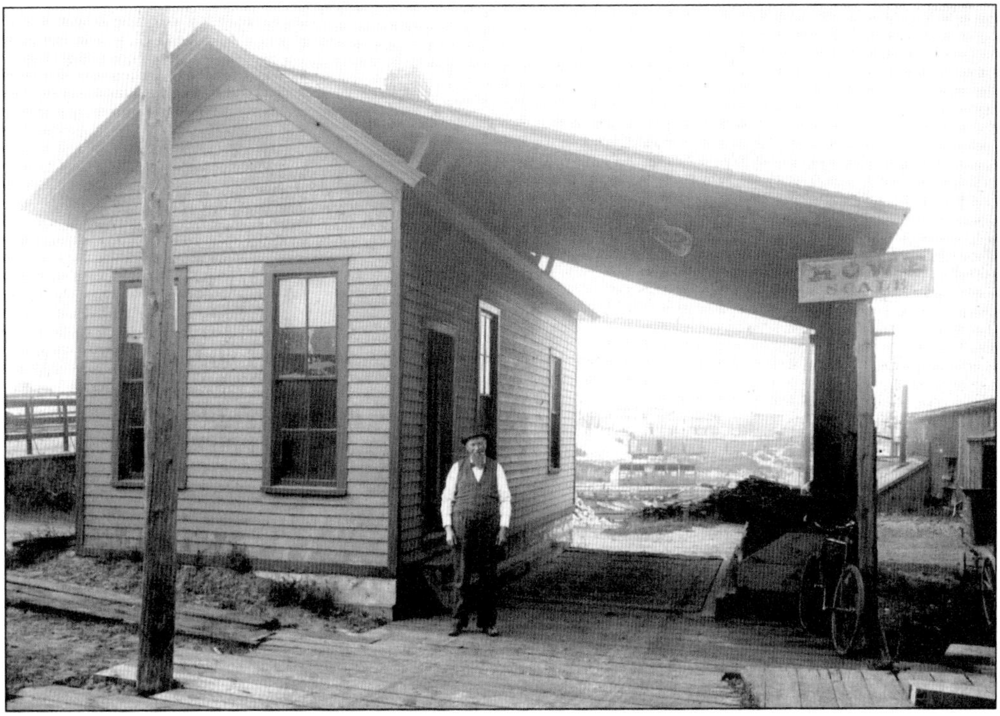

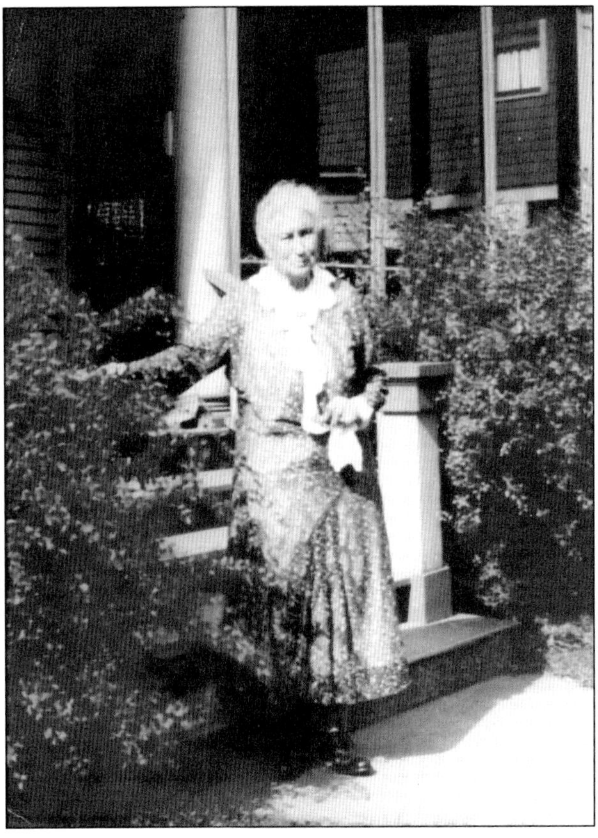

Perhaps with an eye toward the uncertainty of an economy based on a rapidly dwindling resource, Thomas Kenny moved away from lumber-related industries later in life. After three years as president of the newly established Manistee County Savings Bank, in 1894 he established his own coal company on Mason Street, where Manistee Lake empties into the river. In the above photograph, Kenny is pictured in front of his coal company office. The bicycle was probably his, as the office was near his home on Sibben Street. He died in 1910, before his new home on the corner of Bryant and Elm Streets had been completed. His wife Ellen, who moved there after his death, stands outside that home in the image to the left. The current resident claims that her spirit remains there, and he tends her grave every year. (Left, courtesy of Katie Kennicott.)

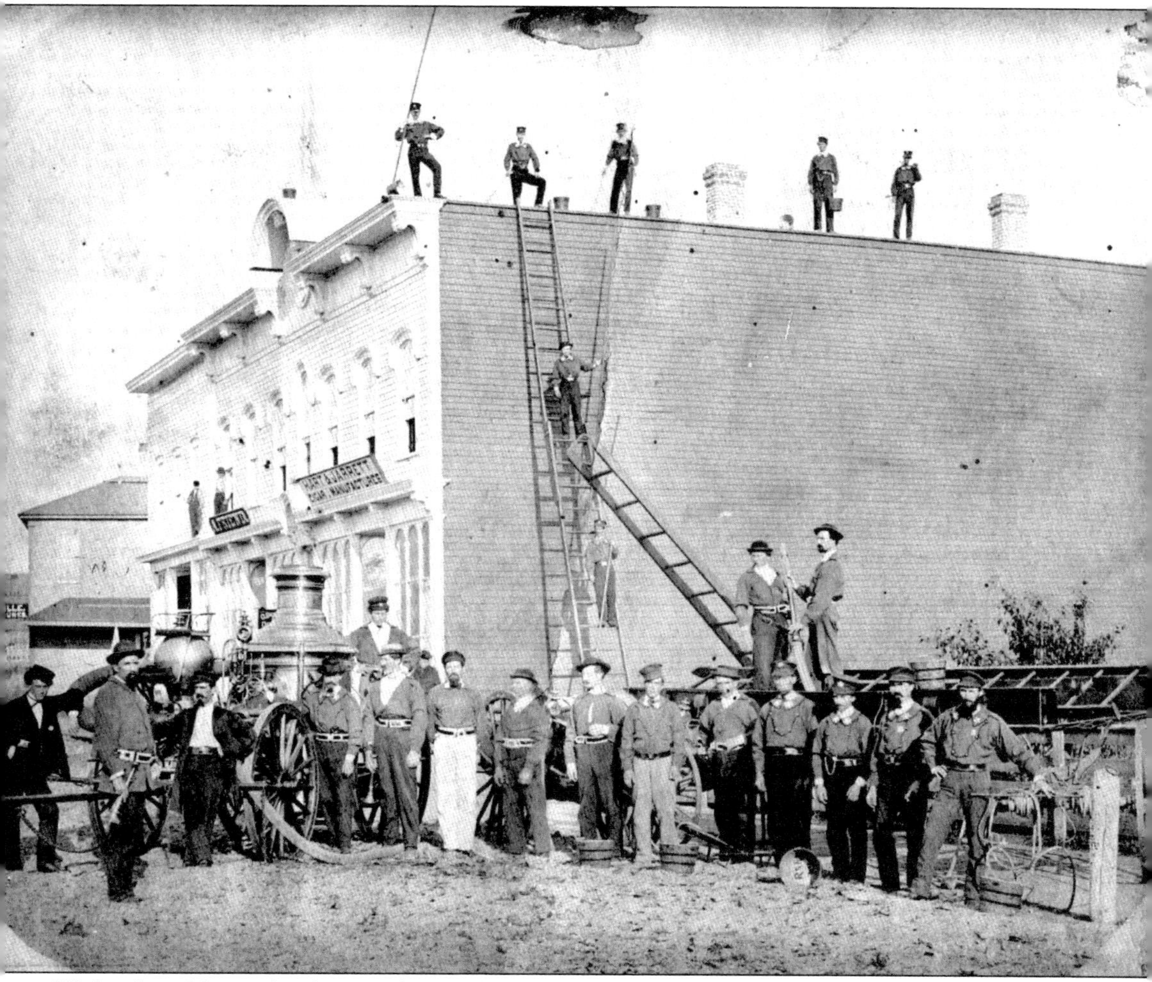

With piles of drying lumber, sawdust, and sparks from the constantly working mills, all inside a city built of wood, Manistee recognized early the necessity of a well-trained fire crew. This scene, recorded in 1869 or 1870 using the daguerreotype process, depicts a fire crew on River Street during an early training exercise. The man to the far left is identified as Tuxworth. Next to him is the crew boss with his bugle, through which he shouts orders, as with a bullhorn. The man in white trousers, standing at the outer corner of the building, is identified as Dan Hornkohl, and farthest to the right is Andrew Jack. The rest of the men in front are the water crew, who in firefighting situations must wait for the ladder crew—shown on the roof of the building and on the ladders—to set up. The roof ladder has a hook for attachment to buildings, hence the term "hook and ladder." (Courtesy of Timm Smith.)

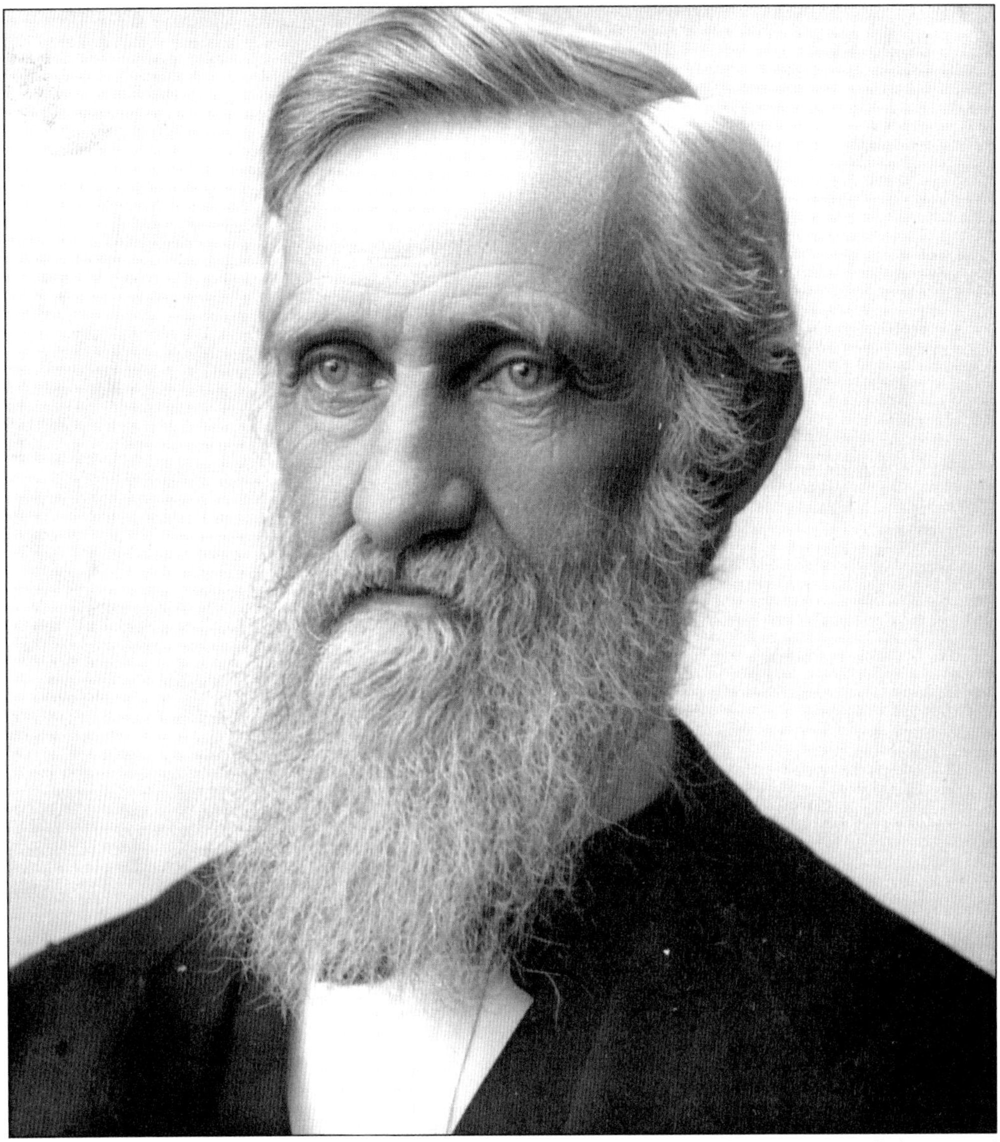

Early Manistee was a frontier town with no established rule of law or any of the social establishments that make for a settled community. If one person could be said to be responsible for bringing civilization to Manistee, that person would be lawyer Thomas Jefferson (T. J.) Ramsdell. Born on a farm near Plymouth, Michigan, in 1833 to a family of Scottish descent, T. J. Ramsdell worked as a schoolteacher before earning a law degree in New York State. He made his way to Manistee from Grand Haven along an American Indian trail during the winter of 1860, with nothing but a horse and cutter loaded with law books. Manistee residents, who had previously had no legal representation when negotiating complex contracts or when arrested for crimes, welcomed his arrival. After the 1871 fire destroyed most of the city, Ramsdell was largely responsible for rebuilding it and shaping it into the grand city it became. His legal ability led to his holding office as secretary or treasurer in most municipal corporations in Manistee.

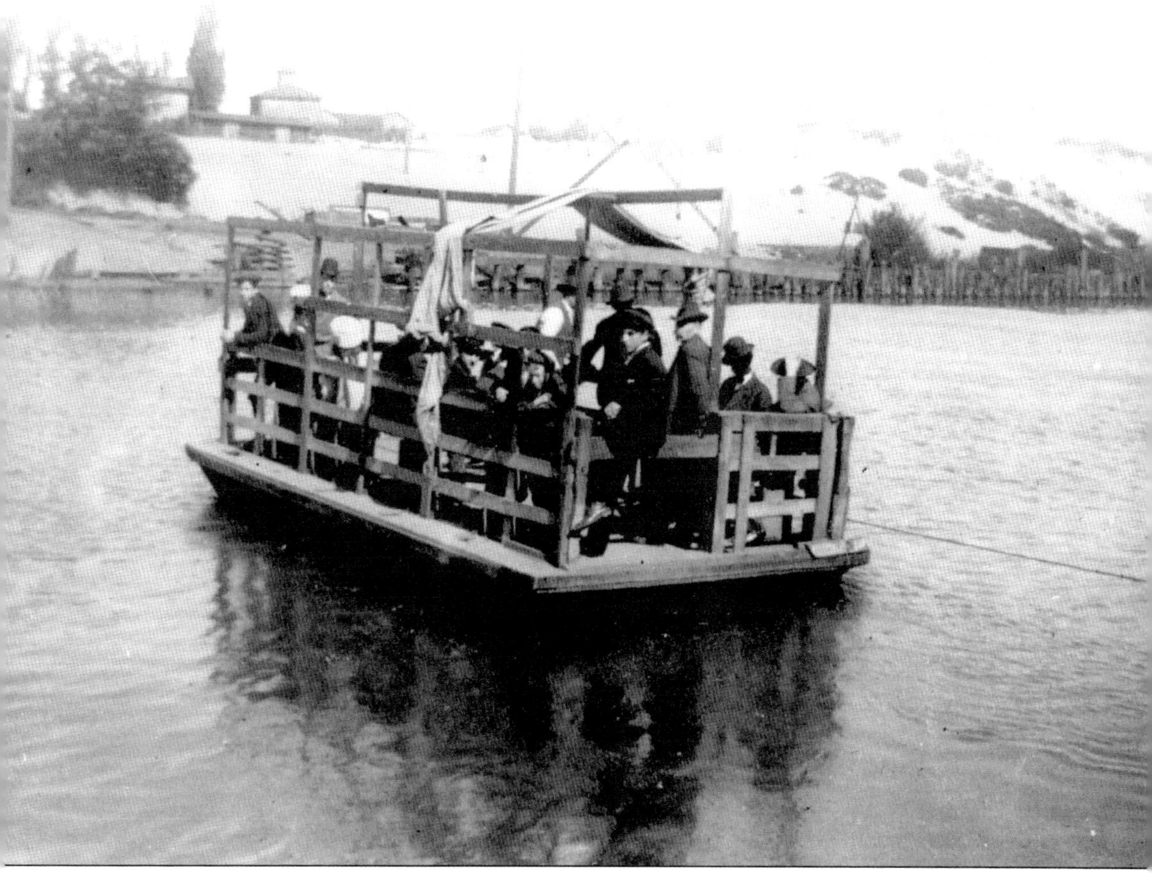

By 1866, the population of Manistee had exceeded 2,000, with the Manistee River dividing the city into communities on the north and south. Crossing the river involved walking over logjams, hiring a dugout canoe, or waiting until winter when roads would be marked out across the frozen water. All of these methods made commerce and communication across the river difficult at best. At some point, ferry service was established between Canfield's Mill and Manistee Village on the north side. That ferry probably resembled this rope-pull scow, which was used to carry passengers across the Manistee River while the Maple Street bridge was being built in 1906. With the organization of a county government in 1855, a franchise was granted to regulate the operation of the ferry.

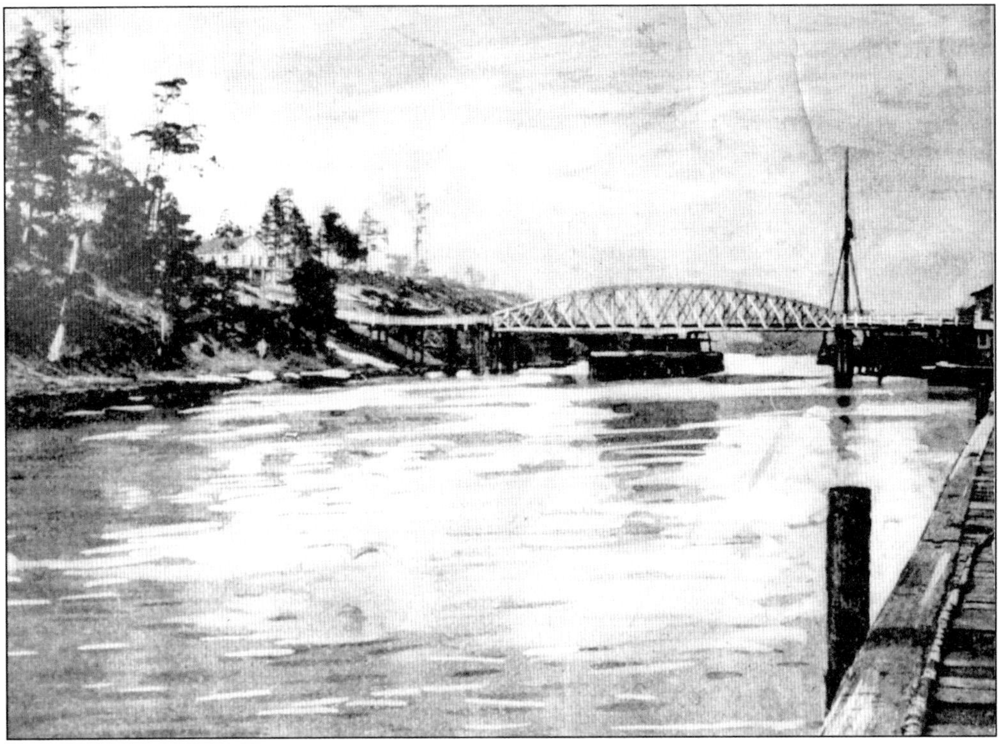

A bridge across the river was clearly required. By now, schooner traffic had become so extensive that the span would have to open to accommodate it. Local businessmen formed the Manistee Bridge Company, which acquired a franchise and raised sufficient funds to build the wooden turn bridge shown above. In 1866, the two communities at Manistee were united. Tension ensued, however, when the Manistee Bridge Company charged tolls for passage—5¢ per person and 10¢ per team, at a time when most laborers averaged 8¢ an hour. Of all the losses incurred in the 1871 fire, Manistee citizens probably regretted the burning of that toll bridge the least. The new swing bridge, pictured below, constructed after the fire, was toll-free.

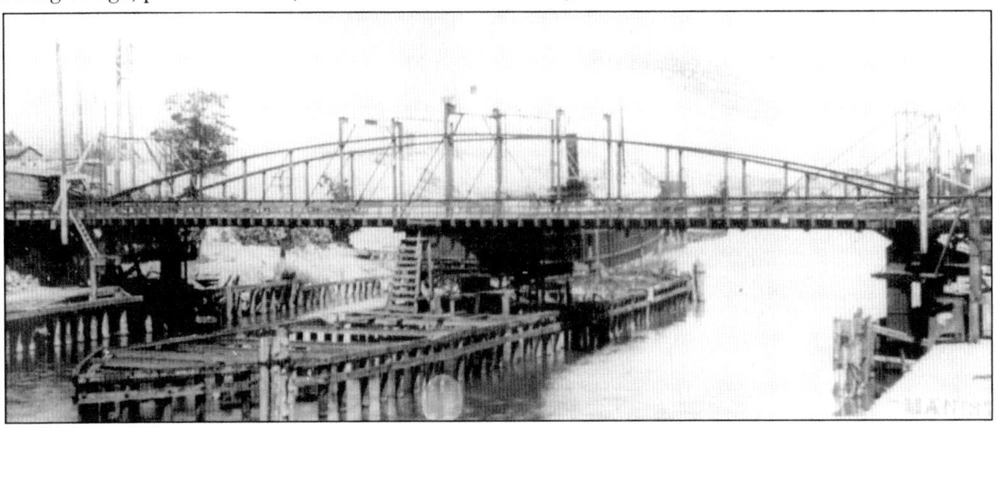

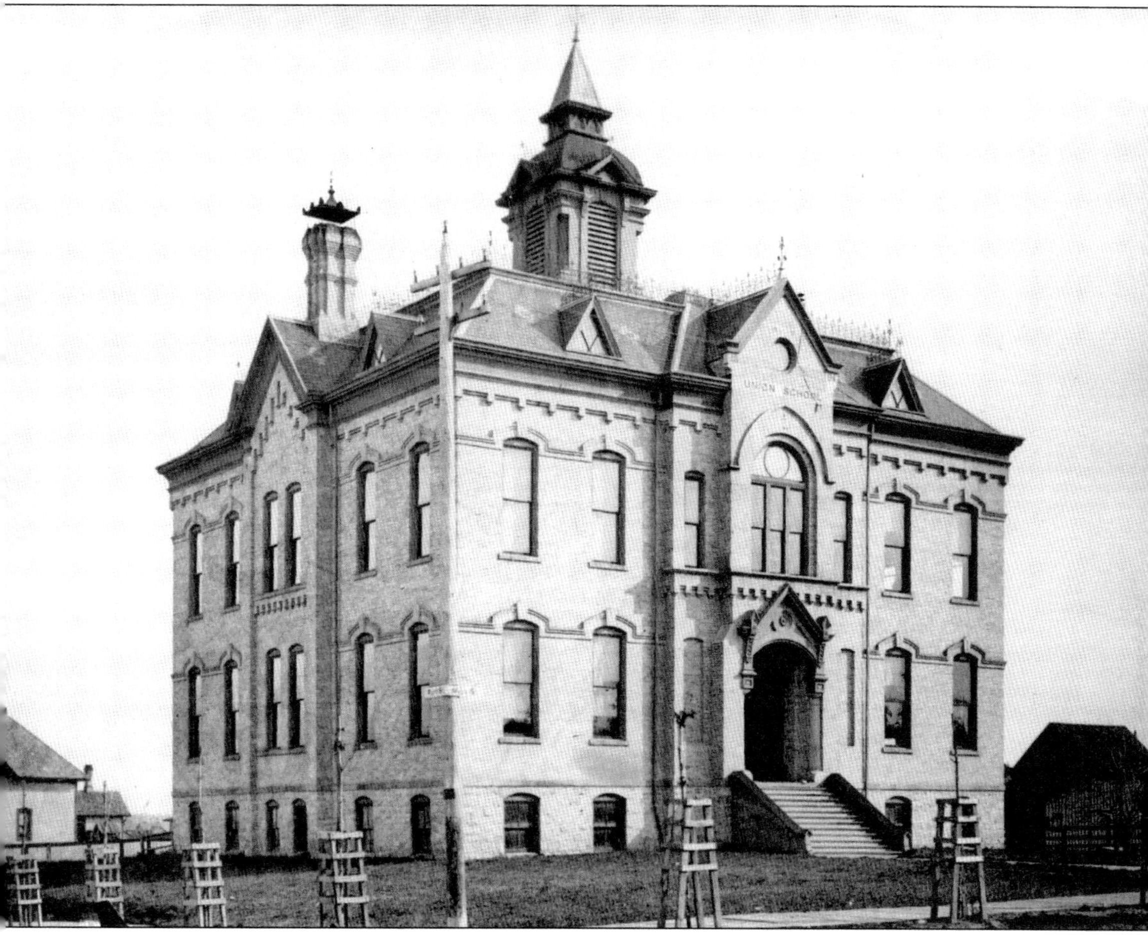

Among the many beautiful public buildings Ramsdell contracted for was the Union School, the first large public school in Manistee. Previous school arrangements had been somewhat makeshift. In 1852, John Canfield had opened a private school near his mill for the children of his employees, and other Manistee children had likely also attended. The first public school in the region was established two years later on the northwest corner of Spruce and First Streets, which sufficed for the next 13 years, until it became inadequate for the growing population. Ramsdell therefore contracted for a four-room school on the southwest corner of First and Oak Streets. This original school was expanded in 1870, and in 1874, high school courses were offered for the first time. The program called for a Latin curriculum and emphasized classical courses. In 1879, two students, Kate Bullis and Kittie Edington, had completed enough courses to graduate. Within four years, the school's curriculum was approved by the University of Michigan, and local students started enrolling at the university.

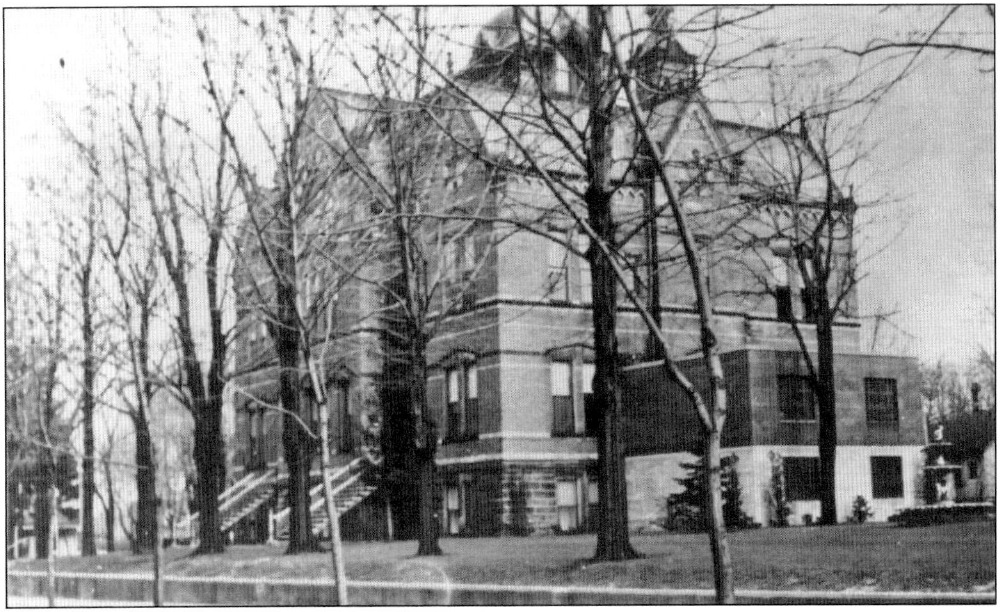

Two other public buildings the growing city required were the courthouse (above) and the lifesaving station (below). Built in 1877 on the corner of Fourth and Maple Streets, the courthouse included the sheriff and the jail on the first floor, public offices on the second, and the courtroom on the third. Increasing incidence of shipwrecks off the coast due to additional shipping traffic necessitated the establishment of a lifesaving service. Constructed in 1879 on the north side of the river, the station was tended by a resident keeper. The main floor stored lifeboats and equipment, with a sliding door at the rear so that boats could be quickly launched in an emergency. Living quarters were on the second floor, and the attic provided storage.

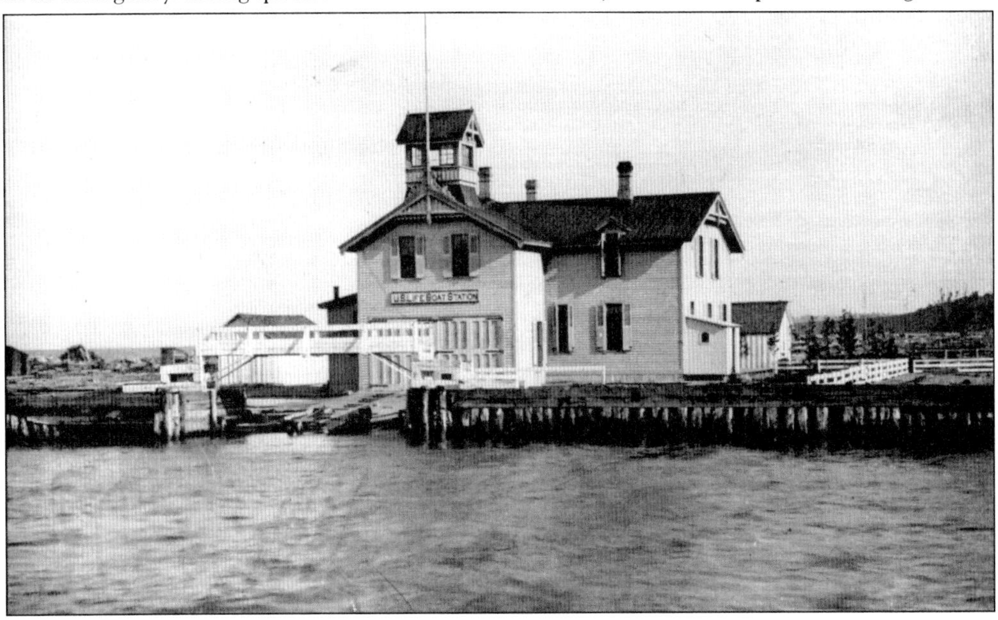

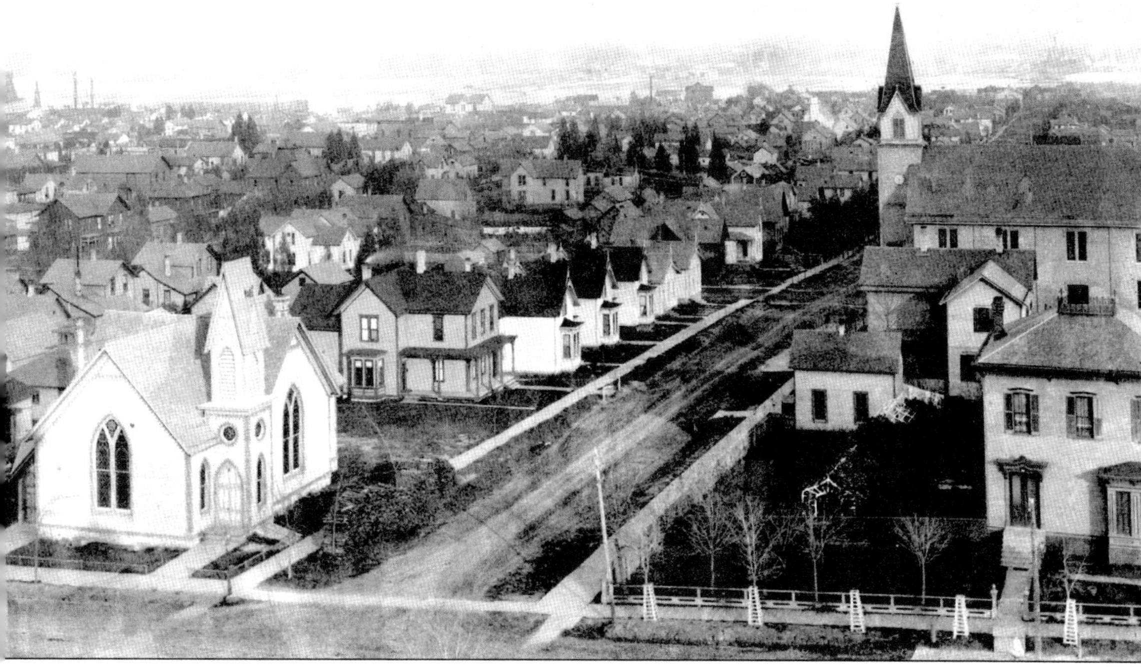

A sure sign that Manistee was developing from a makeshift frontier encampment to an established community was when its citizens began building permanent churches. Before the 1860s, congregations met in whatever rough buildings were available. Religion itself was not new; Jesuits had established Catholic missions in northern Michigan in the 1600s, and subsequent chapels had been built to convert Native Americans. This view, looking northeast along Maple Street from the courthouse, shows two of Manistee's earliest churches. In the left foreground, on the corner of Third and Maple Streets, is the Maple Street Baptist Church. Its first pastor, Rev. J. Snashall, organized its construction, which was completed in 1882. By 1890, the church's membership was about 75. It also housed a Sunday school, a Baptist Young People's Union, and a Ladies Aid Society. To its north, on the right, is the much older St. Mary's Catholic Church. Established in 1863, it primarily served Manistee's earliest Catholic settlers: the French Canadian loggers and their families.

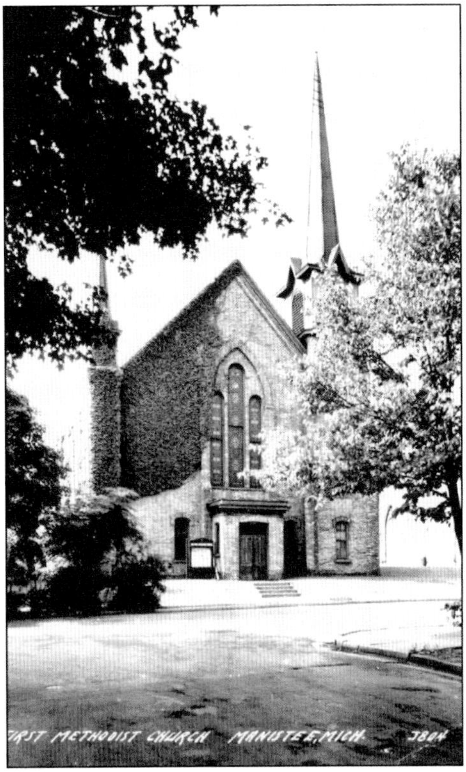

The first church built in Manistee was the Methodist Episcopal Church, seen at left. Organized by Rev. N. M. Steele in 1860, it had an initial congregation of only five members. The building was constructed in 1862 under Rev. H. H. Bement, on a First Street lot given to the society by John Canfield. The Sunday school was organized shortly thereafter. The Trinity Lutheran Church and School (below) was organized in 1870 by a group of German immigrants. Manistee's ethnic churches typically established parochial schools that went up to the eighth grade. Classes in Trinity School were conducted in German. By the 1890s, enrollment had reached a peak of 292 students. Now located on Fourth and Oak Streets, the school still carries out its mission, along with the church, of faith-based education. (Courtesy of Jon Rose.)

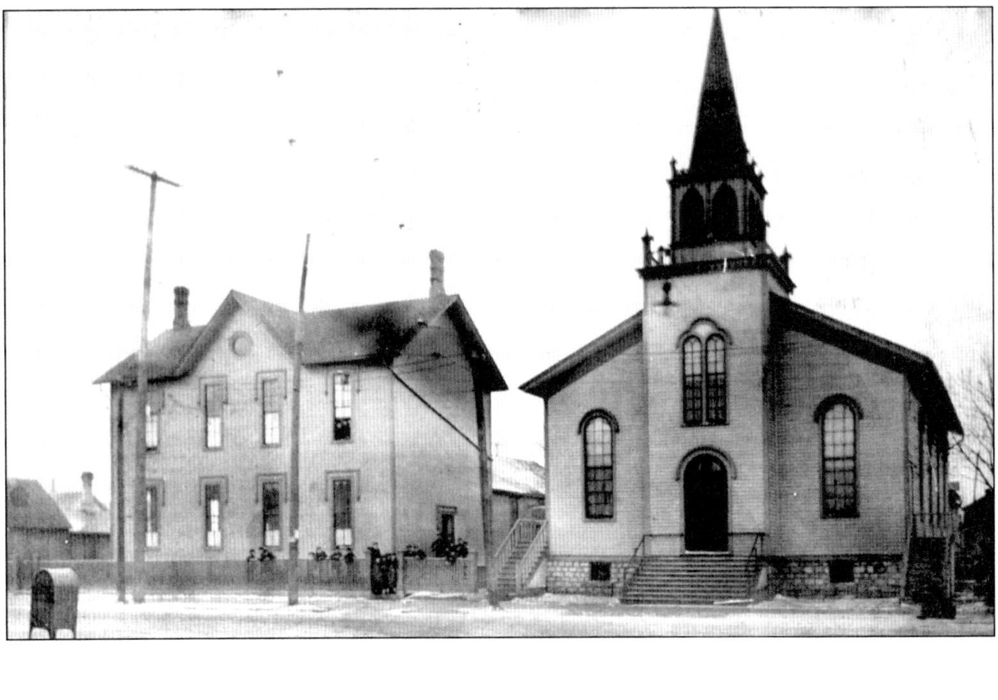

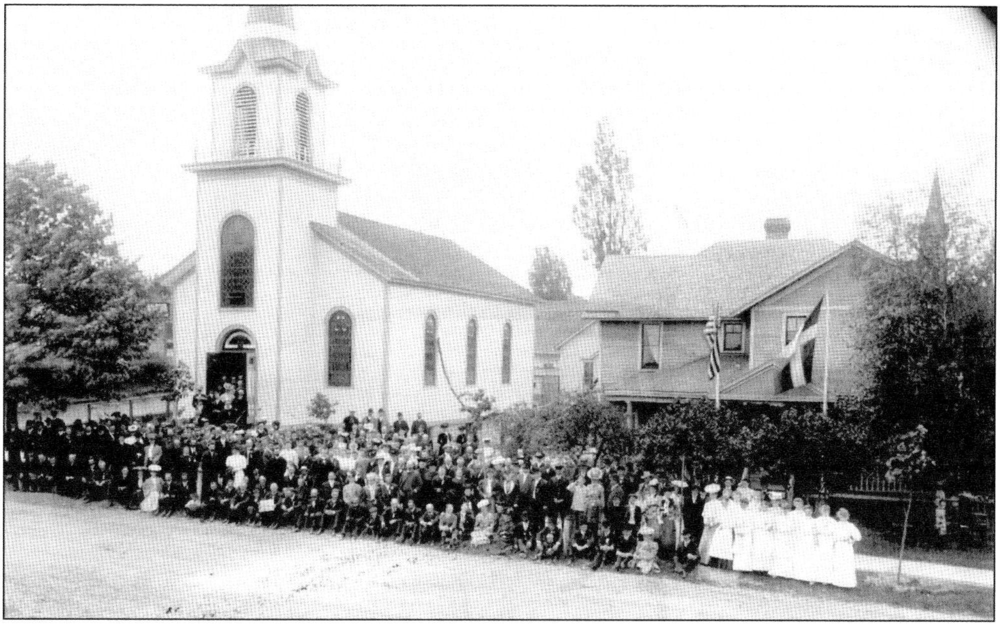

The Danish Evangelical Lutheran Church (above), now called Our Saviour's, is the oldest Danish Lutheran church in America. Funded by Louis Sands, among others, construction began in May 1868, and the first worship service was held the next year. Pictured below, from left to right, are the following original members of the 1869 congregation: (first row) Johan Jensen, Niels Nielsen, Hans Nielsen, and Rasmus Clausen; (second row) Mrs. Johan Jensen, Mrs. Niels Nielsen, Mrs. Jorgen Simonsen, Mrs. Hans Nielsen, Ole Hansen, and Mrs. Rasmus Clausen; (third row) Mr. and Mrs. Christ Larsen, Mads Jorensen, and Jens Nielsen. (Courtesy of Our Saviour's Historical Museum.)

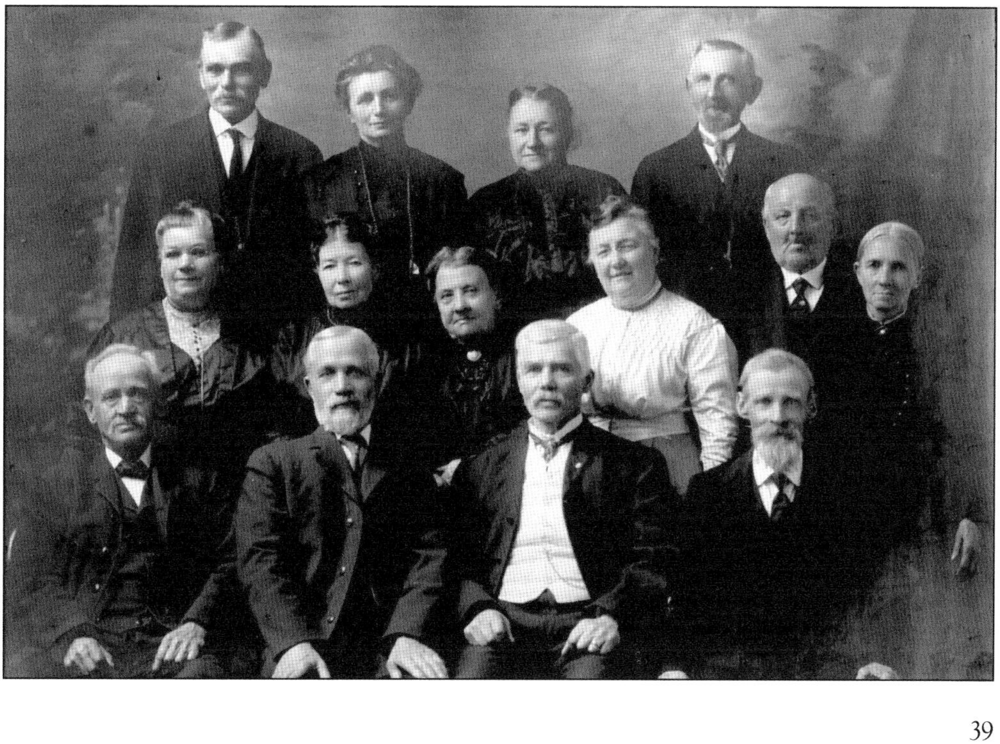

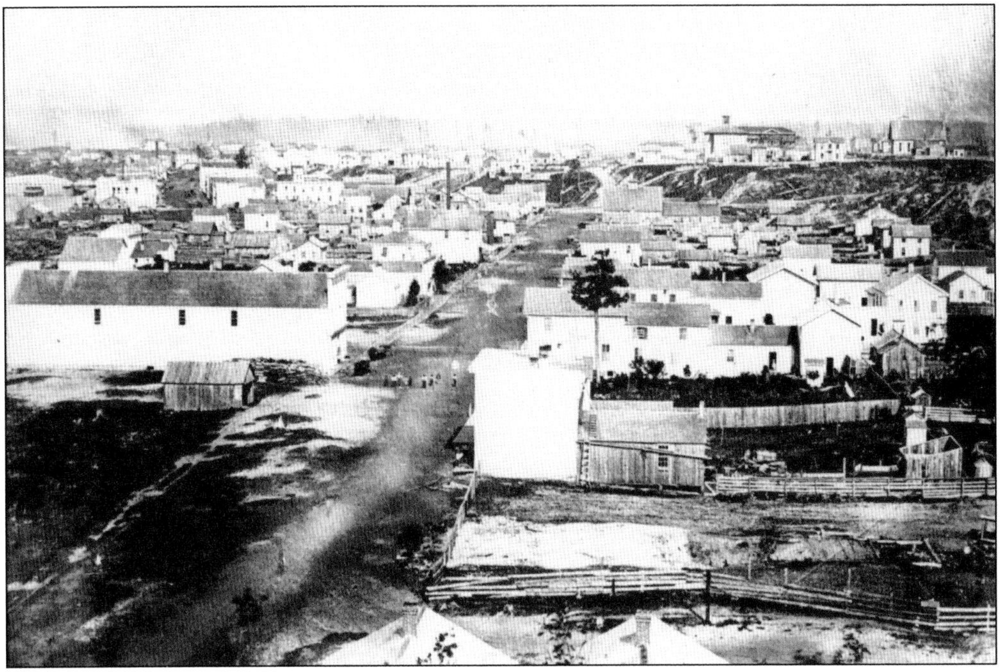

These two views, looking east over Manistee in 1868 (above) and in 1888 (below), taken by Edwin Russell, dramatize the city's phenomenal growth. In 1869, the busy city was still a rough frontier town. The 1888 scene of Manistee at the peak of production shows a city still under construction, with dirt roads and rough dwellings but most major buildings in place. The long unpaved road is First Street. The building in the lower left corner is the waterworks. Central School, with its onion dome, appears above and to the right. The church steeple just to the left of the school is the Methodist Trinity Church; to the other side of the school are, from left to right, the original Congregational Church and the courthouse. The timber visible in the earlier horizon has now been cut.

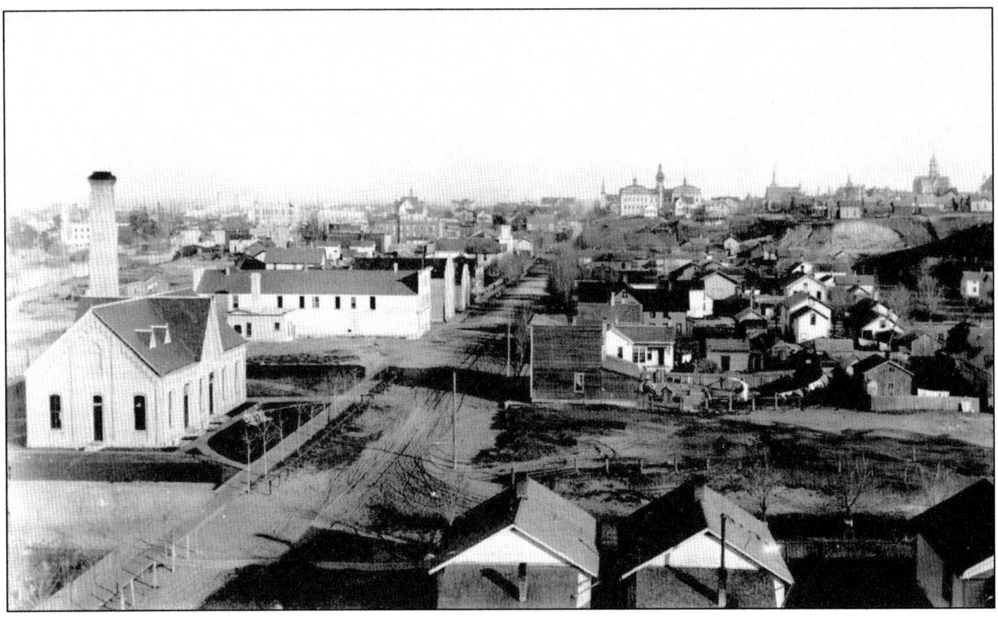

Three

LUMBER AND SALT

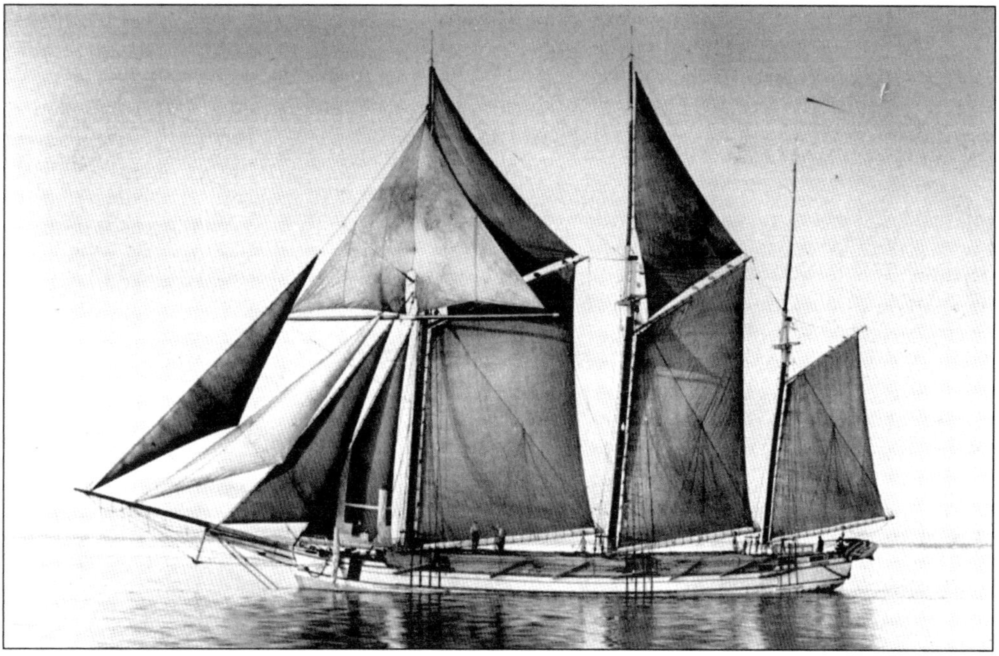

By 1880, Michigan was producing more board feet of lumber than any other state. Schooners like the three-masted *J. B. Newland*, shown here, would transport this lumber, along with other goods, from Manistee across Lake Michigan to Chicago or Milwaukee, where it would be shipped by train to newly established communities throughout the Great Plains. Schooners would typically load their holds to capacity and then add more lumber on deck until it seemed impossible for sailors to work around the cargo. Although the schooners seemed overloaded, the lumber cargo was relatively light; if the schooner filled with water, the lumber provided sufficient buoyancy to keep it afloat. Hundreds of these schooners arrived in Chicago daily until the 1890s, when steamships began to dominate the waterways. The *J. B. Newland* continued its run, however, until 1910, when it was wrecked on the North Manitou Shoal during a fog. The wreck makes a popular diving destination today. (Courtesy of the Portage Point Inn.)

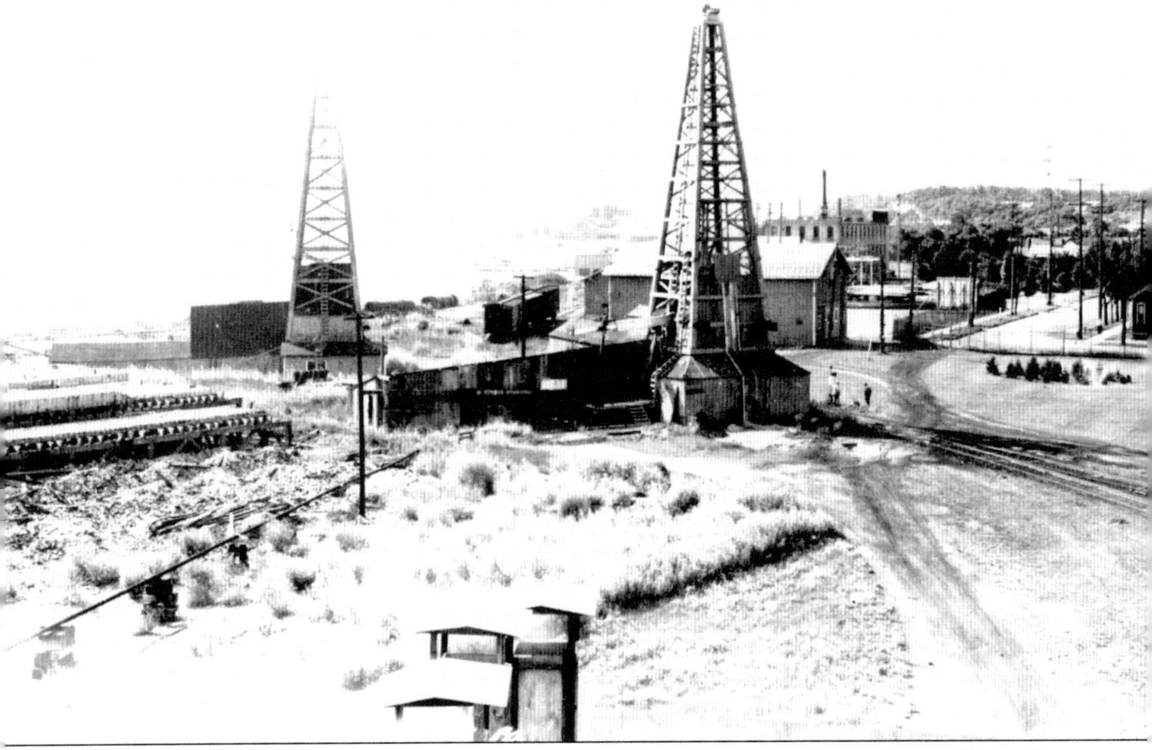

In February 1879, when the lumber industry was nearing its peak, another industry began that boosted the Manistee economy into another boom cycle. Locals knew that salt springs were to be found on the rivers and some inland lakes. Charles Reitz attempted to interest local businessmen in organizing a company to pursue exploratory drilling for salt. Unsuccessful at first, Reitz next contracted with a Chicago firm. This time he succeeded; the first salt vein was reached on February 7, 1881. Unlike lumber, this new resource was nearly inexhaustible. Local lumber companies hastily retooled parts of their mills into salt production plants because it gave them a profitable outlet for all their waste wood and sawdust in evaporating the brine to salt. The salt came from a total of 28 wells, like those pictured here. By 1898, Manistee was producing over 400 million pounds of salt per year. (Courtesy of Jon Rose.)

Edward Buckley (right) and William Douglas (below) were among the most successful in expanding their mill to a lumber and salt operation. Born in England in 1842, Edward Buckley moved to Toronto with his family when he was four. After fighting in the Civil War, he came to Manistee in 1867 and eventually entered into partnership with lumberman Charles Ruggles. William Douglas, another Canadian, was also logging under Ruggles, but his contract proved unprofitable. In 1880, Buckley and Douglas formed a partnership with Ruggles's support. Buckley dealt with all the finances and lumber manufacture, while Douglas was responsible for supervising woods operations, including logging, lumber camps, railroads, and construction. The partnership was so successful that Buckley and Douglas soon became one of the largest concerns in Manistee. (Courtesy of the Manistee Historical Museum.)

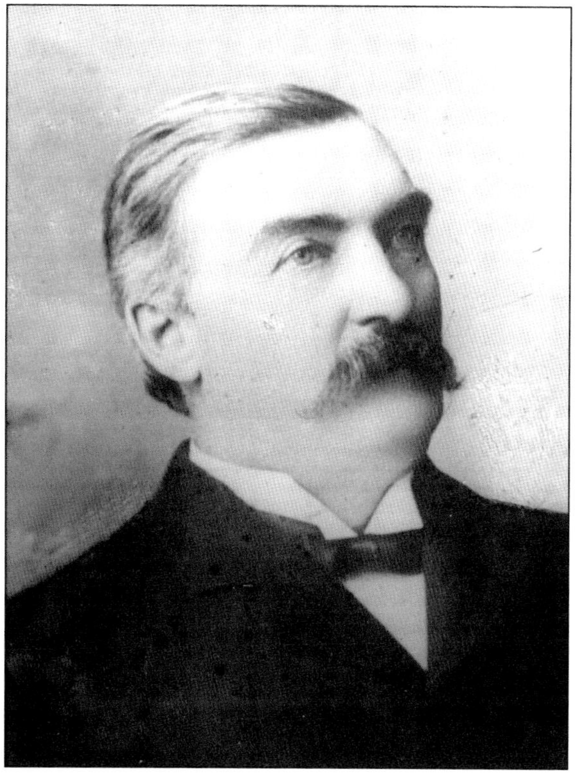

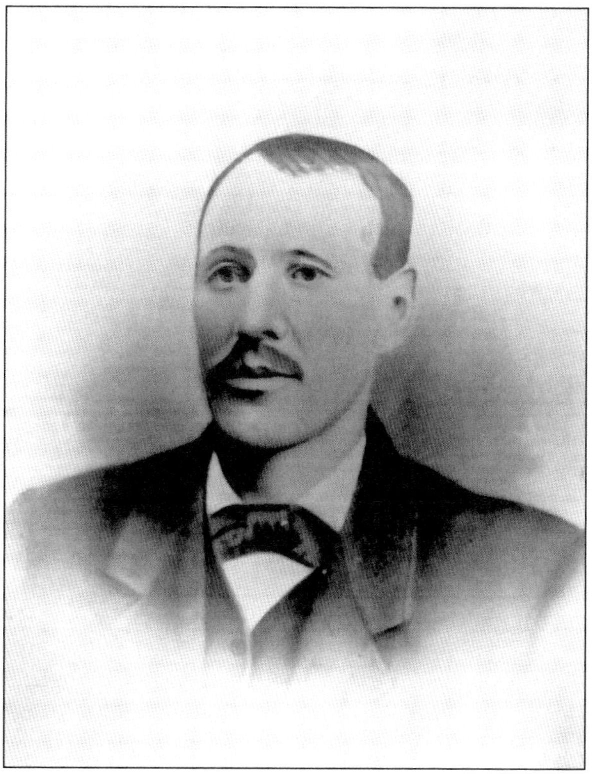

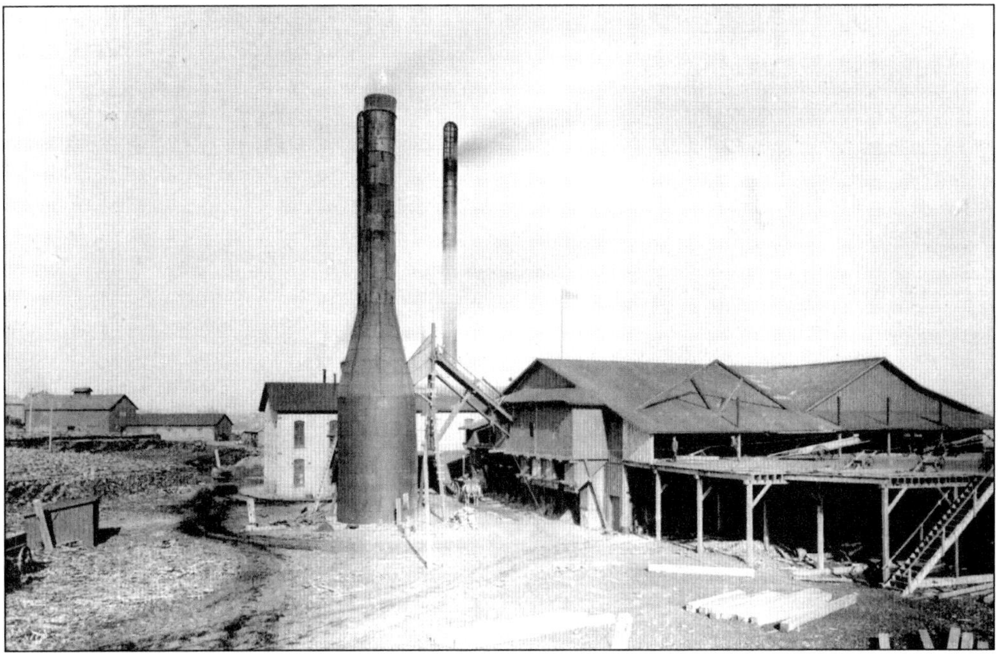

In 1886, Buckley and Douglas purchased the timber interests and mill property on Manistee Lake from Ruddick Nuttall and Company. The original mill, shown above, formed the nucleus of their rapidly expanding operations. Costs for improvement and modernization amounted to over $100,000. In 1896, five salt wells were sunk, and a salt block with a capacity of 2,500 barrels a day was built, covering five acres. By 1905, Buckley and Douglas had the largest salt block in the world and produced half of Manistee's total salt output. Below, workers bring loads of salt from the grainers, which were long, shallow vats with four or five steam pipes at the bottom placed far enough apart for the workers to shovel salt from between them, in order to prepare the product for shipping. (Courtesy of Jon Rose.)

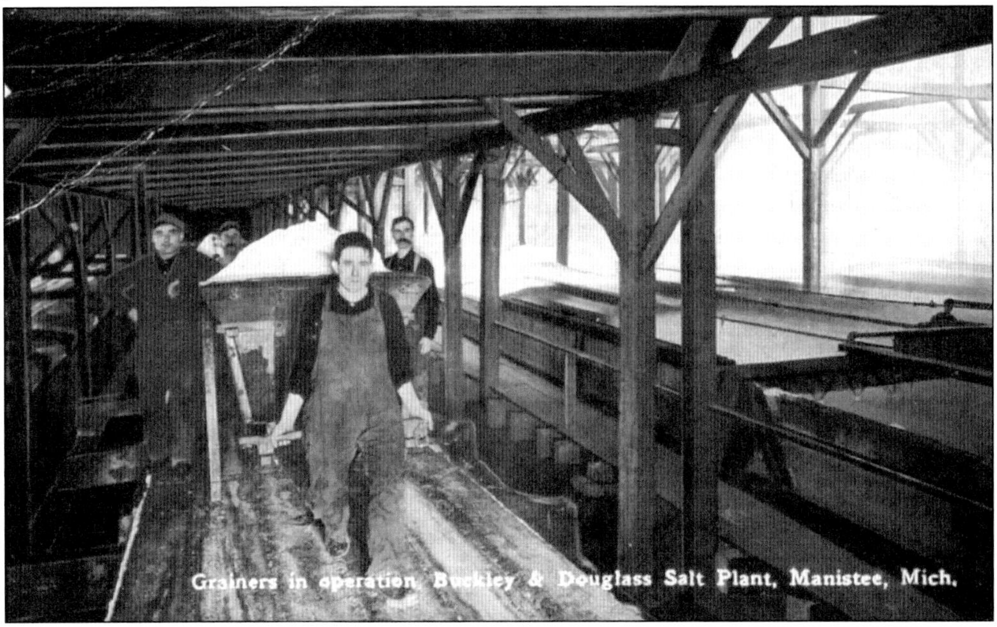

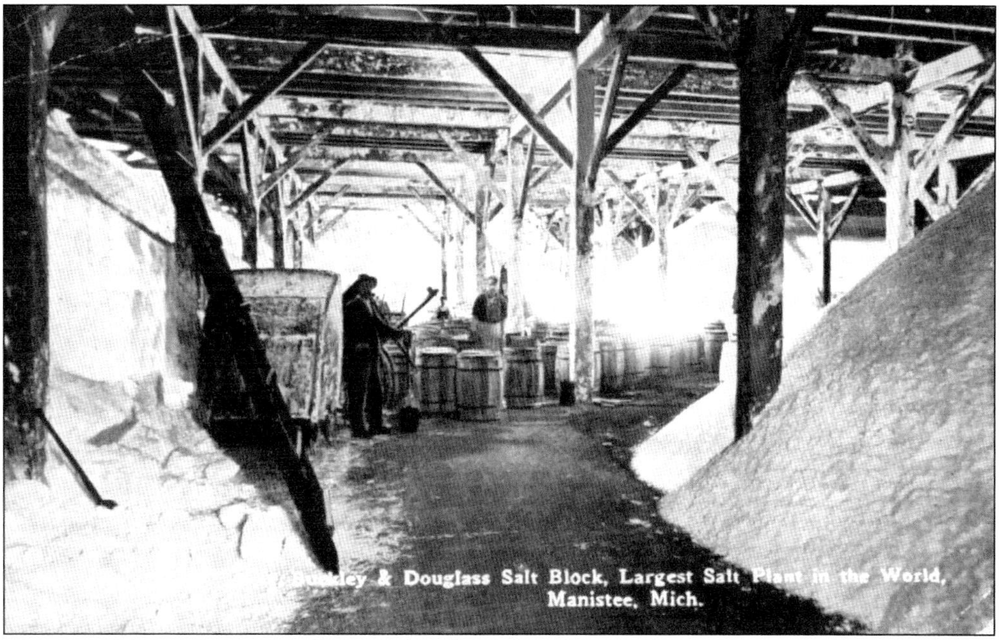

These Buckley and Douglas plant workers held the job of loading salt into barrels. This image was reproduced in a postcard format, indicating that by the early 1900s touring industrial sites had become a popular tourist pastime. (Courtesy of Jon Rose.)

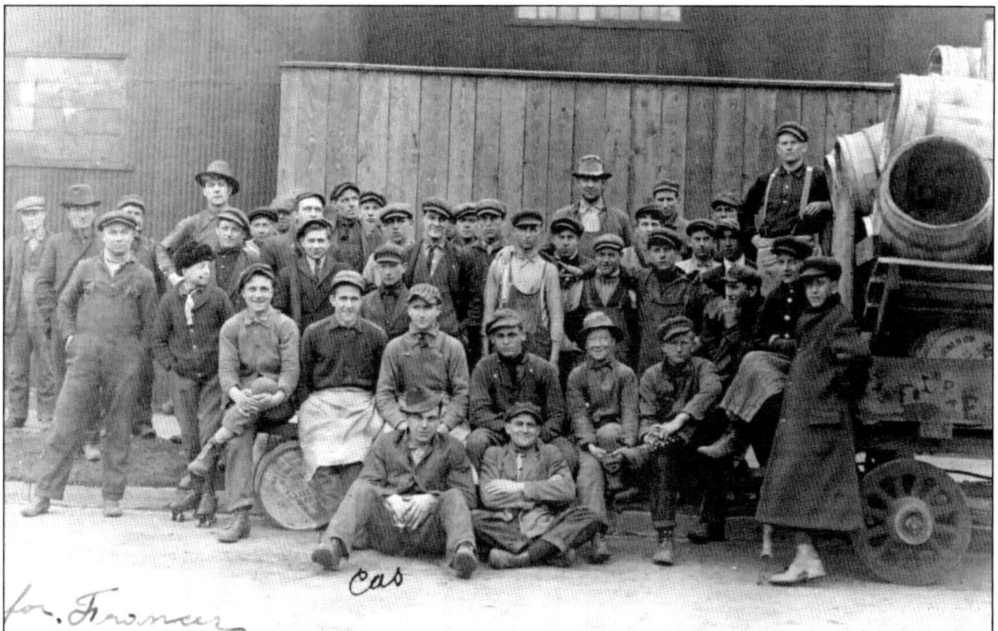

Buckley and Douglas were able to use excess wood for plant operations such as making barrels for product shipment. This photograph was taken in the early 20th century. Pictured on the left in the first row is Casimier "Cas" Chycinski. The other men are unidentified. (Courtesy of Clarence Nowak.)

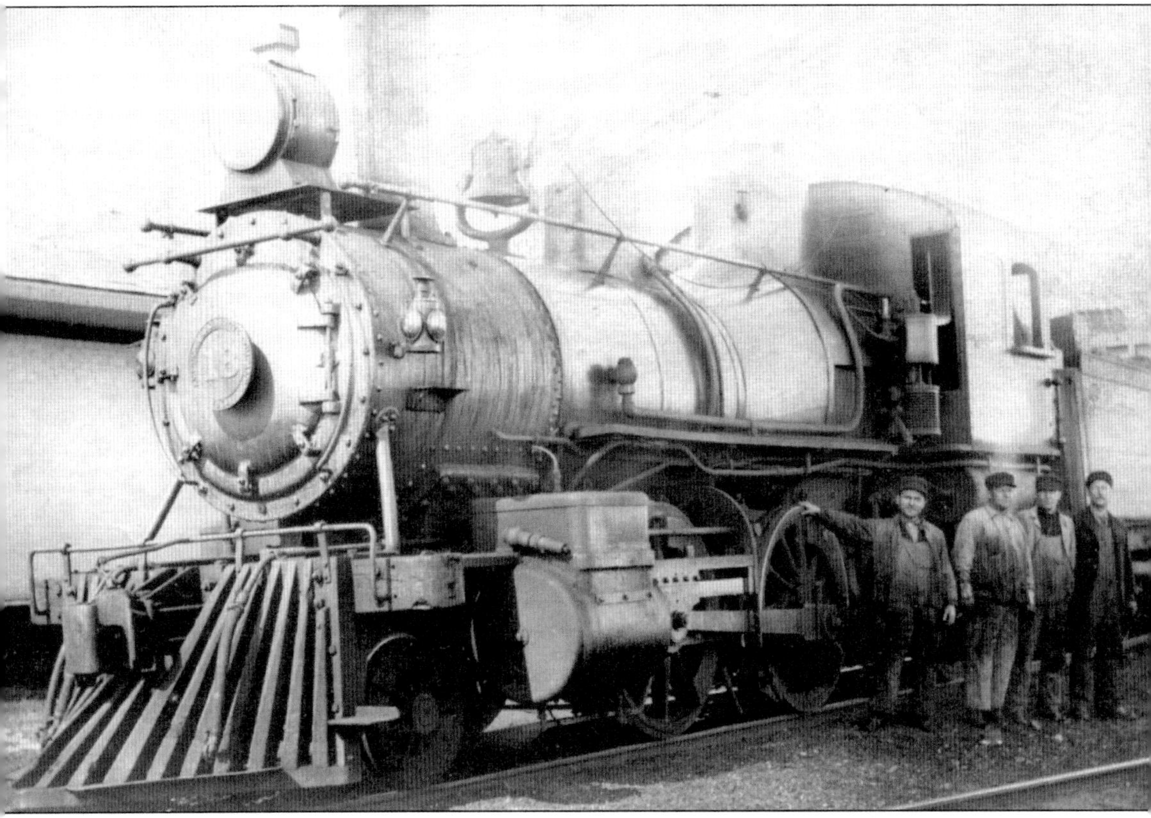

In 1881, Buckley and Douglas built a narrow-gauge railroad north from the Manistee River to Marilla and Maple Grove Townships to facilitate logging operations. Six years later, construction began on a standard-gauge track for the Manistee and Northeastern Railroad. One of the first standard-gauge railroads in Manistee, it was also one of the first to carry passengers along with freight. Locals celebrated the arrival of passenger service as a sign of civilization. Before 1881, when the Pere Marquette line began the first passenger service to Manistee, its residents had had no contact with the outside world except via steamer, and even that was restricted in wintertime. The Manistee and Northeastern also served the outlying towns, carrying fruit and mail as well as lumber and salt. It also came equipped with its own telegraph line. First employed as a fireman on the old steam engines, Stanley A. Nowak, pictured here on the left, eventually worked as an engineer on the diesel engines. This photograph was taken sometime in the early 1900s. (Courtesy of Clarence Nowak.)

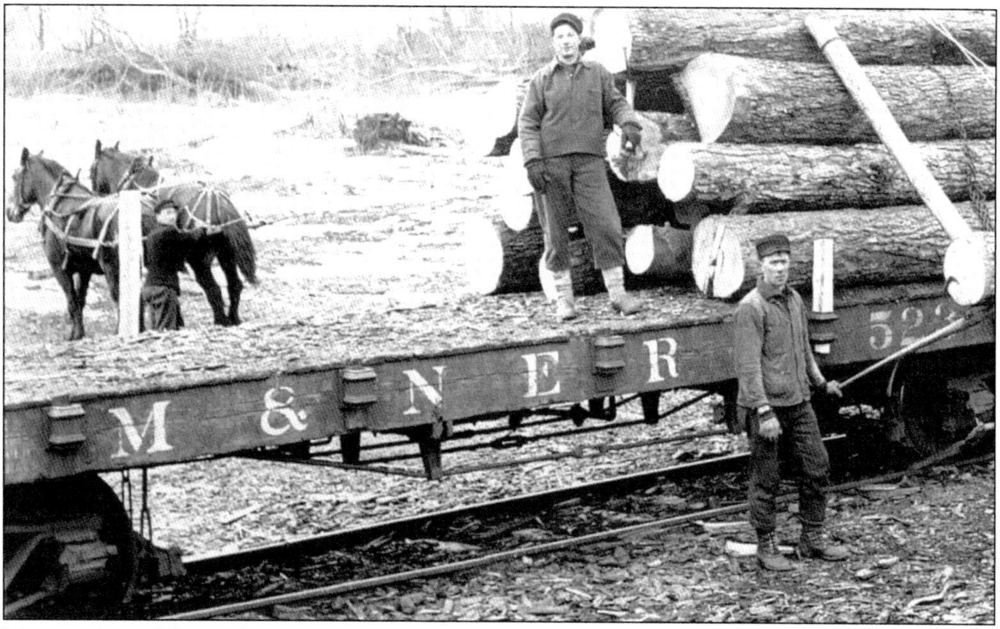

Manistee's wealthiest plant owners came to control all operations of their production—including transportation. With the aid of the Manistee and Northeastern Railroad, the Buckley and Douglas plant continued its logging operations well into the 20th century and extended them far beyond the county line. Above, Albert Meister stands alongside a railroad car. The real-photo postcard is dated 1913 and postmarked Harlan, Michigan. Most owners of private railroad lines also owned or affiliated with a steamer fleet, running ships such as the SS *Manistee*, below. Plant owners found shipping salt by boat to be more economical because local railroads at the time were controlled by the salt industry of Saginaw, which maintained exorbitant rates on rail freight of salt to and from Manistee. (Above, courtesy of Carol Schimke; below, courtesy of Jon Rose.)

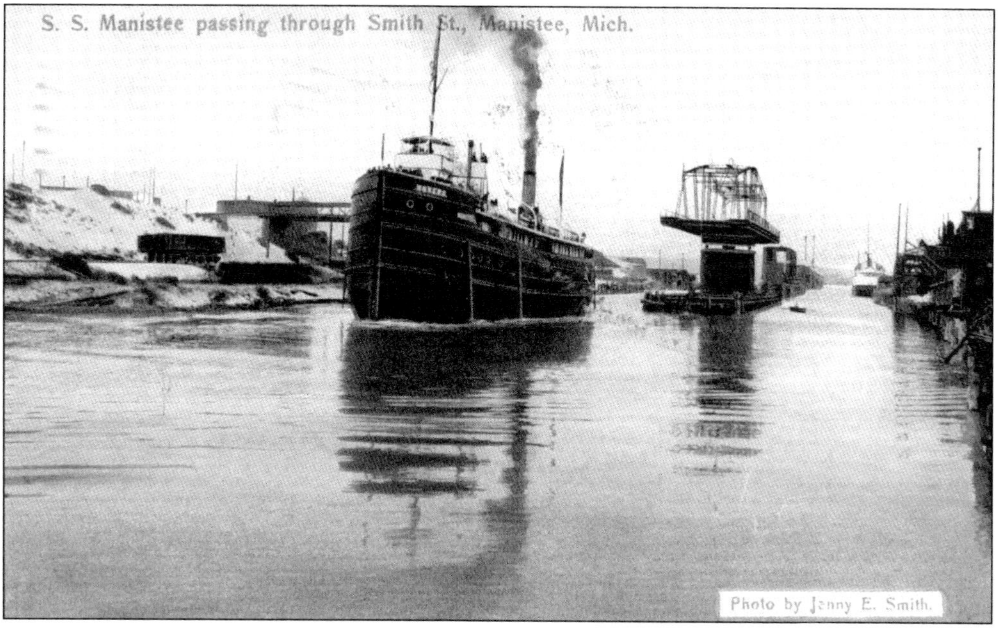

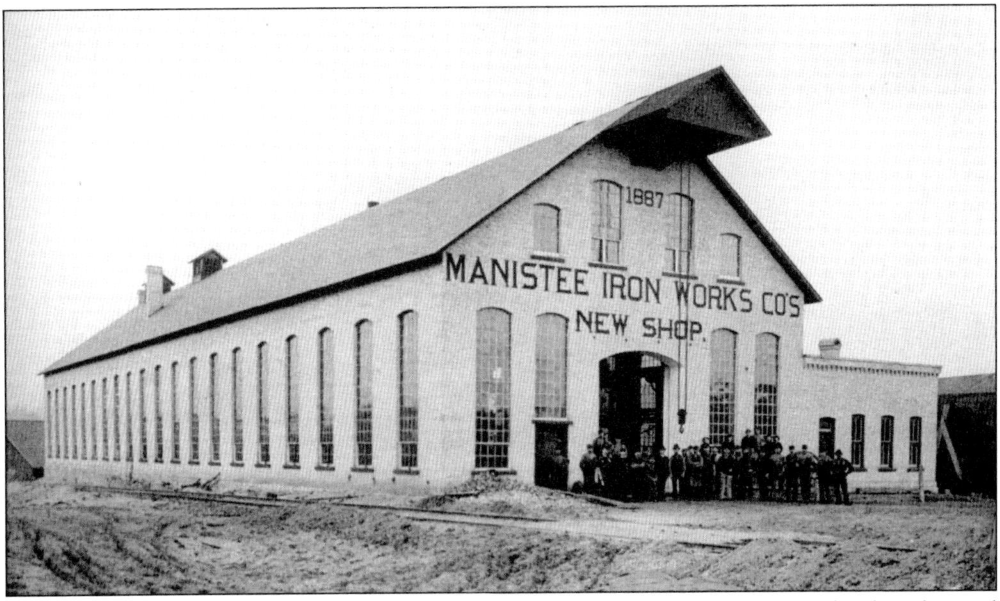

When John Bowie opened the Manistee Iron Works in 1871, he had planned a foundry and machine shop. By 1886, however, the salt industry was creating a demand for heavy processing machinery. The firm consequently began manufacturing pumps, vacuum pans, and salt production equipment. Also manufactured were railroad cars, engine cylinders, feed machines, and other industrial items. The plant (shown above) expanded and moved in 1897 to a new location just north of the 1907-built plant that stands today on Jones and River Streets. When those industries waned in the 20th century, the Manistee Iron Works expanded into marine machinery. The works also made pumps for the British firm of Rees Roturbo. The erecting shop for that firm appears below. (Courtesy of Jon Rose.)

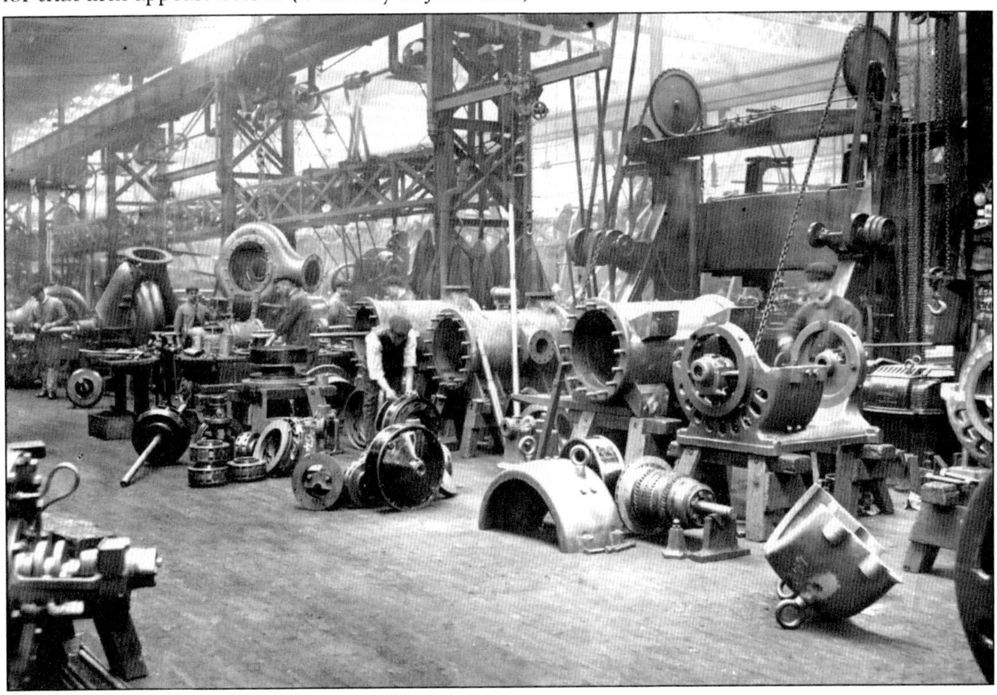

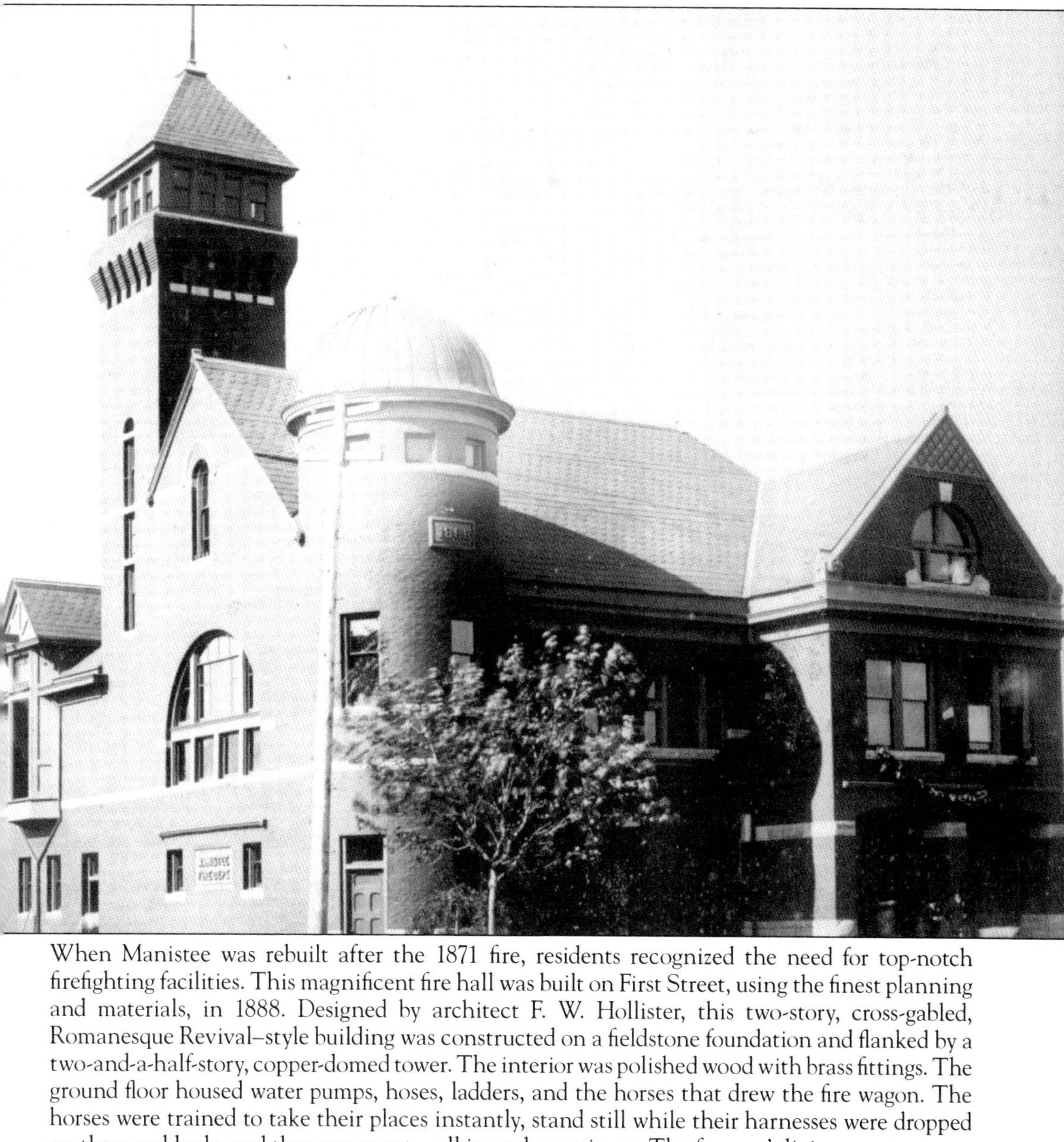

When Manistee was rebuilt after the 1871 fire, residents recognized the need for top-notch firefighting facilities. This magnificent fire hall was built on First Street, using the finest planning and materials, in 1888. Designed by architect F. W. Hollister, this two-story, cross-gabled, Romanesque Revival–style building was constructed on a fieldstone foundation and flanked by a two-and-a-half-story, copper-domed tower. The interior was polished wood with brass fittings. The ground floor housed water pumps, hoses, ladders, and the horses that drew the fire wagon. The horses were trained to take their places instantly, stand still while their harnesses were dropped on them suddenly, and then move out—all in under a minute. The firemen's living quarters were above. Early fire alarms were telegraphic, with a switch panel inside the station to indicate the district in which an alarm had been tripped. One of the oldest continuously operating fire halls in Michigan, the structure, still in use by professional firefighters, has not undergone any design alterations since it was built. (Courtesy of the Manistee Historical Museum.)

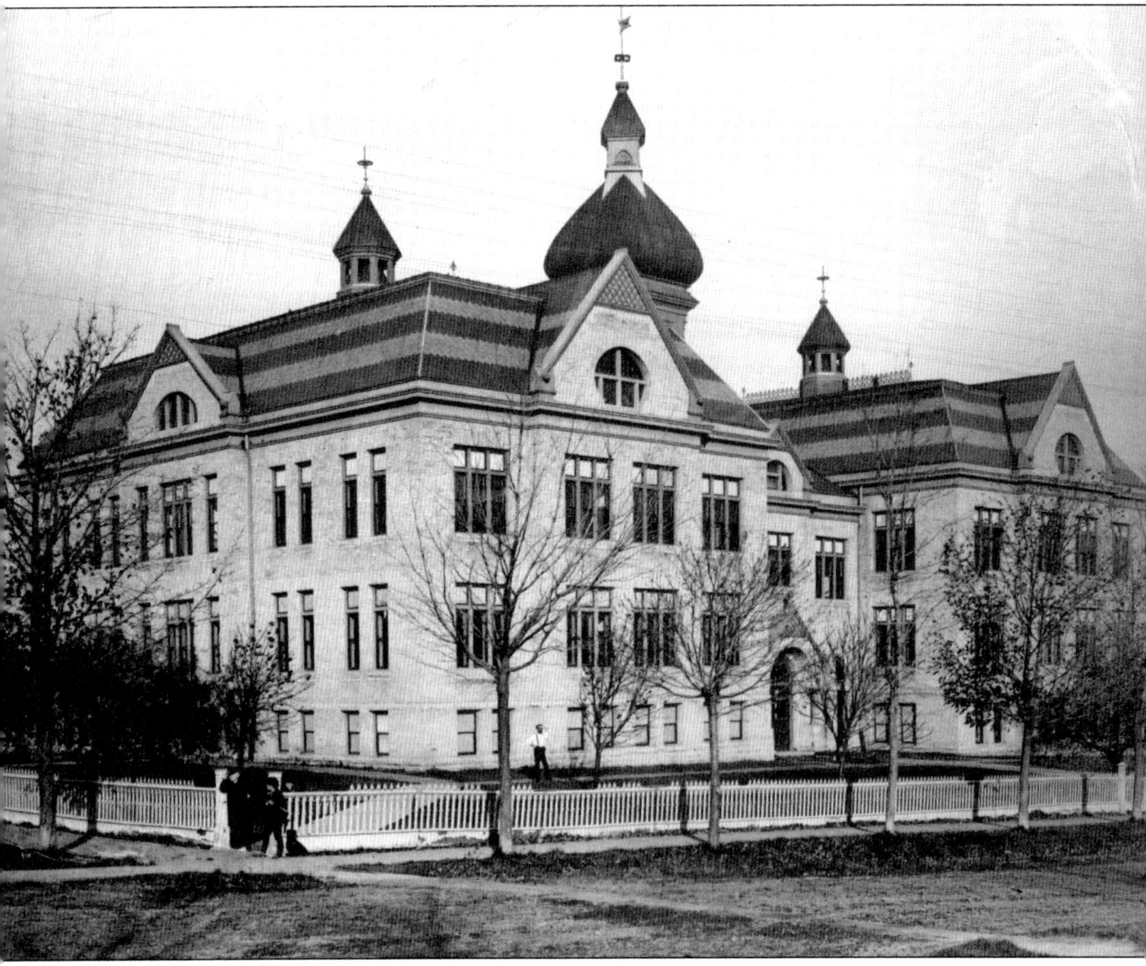

On May 1, 1886, Manistee's grand and expensive Union School was destroyed by fire. Fittingly, F. W. Hollister, the same architect who had designed the fire hall, was commissioned to design the new high school. The result, two years later, was the palatial Central School. With a foundation three and a half feet thick, solid brick walls, a slate roof, and hard maple floors, this new building was meant to last. In keeping with the spirit of modernity that characterized public building during this period, every schoolroom was built with good light and proper ventilation. The basement even featured marble sinks and 13 "water closets" equipped with running water. On the first floor were eight lofty classrooms, a marble drinking fountain, and an especially fine large library. The second floor housed four classrooms, a laboratory, and the superintendent's office. A recitation room was also located in the front part of the building. The building remained in use as Woodrow Wilson School until the mid-1950s, when it was finally torn down.

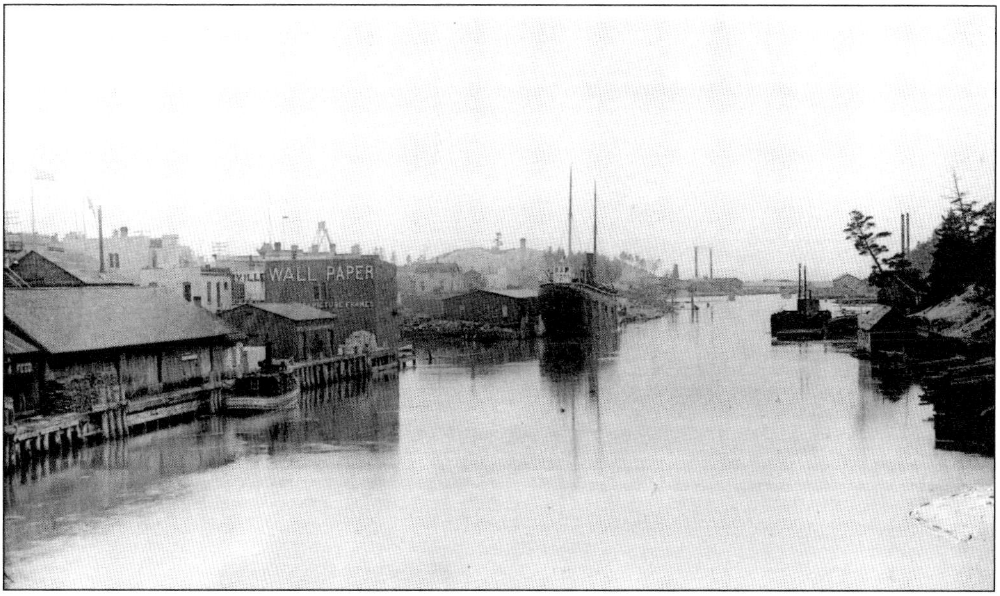

By 1885, Manistee's population was 10,000. With 40 sawmills, it was among the top producers of lumber in the country and possibly the largest shingle manufacturer in the world. Even with the coming of the railroads, shipping represented a vital means of transportation essential to the Great Lakes economy. The photograph above, a view of the river from the Maple Street bridge, shows an energetic riverfront district of warehouses and supply stores. The smokestacks in the distance are the Canfield and Wheeler Mills. The steamer at left center is possibly the *Petoskey*, and the small structures on the right are boathouses. As suggested by the drying nets below, Manistee was also home to a thriving fishing industry, which was traditionally a family enterprise. (Courtesy of Jon Rose.)

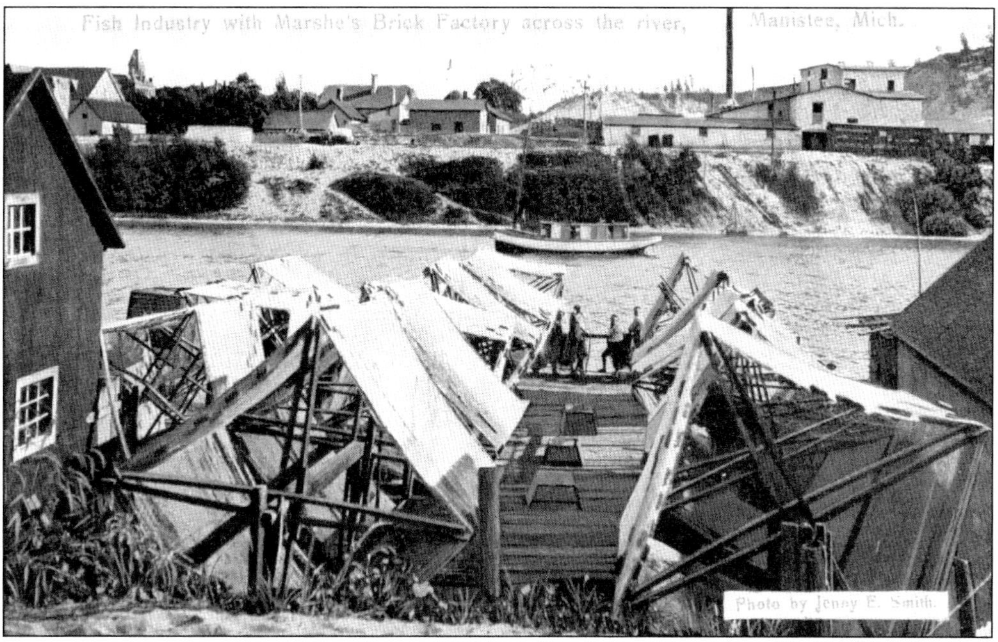

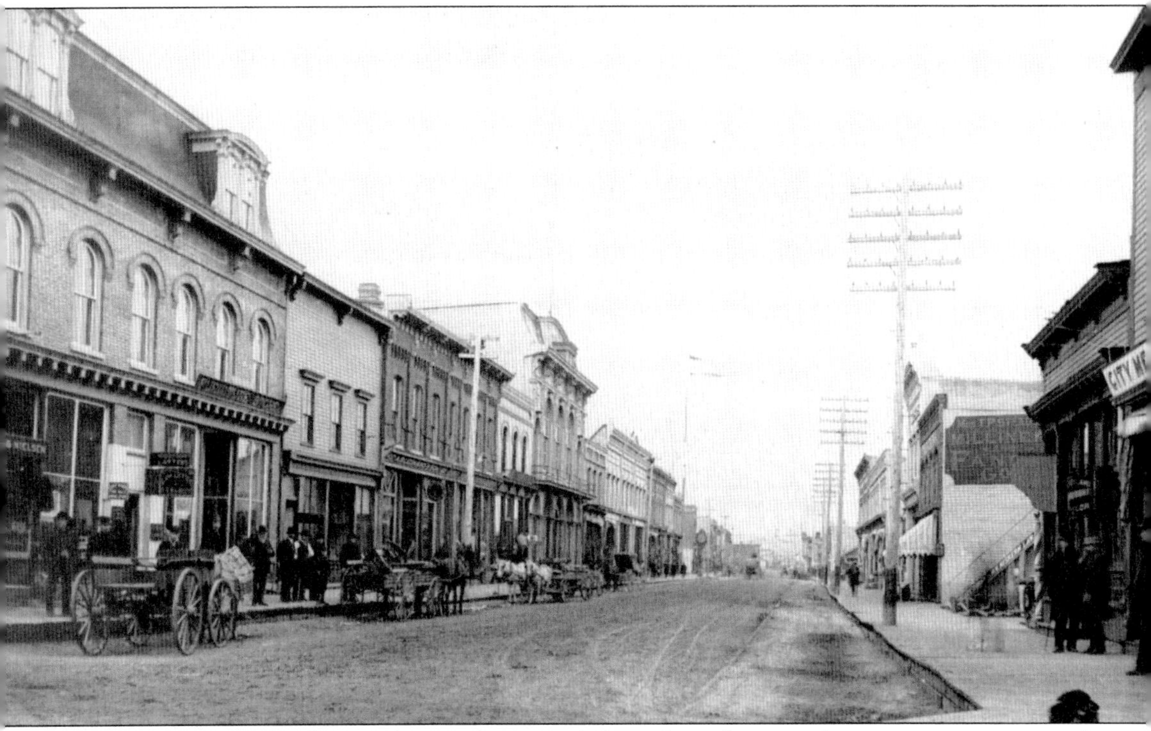

When the 1871 fire destroyed most of Manistee's River Street business district, citizens got to work rebuilding. The town's now-booming economy allowed the row of rough wooden structures from the early days to be remade into a curving avenue of elegant brick buildings. Small grimy windows gave way to glimmering sheets of glass, allowing citizens strolling along the wooden sidewalks to peruse any number of high-quality items displayed behind them. River Street featured grocery stores, meat markets, banks, legal and business offices, dry goods shops, millineries, dress goods establishments, and retailers of the luxury items that city residents previously had to journey all the way to Milwaukee to obtain. In less than half a century, Manistee had transformed from a rough, remote mill town into a glittering showplace.

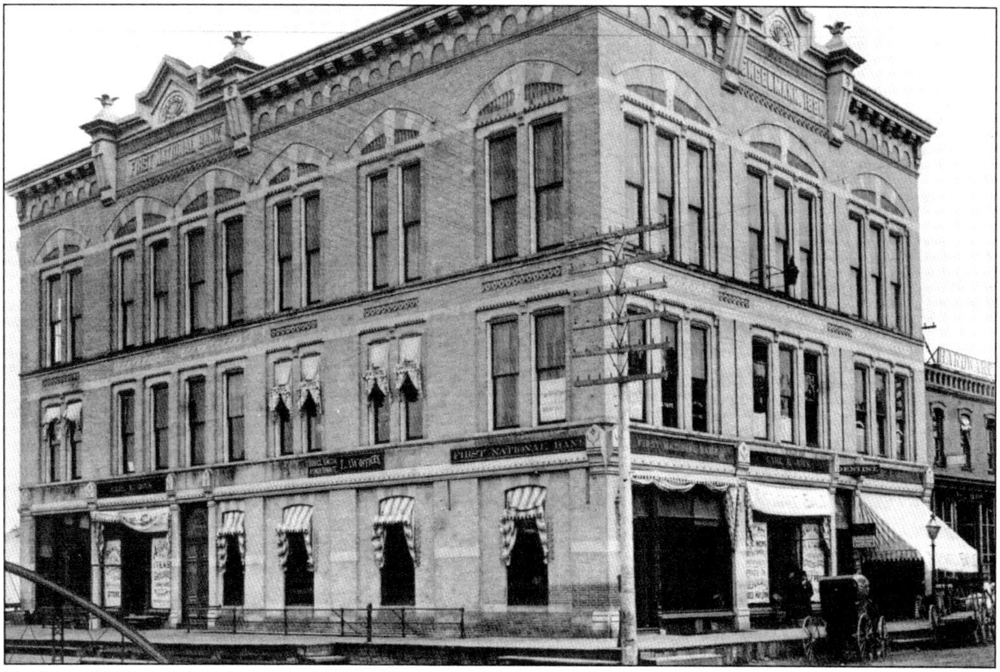

Built in 1883 on the corner of River Street and Maple Street, the Engelmann Block (above) was one of the finest buildings on River Street. The ground floor housed the First National Bank; the firm of Friend, Joys, and Company occupied its three other business fronts. An early department store, that firm sold among other things quality dress goods, luxury fabrics, footwear, and some ready-made clothing. Offices and meeting halls, including a Masonic lodge, occupied the second and third floors. Featuring ceilings 15 feet high and rows of French plate-glass windows, the building was likened to "a crystal palace" in early reports. Unfortunately, it was destroyed by fire on May 10, 1909. Although the loss was tragic and images of the wreckage (below) were dramatic, an out-of-town newspaper exaggerated the incident into yet another city-wide conflagration. (Courtesy of Jon Rose.)

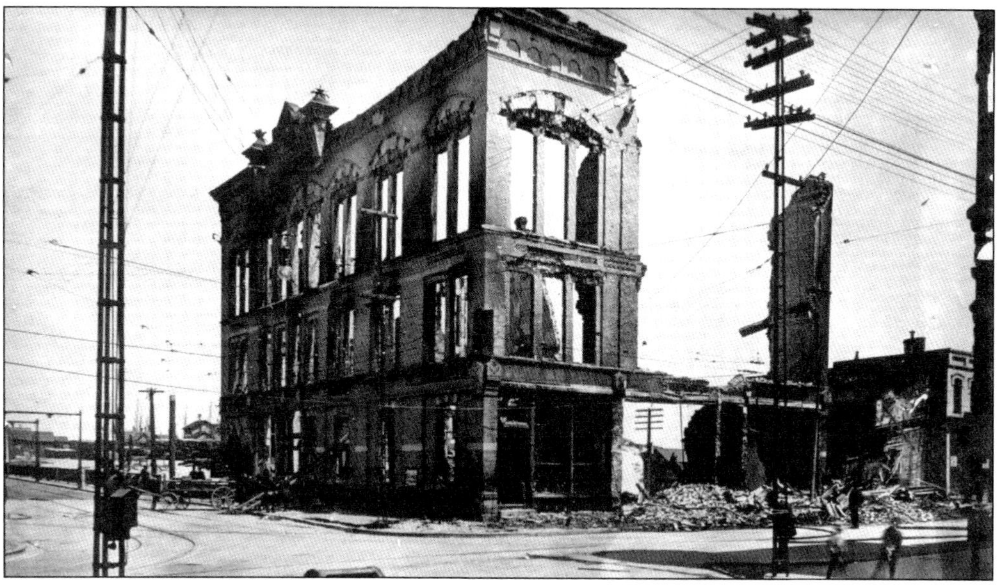

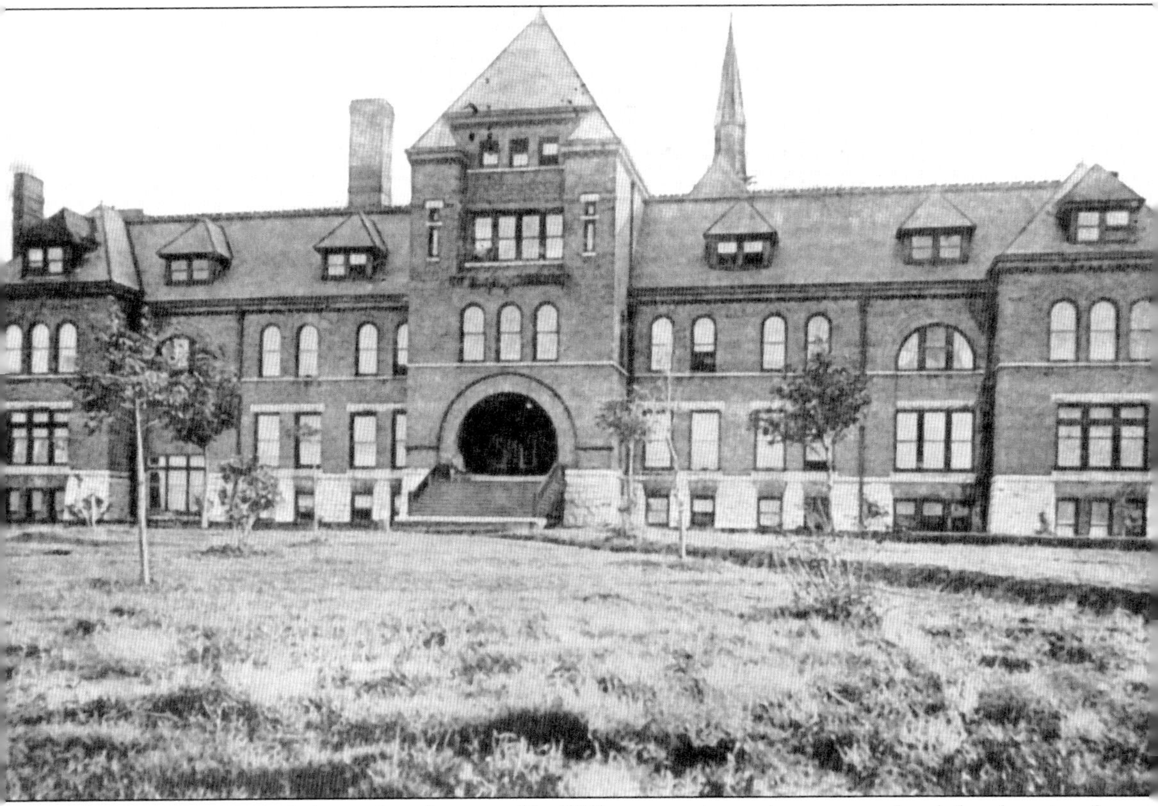

Mercy Hospital, dedicated on January 10, 1890, was perhaps the most truly philanthropic of Manistee's grand public buildings. John Canfield funded most of the building itself, while T. J. Ramsdell provided the grounds upon which it was built. Michael Engelmann took charge of collecting other subscriptions for its construction. Staffed by the Sisters of Mercy, the hospital was to provide excellent medical care to all persons, even those who could not afford it. To fund this, lumbermen paid $1 per year for each employee, thus creating one of the first health insurance programs in America. Wealthy families also funded private rooms for themselves and made regular contributions to the hospital. Designed by Chicago architect William LeBarron Jenney (who also designed the First Congregational Church), the Romanesque building was planned to maximize fresh air, good light, and proper heating—features that previously were unheard of in most public hospitals. (Courtesy of Jon Rose.)

Four

SPIRITED LIVES

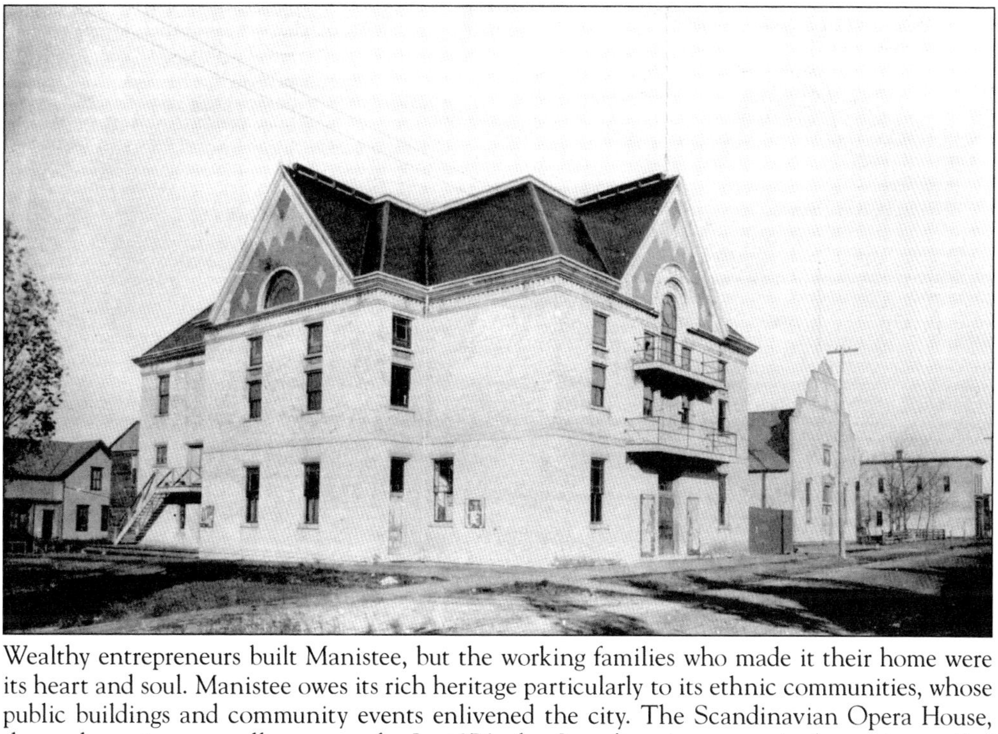

Wealthy entrepreneurs built Manistee, but the working families who made it their home were its heart and soul. Manistee owes its rich heritage particularly to its ethnic communities, whose public buildings and community events enlivened the city. The Scandinavian Opera House, shown here, is an excellent example. In 1876, the Scandinavians organized a society called *Nordisk Fremskridts Forening*, in order to conduct discussions and enjoy music and theatrical performances rooted in Scandinavian culture, and as a community center. For this purpose, they built the Opera House in 1883 on the northwest corner of First and Greenbush Streets. The auditorium sat nearly 1,000 people. Because the building was the only thoroughly equipped playhouse in Manistee at the time, other groups rented the facility as well. Around 1900, the structure was destroyed by fire, leaving no adequate space for public gatherings, until T. J. Ramsdell built a new theater and hall on the corner of First and Maple Streets.

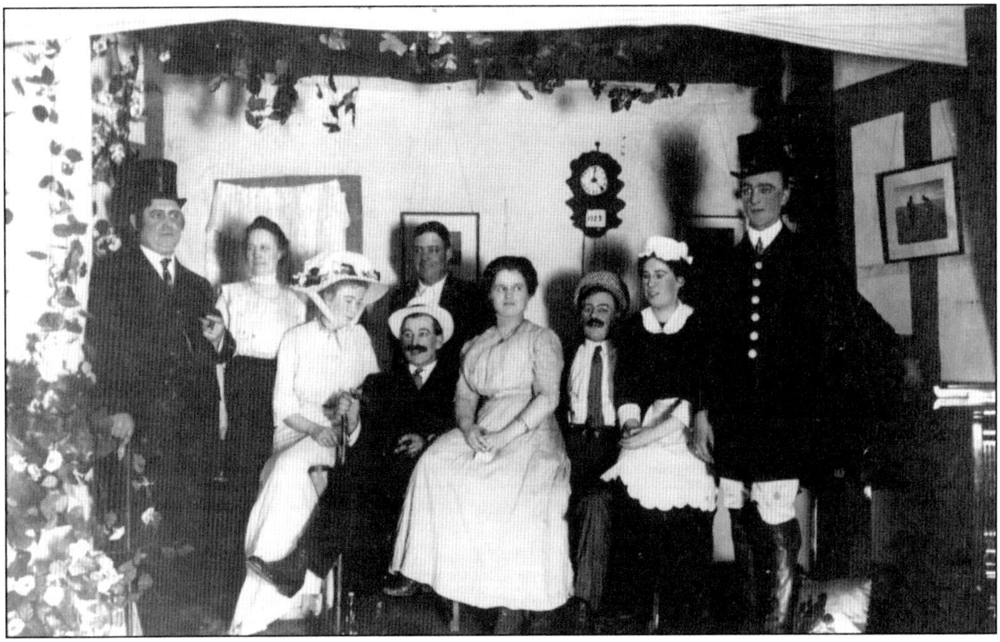

The Danish School also hosted amateur dramatic performances. Above, on a temporary stage in front of the school about 1912 are, from left to right, Thomas Knudstrup, Anna V. Nielsen, Rigmor Nielsen, Carl Frederiksen, Magus Petersen, possibly Anna Nielsen of Greenbush Street, two unidentified people, and possibly Jim Sorensen. Although the school was constantly used since its founding, financial constraints halted full completion of the church complex until 1896. Below is the newly improved interior as it looked in 1903. Daniel Jensen of Manistee carved the pulpit in 1896. The altar was brought in by boat from Milwaukee in 1898, and the marble baptismal font was shipped from Denmark. Also added was a hand-carved Viking ship—a special symbol frequently found in coastal churches in Denmark—which represents the second ark of Christ, and safe harbor. (Courtesy of Our Saviour's Historical Museum.)

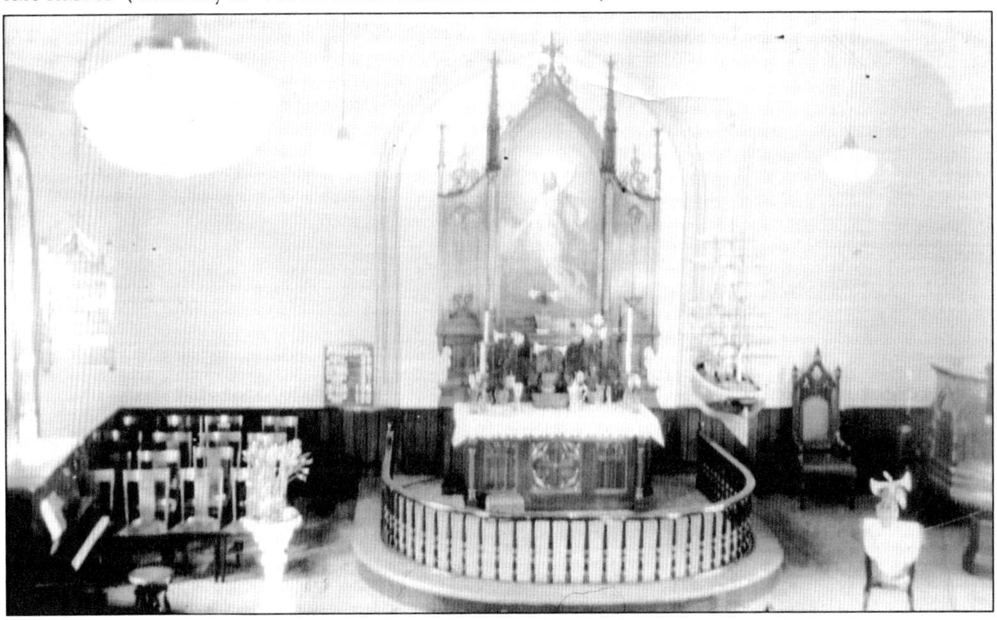

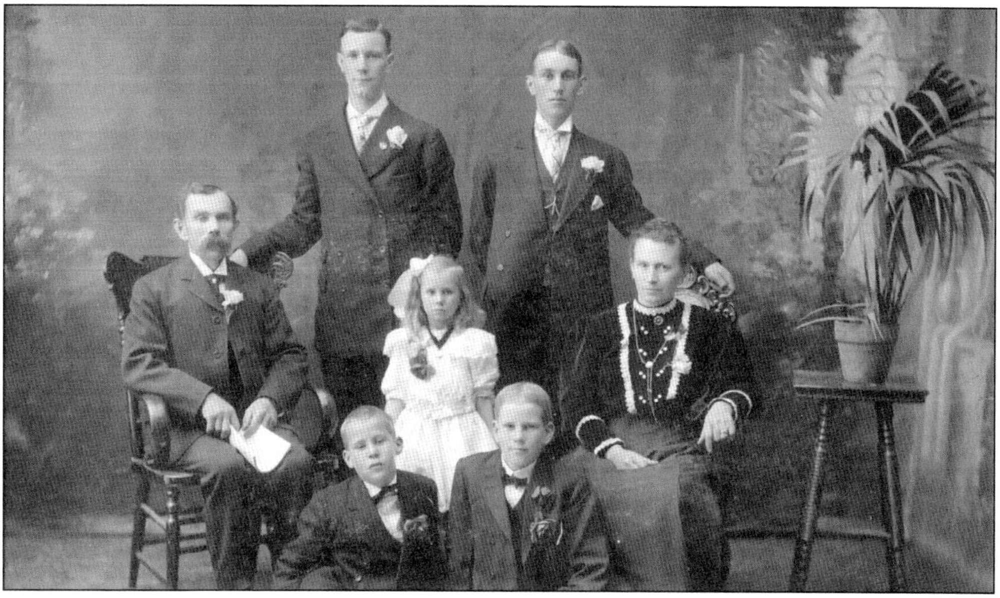

Thomas E. and Hansine Andresen came to Manistee from Denmark in the late 1800s with their daughter Elna. The Andresens quickly became active community members; father and sons founded a number of small family businesses. This formal family portrait was made in 1907, on the occasion of the couple's silver anniversary. Pictured here, from left to right, are the following: (first row) younger sons Edgar and Thomas W.; (second row) Thomas E., daughter Ella, and Hansine; (third row) older sons Thorwald and Harry. (Courtesy of Sandee Jones.)

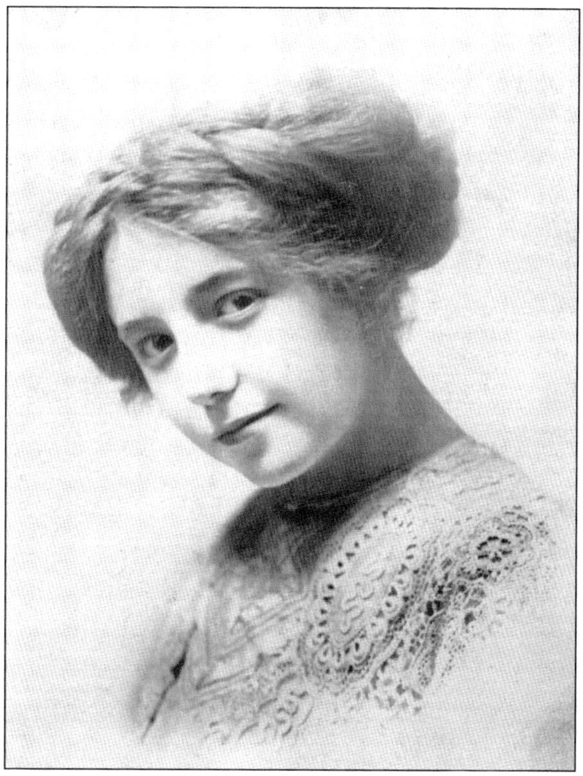

In the later 19th century, families wishing to resettle in America were required to have resident sponsors. The Andresens were sponsored by the Sorensons of Manistee. The two families developed a close friendship. This image depicts a young Agnes Sorenson, a daughter of the sponsoring family. (Courtesy of Sandee Jones.)

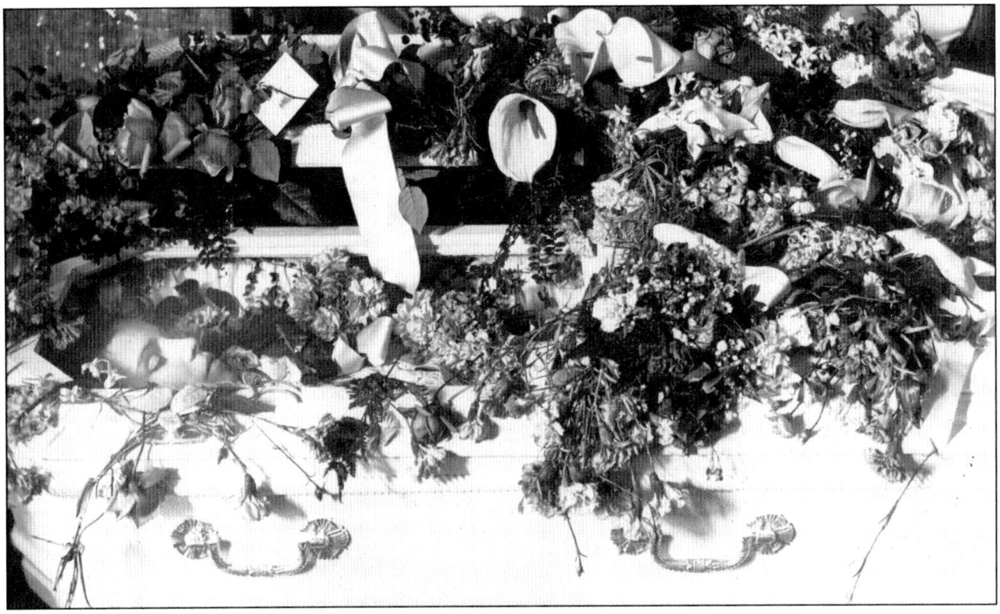

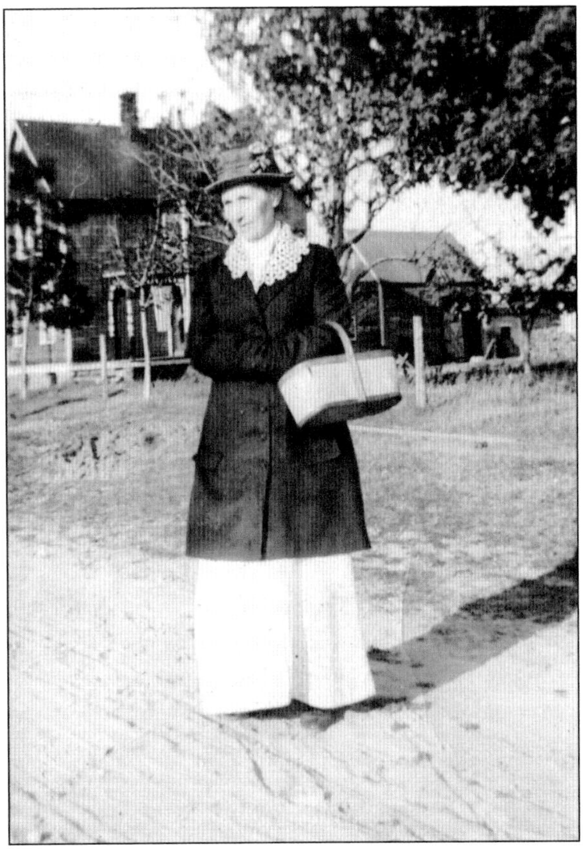

Unfortunately, young Elna Andresen died soon after the family's arrival. She is shown above on the day of her funeral in 1898. Images of the newly deceased were common in the 19th century when photography was new; they offered living relatives a memory of the ones lost. The practice of preserving such memories faded in the 20th century. Family members remember their loved ones in many other ways. To the left, Elna's mother, Hansine Andresen, stands on an as-yet-unpaved Maple Street after visiting her daughter in the cemetery. (Courtesy of Sandee Jones.)

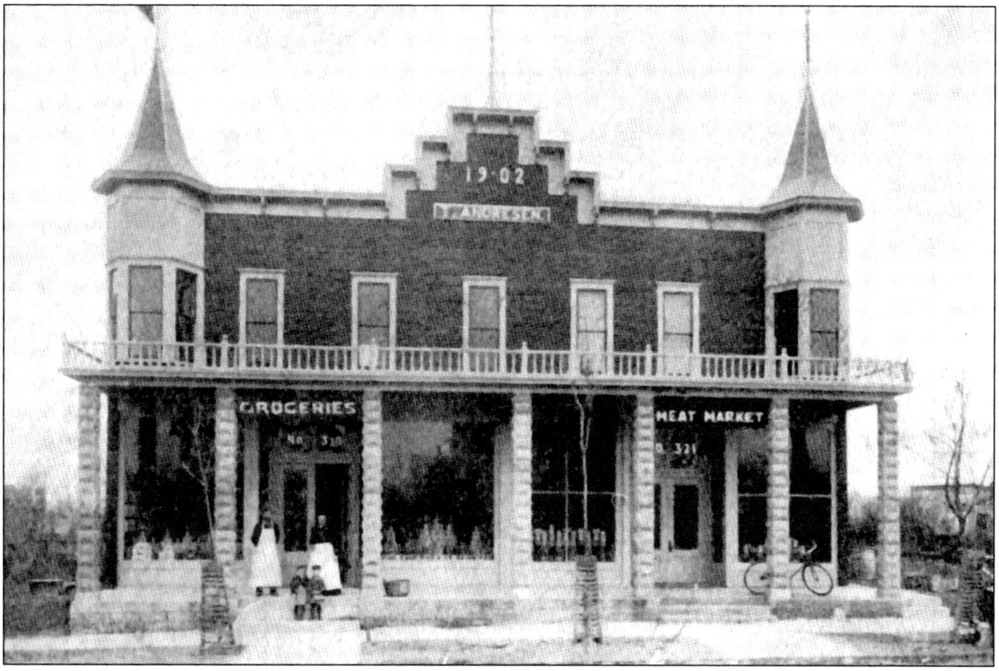

Like most young men, Thomas E. Andresen likely worked in the lumber camps until he had earned enough money to support his family more comfortably. In 1902, he opened his own business, a grocery store on Sixth Street, just off of what is now U.S. 31. The concern, which featured two front entrances, as shown in the advertising postcard above, was known as a "three-in-one" store. It sold groceries, meat, and baked goods, among other items. Shown below is the store interior on the grocery side, with Hansine standing to the front left. The couple's son Harry also ran a grocery store on Fifth Street, where Albright Sheet Metal is now located. (Courtesy of Sandee Jones.)

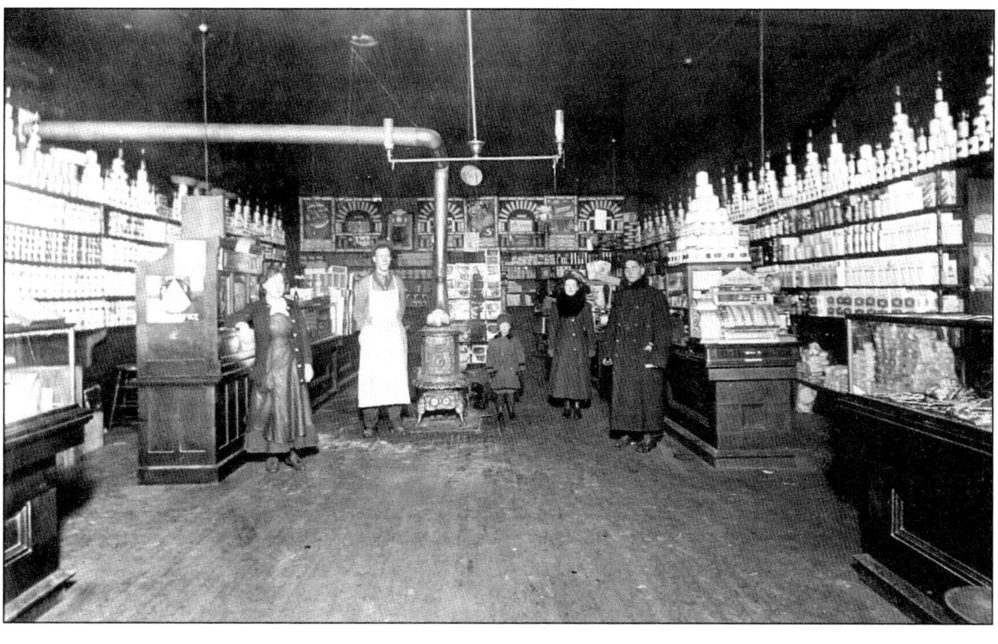

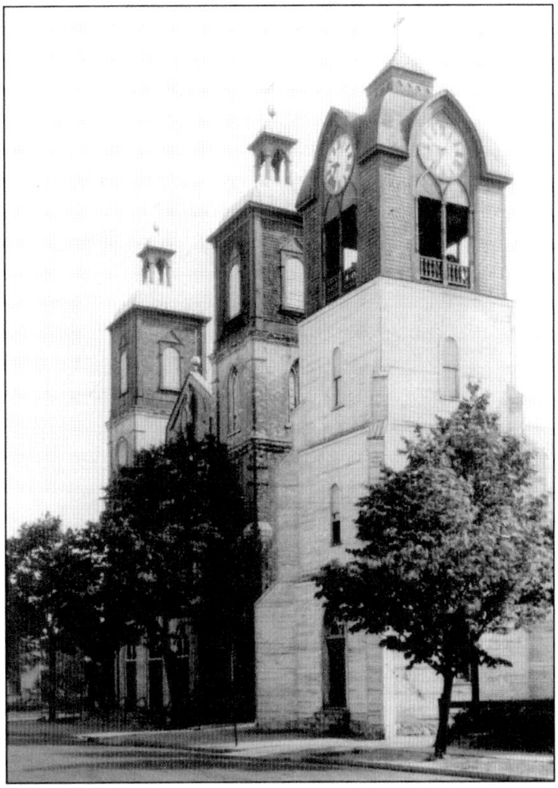

In the 1870s, thousands of Polish families, mainly from Poznan province, sought refuge from an oppressive regime and forced conscription into the German army. Several of those families settled in Manistee. Up until this time, St. Mary's parishioners—mainly French Canadian, Irish, and German—were accustomed to hearing Mass in French or English. As the new arrivals spoke only Polish, ethnic tensions arose in the then extremely overcrowded parish. The Polish congregation requested its own church, and the missionary Father Szulak created St. Joseph's Parish on May 19, 1882. Destroyed by wind before completion, the church on Hopkins and Sixth Streets was quickly reconstructed. Fr. Joseph Barzyski said the first Mass on May 17, 1884. To the left is St. Joseph's Church shortly after completion. Below is a view of its magnificent interior. (Left, courtesy of Clarence Nowak; below, courtesy of Jon Rose.)

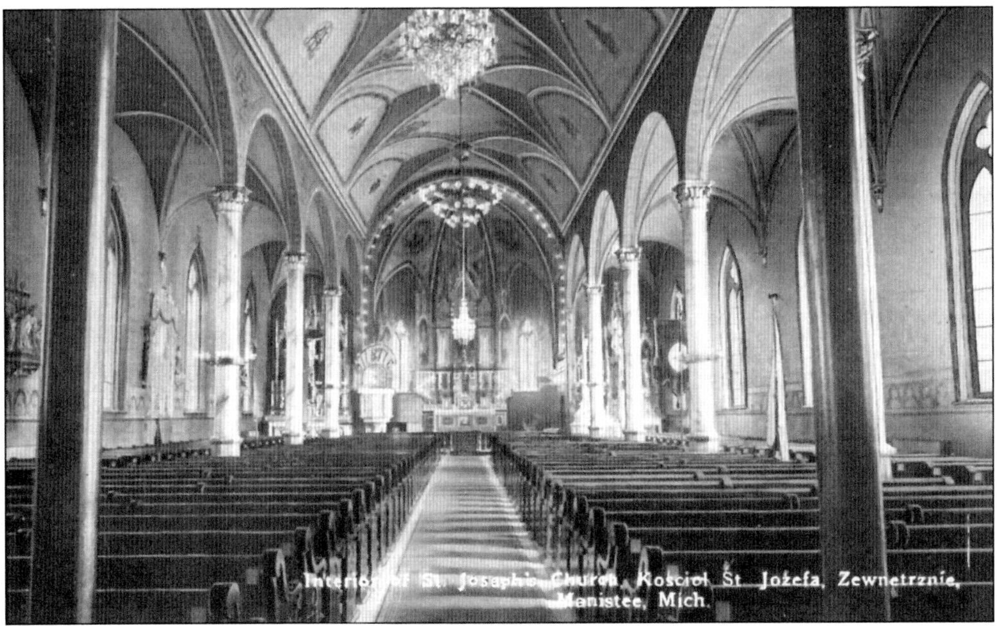

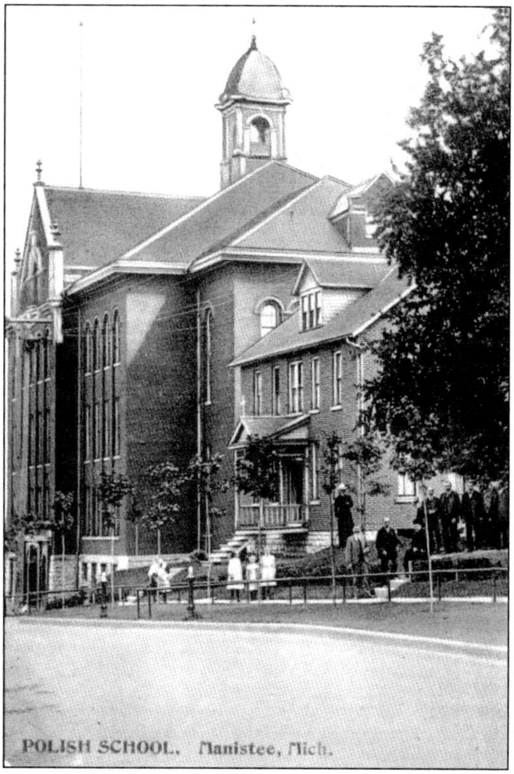

Like Manistee's other ethnic churches, St. Joseph's operated a parochial school, shown at right. The school building included a great hall, where community members produced Polish-language plays, staged musical performances, and held social events. In 1909, St. Joseph's School had 741 pupils. Below, third-grade class 3A assembles in 1909. (Right, courtesy of Jon Rose; below, courtesy of Clarence Nowak.)

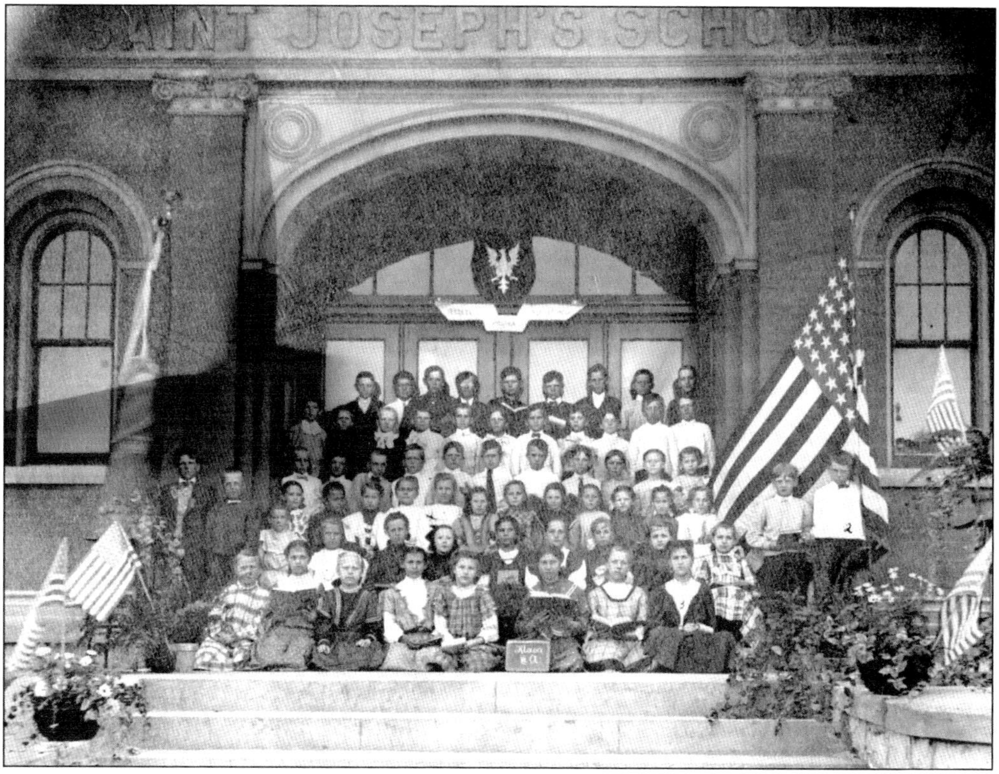

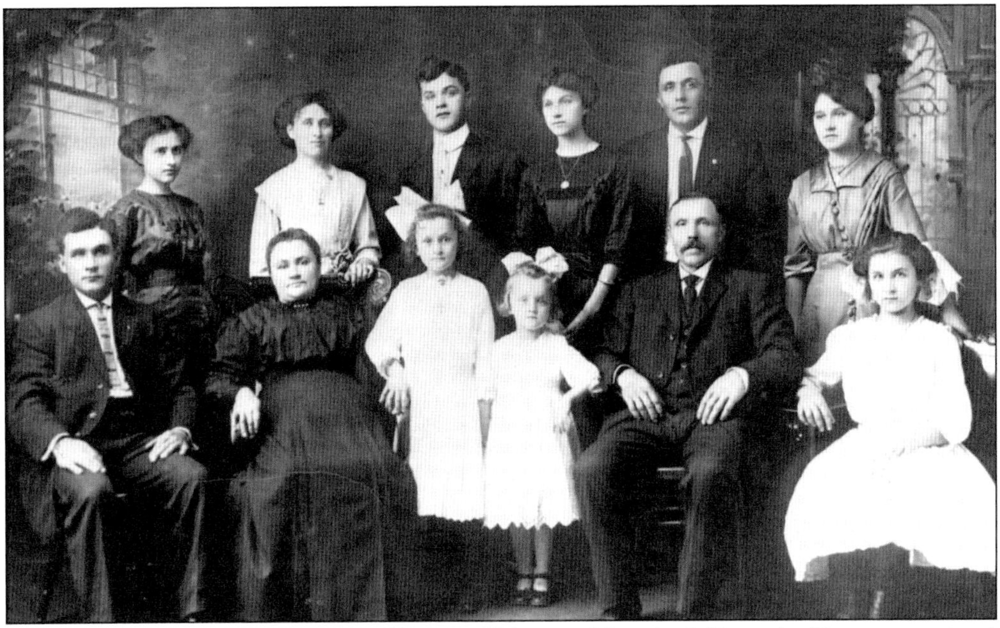

Forced to serve two years in Bismarck's army, Valentine Nowak of Oborniki (Poznan province) escaped to America in 1884, found work with the Buckley and Douglas salt factory, and started a family. This 1912 family portrait includes the following, from left to right: (first row) Stanley, Mary (née Golembowski), Irene, Cecile, Valentine, and Clara; (second row) Helen, Sadie, Cas, Ursula, Joseph, and Sophie. (Courtesy of Clarence Nowak.)

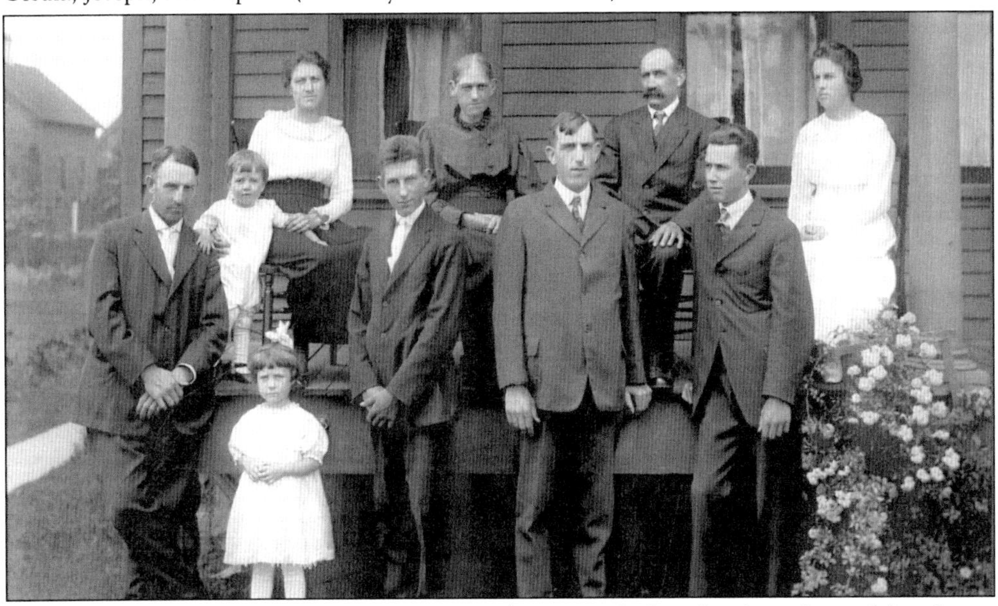

Also from Poznan, Frank and Marcianna Wicinski pose with their family in front of their home on Eighth Street near Hopkins. Pictured here, from left to right, are the following: (first row) son-in-law Frank Newman, who worked for many years at Foyes Bakery; grandchild Evelyn; and sons Aloysius "Ollie," Louis, and John; (second row) grandchild Frank Jr.; daughter Mary; Marcianna; Frank; and daughter Helen. Mary was the only family member who married. (Courtesy of Janet Newman-Graham.)

Weddings were grand occasions in St. Joseph's Parish. Adam Kubacki of Filer City and Theresa "Tracy" Paprocki of Oak Hill were married in 1915. Adam was a day laborer whose parents were farmers. Tracy worked for many years in a salt plant and was known for her fine work as a seamstress. Also in the photograph are Tracy's unidentified parents and siblings. The Kubacki couple had five children. (Courtesy of Janet Newman-Graham.)

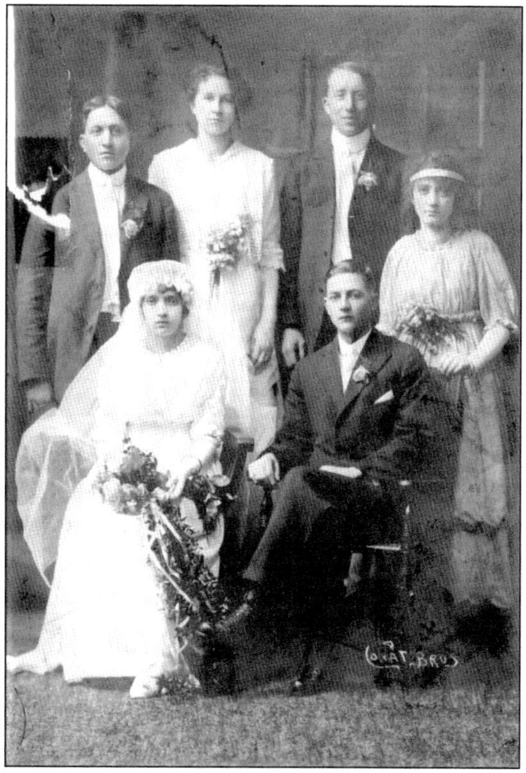

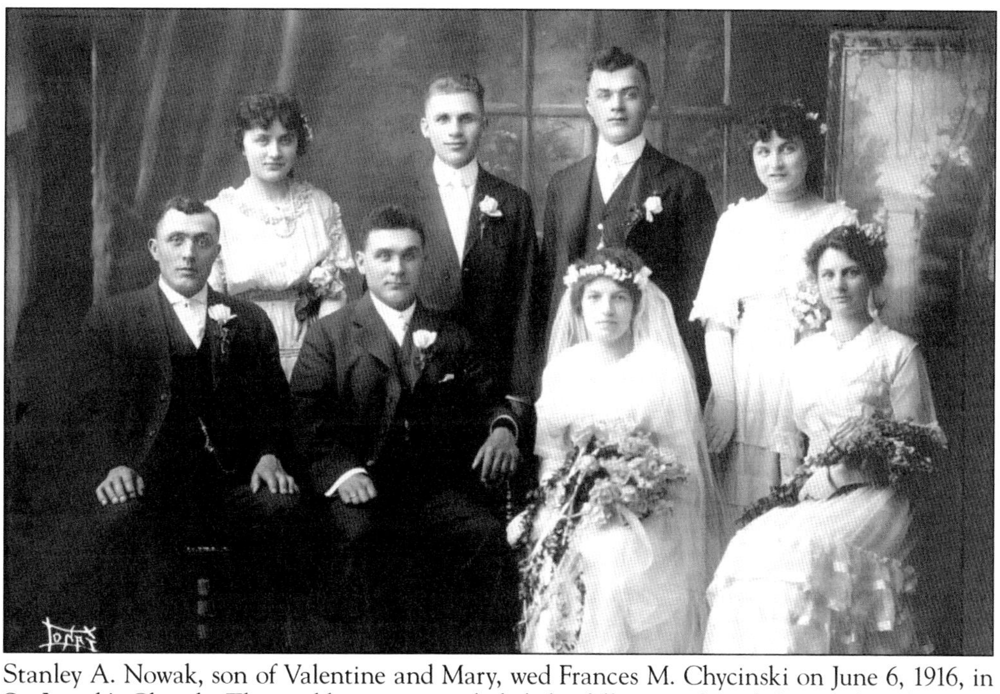

Stanley A. Nowak, son of Valentine and Mary, wed Frances M. Chycinski on June 6, 1916, in St. Joseph's Church. The wedding party included the following, from left to right: (first row) Joseph Nowak, Stanley, Frances, and Julia Jaitner; (second row) Sophie Nowak, Frank Chycinski, Casimer Nowak, and Clara Nowak. (Courtesy of Clarence Nowak.)

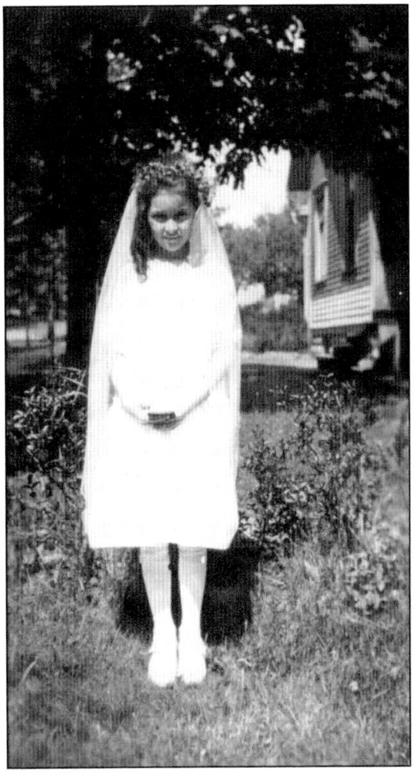

First Communion is an essential rite and one of the most special days for Catholic children. Held when they are six or seven years old, a time when the church considers them capable of reason and conscious participation in their faith, candidates receive several weeks' worth of training and moral instruction prior to the ceremony. The occasion is marked with many symbolic traditions. One of those is to dress the young communicant in clothing similar to that worn by a bride or groom, as shown in these photographs of Dorothy Ferguson and Frank Newman in 1927. (Left, courtesy of Mary Ann Kaczmarek; below, courtesy of Janet Newman-Graham.)

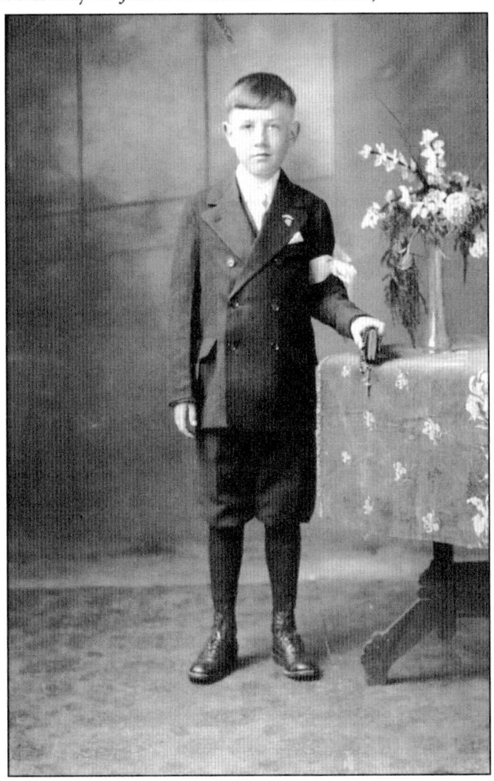

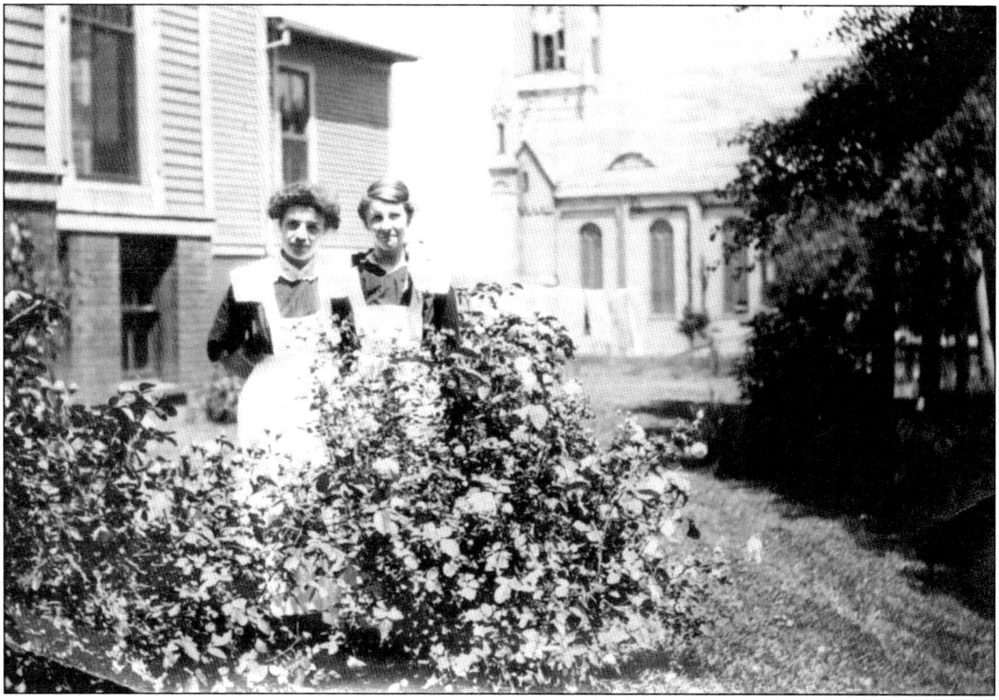

As was typical in working-class families in the late 19th century, Manistee's Polish women often worked outside the home in order to help make ends meet. In the above photograph are Frances Chycinski (left) and Clara Ello (right). Both worked as domestics for shipping industrialist Gus Kitzinger. They are seen on the south side of Kitzinger's residence at 515 Maple Street. Note Guardian Angels Church in the background. Once Frances married, her husband supported the family. The two girls at right are Pauline "Lottie" Paprocki of Oak Hill (left) and possibly her sister Sylvia. Lottie married William Zawacki, and the couple ran a River Street tavern called Buja's. A workingman's bar, Buja's featured a colorful crowd of regulars whose exploits live on in local legend. (Above, courtesy of Clarence Nowak; right, courtesy of Janet Newman-Graham.)

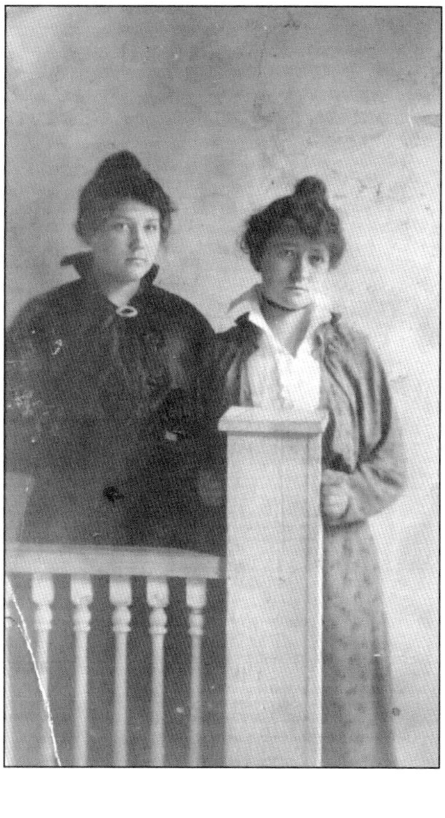

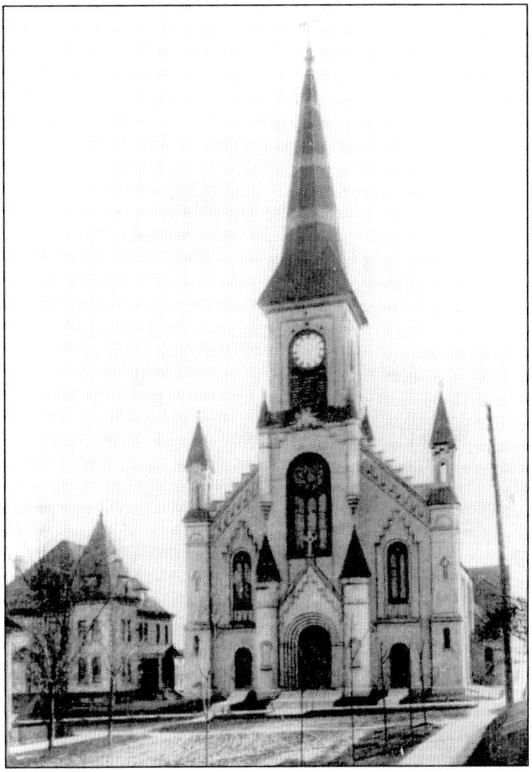

The Polish departure to St. Joseph's did little to ease the overcrowding at St. Mary's, or the tension between the remaining ethnic groups. Eventually, the Germans and the Irish also formed their own church—Guardian Angels Parish—in 1888. Finally completed in 1890, the church featured a 170-foot-high spire. One of the most visible features on the Manistee skyline, the spire was intended to represent a beacon and thus become a symbol of safety, protection, and homecoming for parishioners. (Courtesy of the Manistee Historical Museum.)

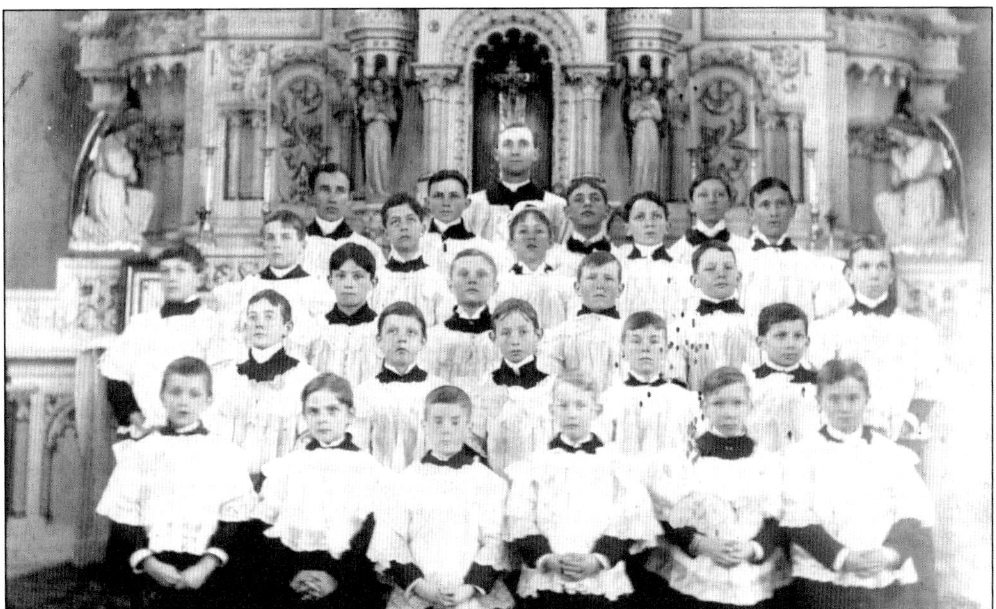

Father Steffes, shown here with his altar boys in 1910, became pastor of Guardian Angels on September 1, 1892, succeeding parish founder Fr. H. W. Grimme. Young, liberal, energetic, and much beloved by the parishioners, Father Steffes was responsible for installing the beautiful altars and statuary inside the church. (Courtesy of Clarence Nowak.)

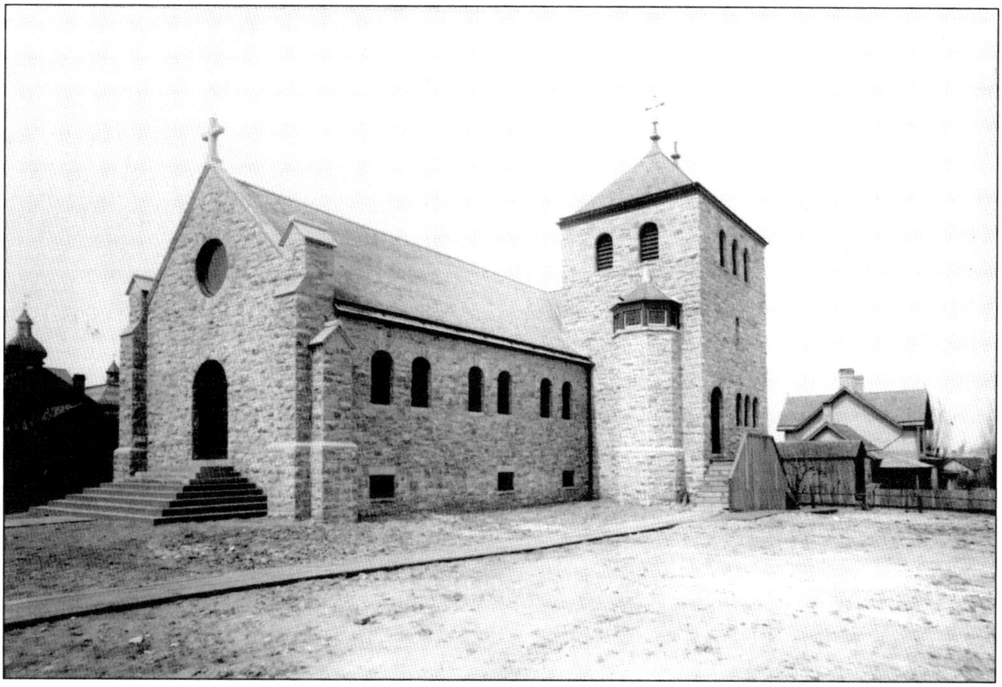

The Episcopalian church in Manistee dates as far back as 1869. Most services were conducted by traveling missionaries, until Rev. William Stone Hayward arrived in 1881 and stayed on to hold regular services. Constrained by lack of permanent space, Reverend Hayward first held his services in the courthouse and later in the Temperance Hall, until funds were successfully raised for a permanent building. The Norman-style building, designed by Richard Upjohn and constructed of hewn stone on 410 Second Street, is pictured above shortly after its completion in 1888. In October 1887, Rev. H. E. S. Somerville took charge of the church and saw to its completion. He led the first worship service inside the new building on December 16, 1888, and served as pastor until 1891. (Courtesy of the Holy Trinity Episcopal Church.)

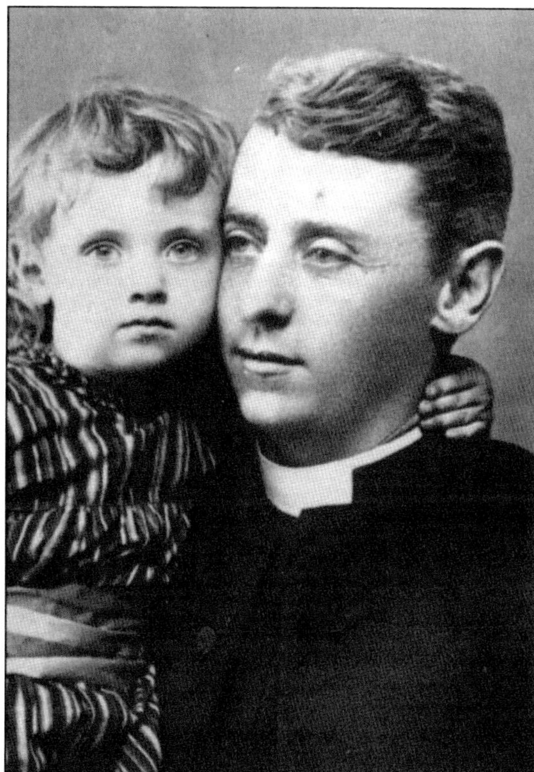

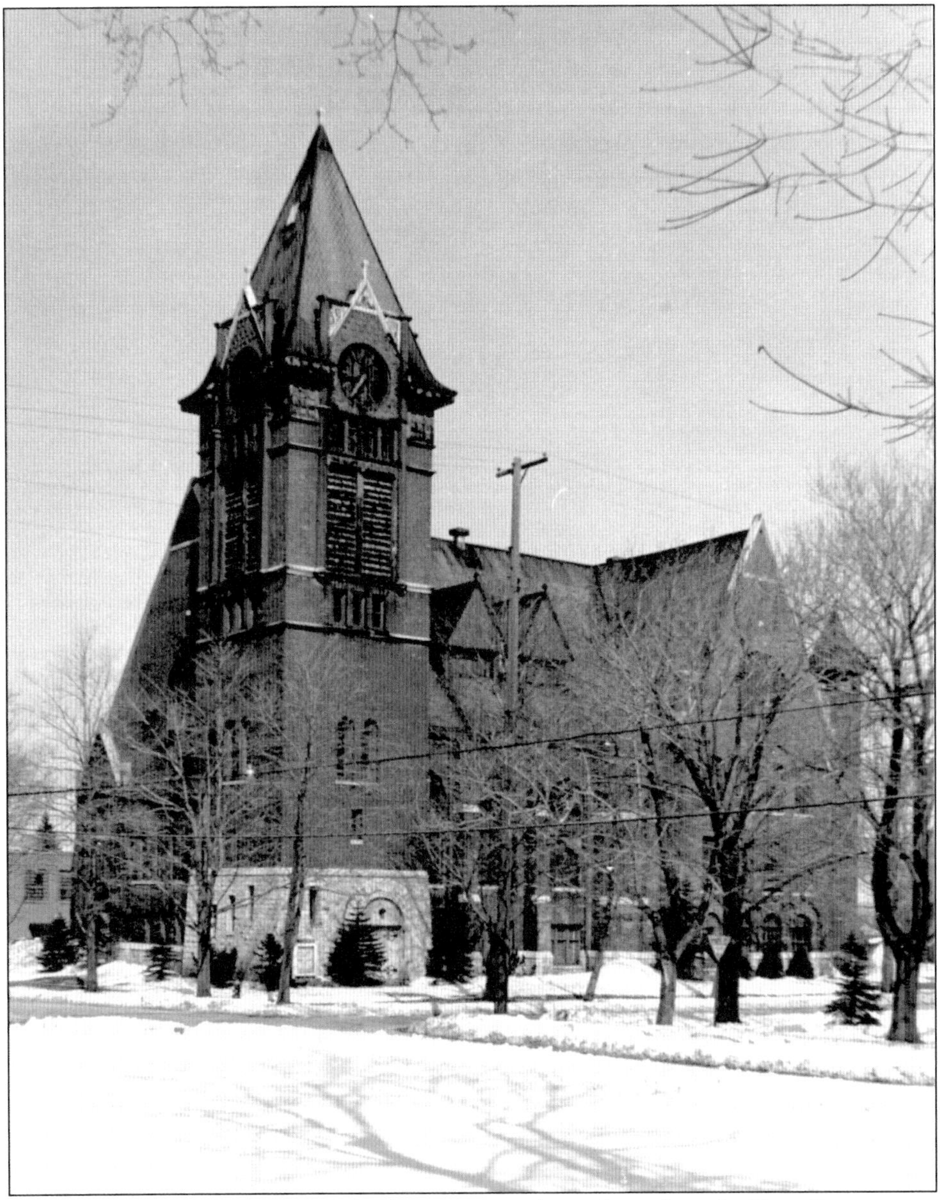

As much a monument to Manistee lumbermen as a place of worship, the First Congregational Church is an architectural marvel designed by Chicago architect William LeBaron Jenney, known as "the father of the American skyscraper." Among all its extraordinary features, the clock tower, shown here, is perhaps the most quietly spectacular. Its maker, Nels Johnson, was born in 1838 on the Danish island of Sjeland and immigrated to America, where he opened a machine repair shop in Manistee in 1871. On a trip to Ann Arbor in aid of his blind wife, he passed time in the observatory. There, he became acquainted with University of Michigan professors, who introduced him to astronomy and higher math and informed him that it was possible to calculate perfect time from the stars. His quest to find a machine that would keep perfect time drove him to build his Century Tower Clocks, beginning around 1886. One such clock was at the Columbia World's Fair in 1893. Another working Century Tower Clock in Michigan is located in Arcadia. (Courtesy of the First Congregational Church.)

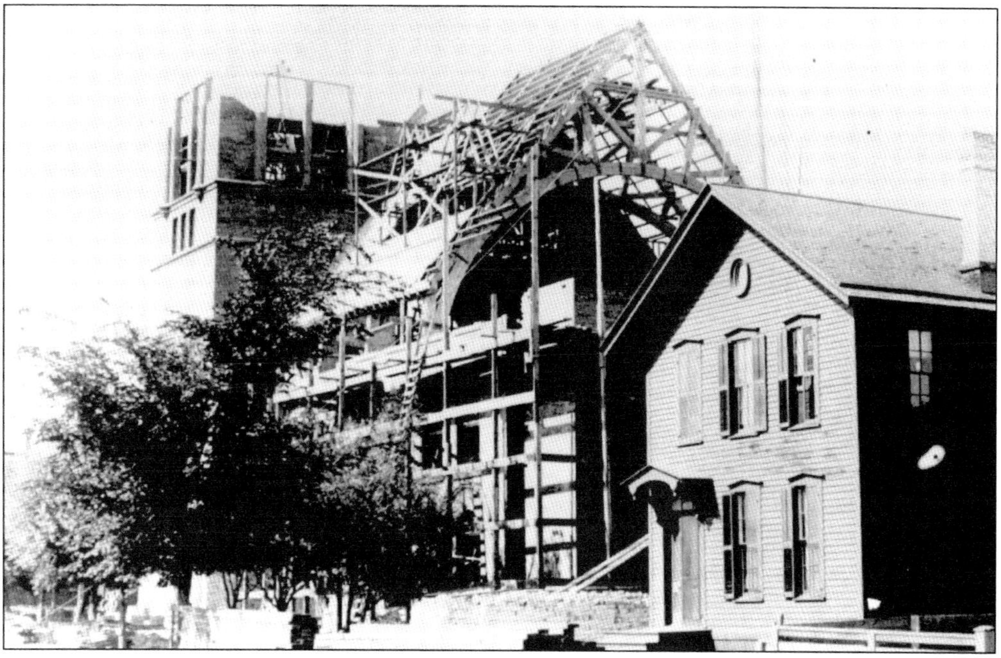

This is a rare photograph of the First Congregational Church under construction, before its completion in 1892. Note the Romanesque vault construction of the roof. This was accomplished with top-quality local timber using shipbuilding techniques, to commemorate Manistee's major industries. (Courtesy of the First Congregational Church.)

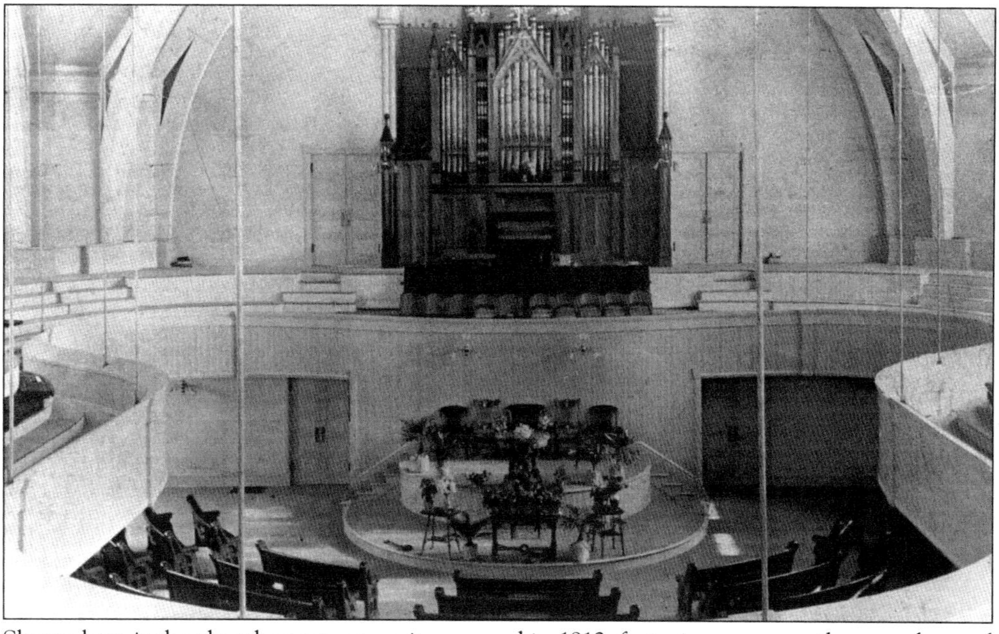

Shown here is the church sanctuary as it appeared in 1912, featuring an organ that was donated by Filer family in 1911. Built by Kilgren Organ Works of Chicago, it was a direct-action tracker organ, its console located directly below the pipes. The church also features 43 stained-glass windows, most of which date to the beginning of the 20th century. (Courtesy of the First Congregational Church.)

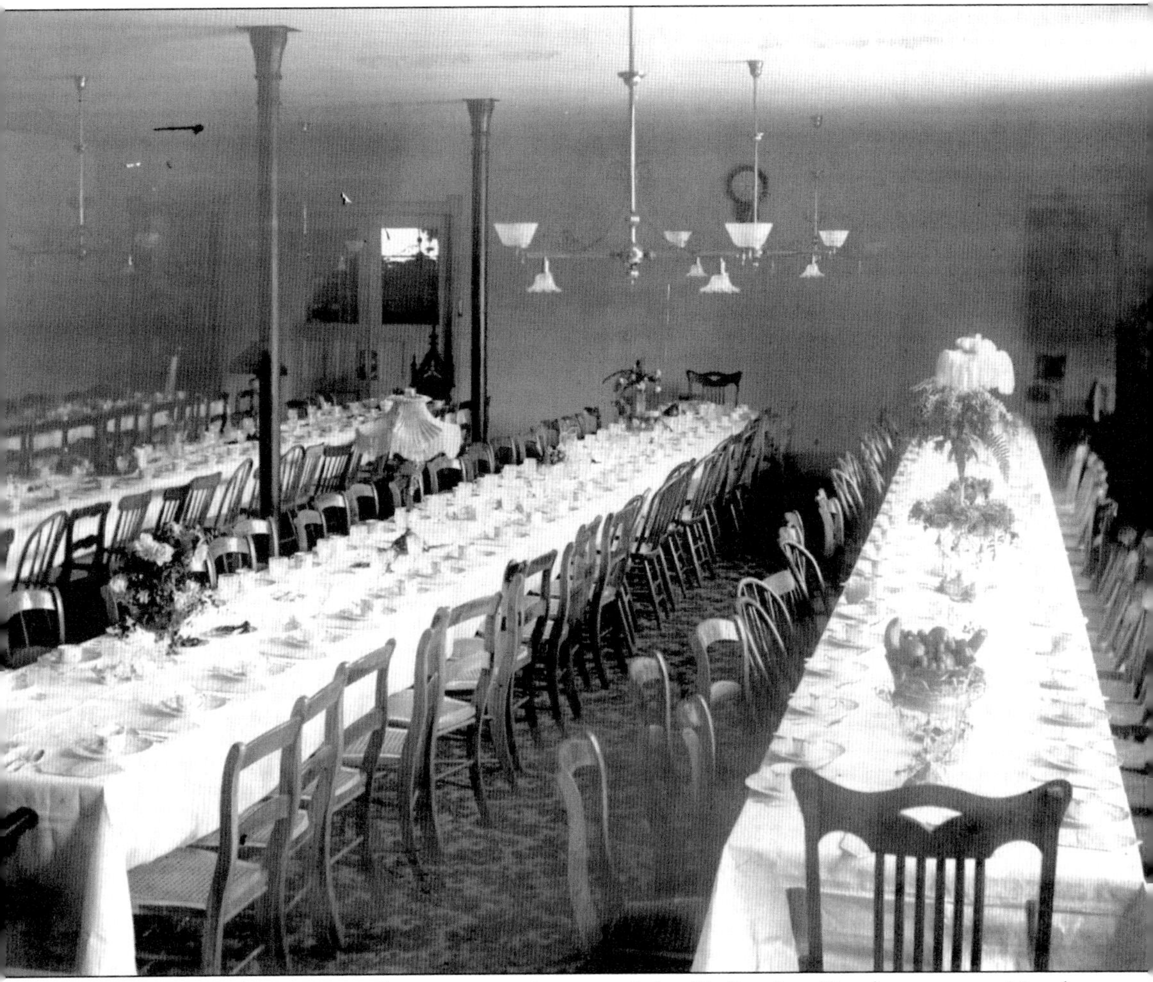

The church basement auditorium was the site of the Dedication Day banquet on Monday, December 12, 1892. Prepared by the ladies of the church in honor of the building committee, the banquet was the last in a series of Dedication Day festivities. The Hon. B. M. Cutcheon of Grand Rapids read historical letters. On Monday, the assembled retired to the auditorium at 5:30 p.m. for the reception and the 6:30 p.m. banquet. Built to seat 1,800, the room was filled beyond capacity. The menu included scalloped oysters, sliced ham, chicken salad, ice cream, cake, and fruit. Rev. A. O. Wheeler was toastmaster, and Miss Jessie Wing provided music. As grand as this event was, the church was not consecrated for official services until 1894, when the pattered slate roof was completed and the $60,000 cost of building was paid in full. (Courtesy of the First Congregational Church.)

Five

Women's Works

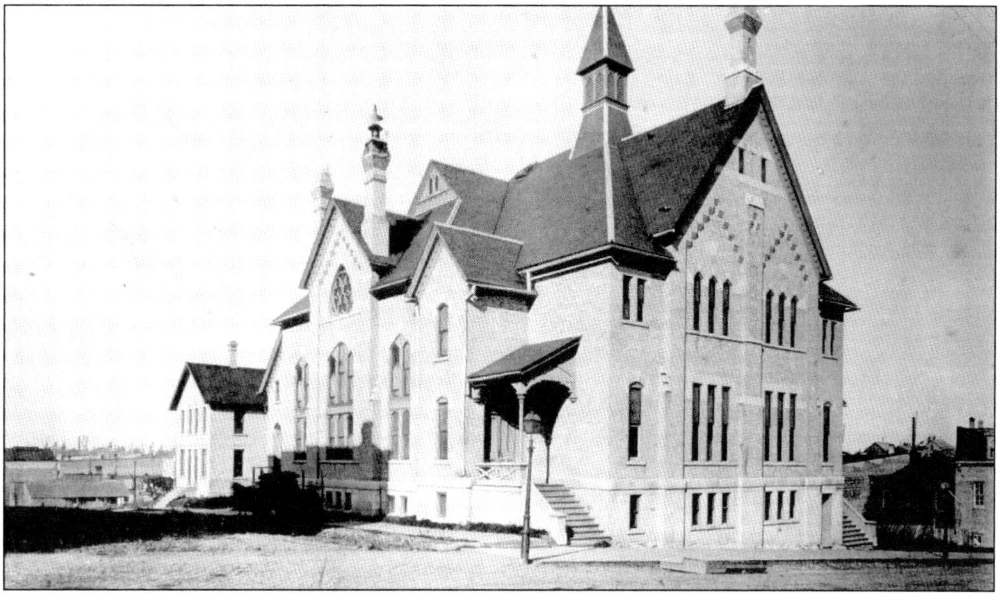

Although geographically isolated, Manistee women were remarkably engaged in the issues of the day. In fact, the town's development coincided with the national rise of the Women's Movement. Three separate concerns converged in this mid-19th century movement: a Victorian ideology that held women as society's moral center, the Enlightenment ideal of equal rights that led to agitation for female suffrage, and Abolition. Of these, moral activism took the greatest hold in Manistee. The Women's Christian Temperance Union (WCTU), a local chapter of the immensely popular national movement, first emerged in Manistee in the mid-1870s as a faction of an earlier Women's Temperance Association (WTA). The Manistee WCTU seceded from the WTA over the issue of dancing in the Temperance Hall, preferring less frivolous activities like revival meetings. To that end, they built a new hall. Funded by R. G. Peters, the Women's Christian Temperance Union Hall was the largest public building in Manistee. When it burned down within a year of its 1879 completion, Peters financed another exactly like it, shown here. The building remained in wide public use throughout the 1890s.

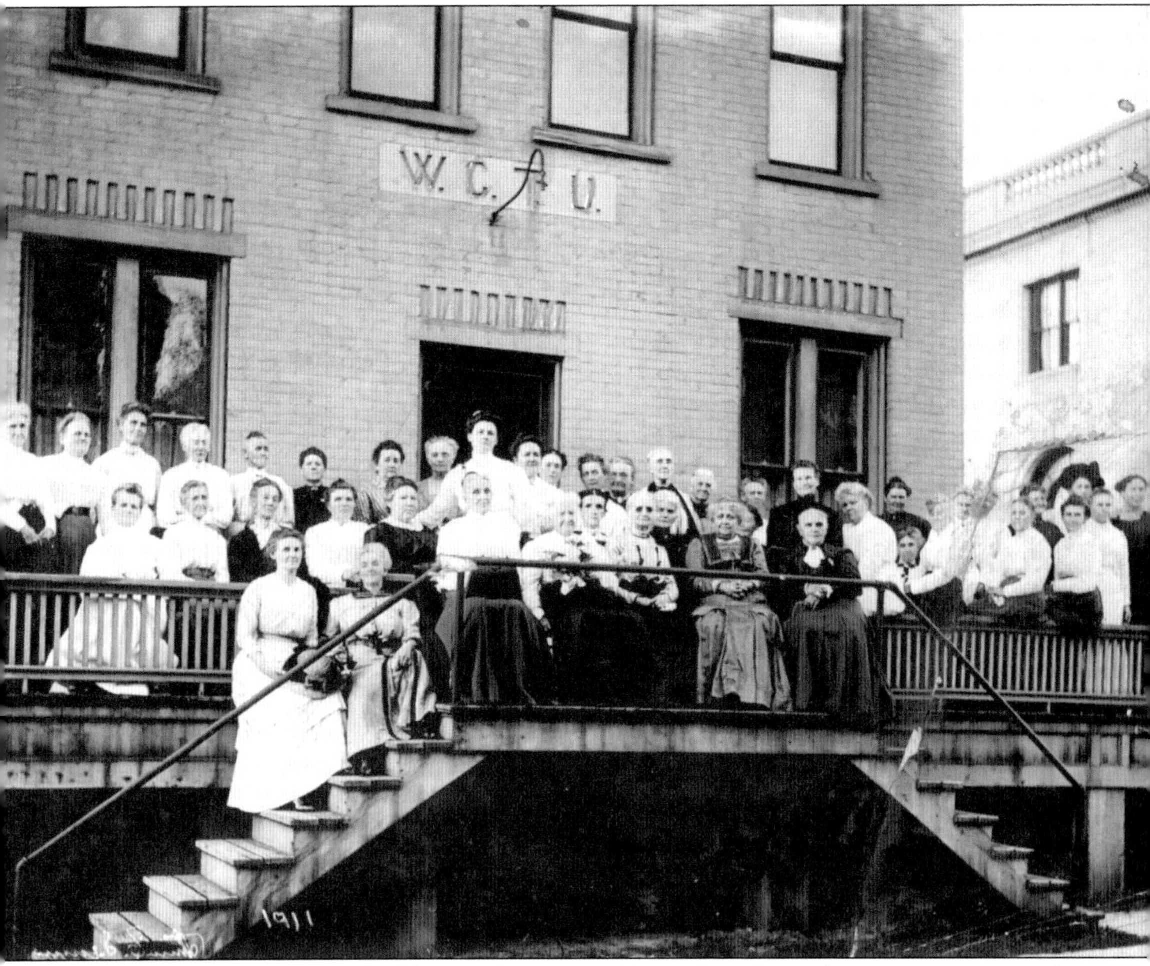

Newly empowered, the highly moralistic WCTU conducted a militant, sometimes violent campaign to close down every Manistee saloon. They soon conducted a militant—sometimes violent—campaign to close down every Manistee saloon. In 1886, the organization had 83 paying members and concerned itself with the maintenance of Manistee's health, hygiene, and moral rectitude on multiple fronts. To the group's credit, one campaign was for women's voting rights, at least in certain municipal elections. Other works included evangelizing to prisoners; juvenile temperance; the distribution of uplifting literature to logging camps, boardinghouses, hotels, and the jail; hygienic homes; Scandinavian literature; suppression of the use of tobacco; scientific instruction; and the suppression of impure literature. This last involved burning public school library books deemed unfit for children. Additional missions included observing the Sabbath and delivering flowers to soldiers, jails, and hospitals. The organization survived for a remarkably long time. This photograph, taken by Jessie Smith, shows a meeting of the active Women's Christian Temperance Union membership in 1911. (Courtesy of the Manistee Historical Museum.)

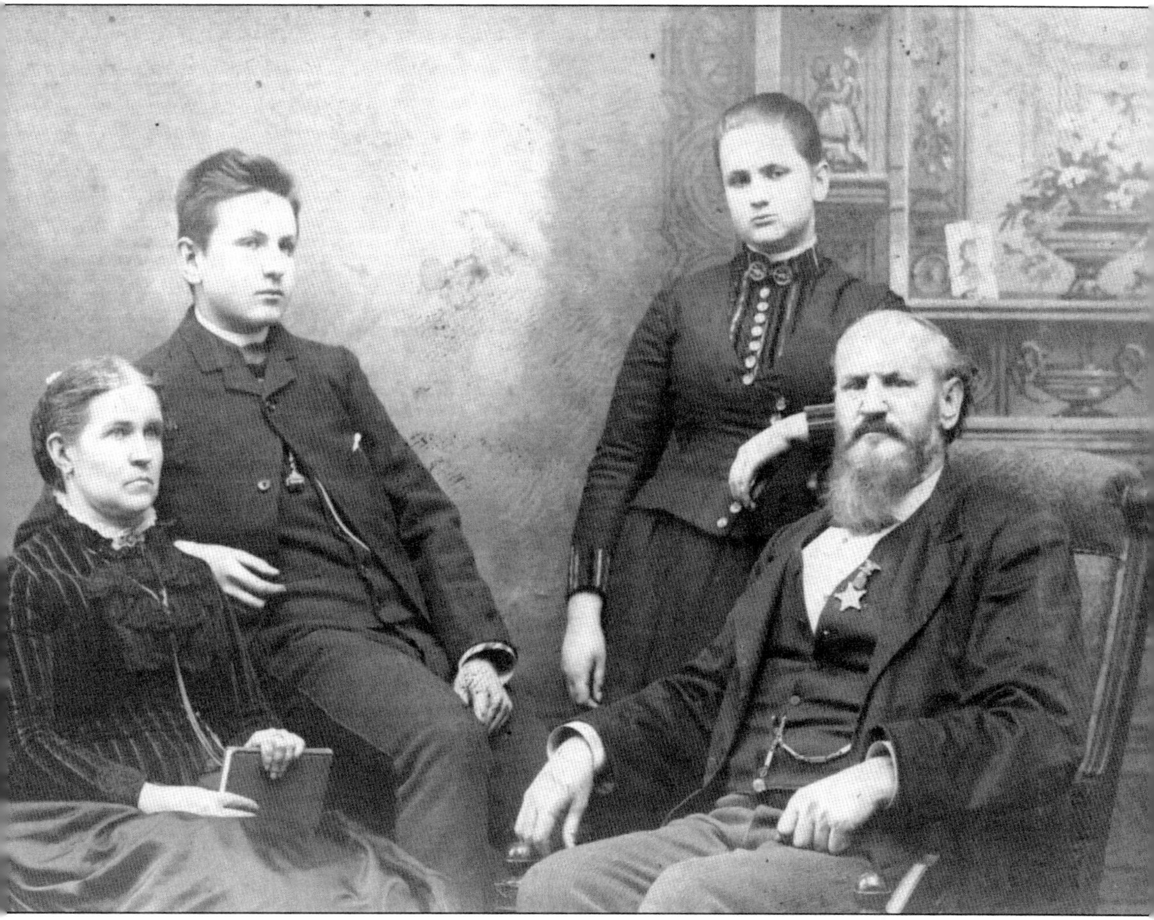

Largely because of Fannie Fowler, wife of newspaperman Smith W. Fowler, Manistee became a significant front in the larger nationwide campaign for women's suffrage. On March 16, 1874, the Michigan legislature voted to submit a suffrage amendment at the November election. The State Suffrage Association appointed a committee that included S. W. Fowler, who along with his wife, campaigned throughout Manistee County. The amendment failed that year despite its popularity. Sponsored by the Fowlers in their continuing campaign, Susan B. Anthony stopped in Manistee on her way from Traverse City to Ludington, giving her lecture "Bread, not the Ballot." In April 1880, the Temperance Association heard Elizabeth Cady Stanton's "Our Girls." This activity resulted in the formation of the Manistee Woman Suffrage Association on June 8, 1880. The organization enjoyed partial success: they began taking part in school elections and serving on local boards of education around 1880. This photograph of the Fowler family shows, from left to right, Fannie, her son Frank, her daughter Angeline, and Smith W. Fowler. (Courtesy of the Manistee Historical Museum.)

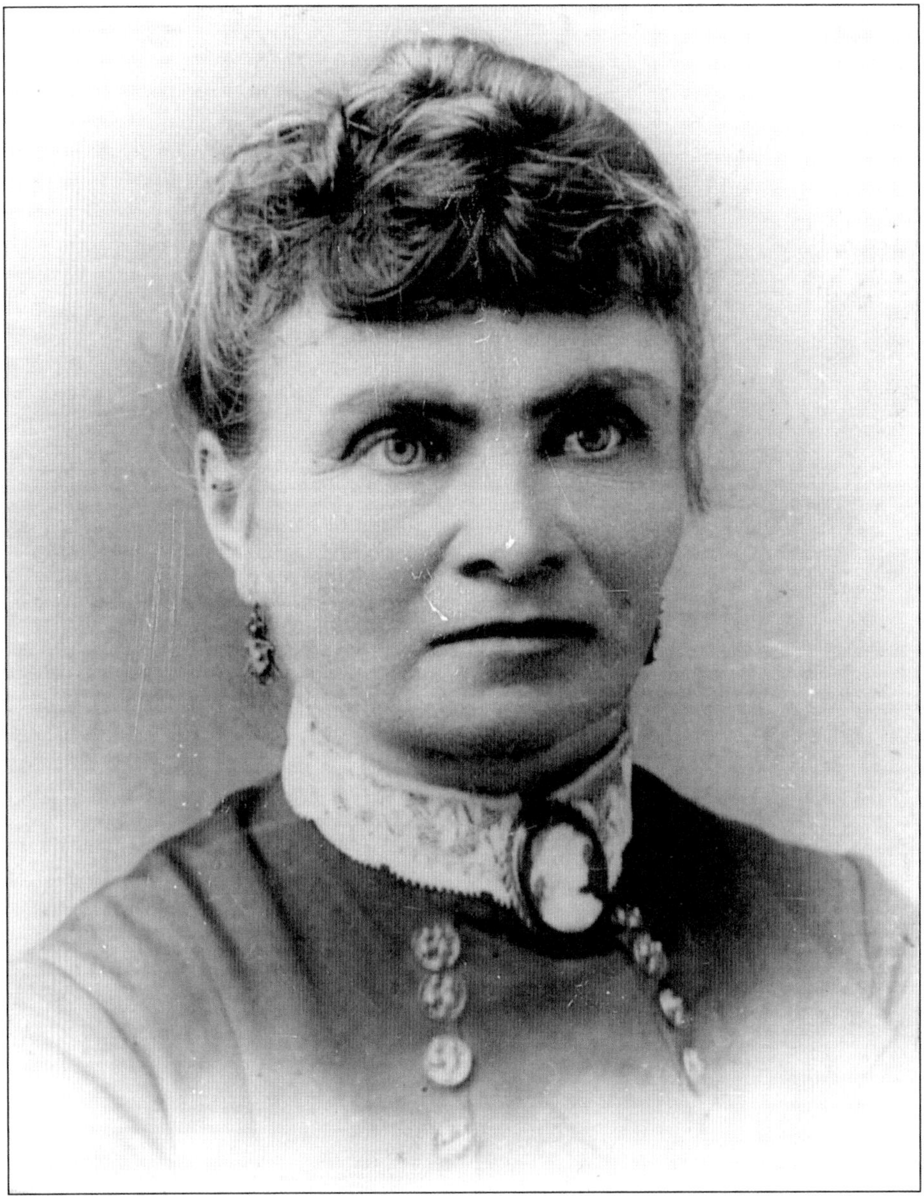

Cecelia Sorenson was an activist of a different order. Coproprietor of a boardinghouse for loggers and laborers off Jones Street (with her husband, John), she halted construction of tracks for a Manistee and Northeastern freight train for two solid days by holding a one-woman sit-in on the site. The Sorensons were not pleased when the company proposed to build the tracks for its new freight train within 10 feet of their boardinghouse. The railroad offered the Sorensons $100 in gold as compensation for the anticipated loss of business, which the Sorensons refused as insufficient compensation. When construction began on October 10, 1888, Cecelia sat down in the path of the proposed rails, effectively halting construction and creating a spectacle. While John sought a lawyer, his wife stayed on the tracks all night and the next day until about 4:00 p.m., when the railroad had her arrested for trespass. Easily acquitted the following Monday, she successfully sued the railroad company for damages. Several weeks later, all the Sorensons' neighbors filed their own suits against the company. (Courtesy of the Manistee Historical Museum.)

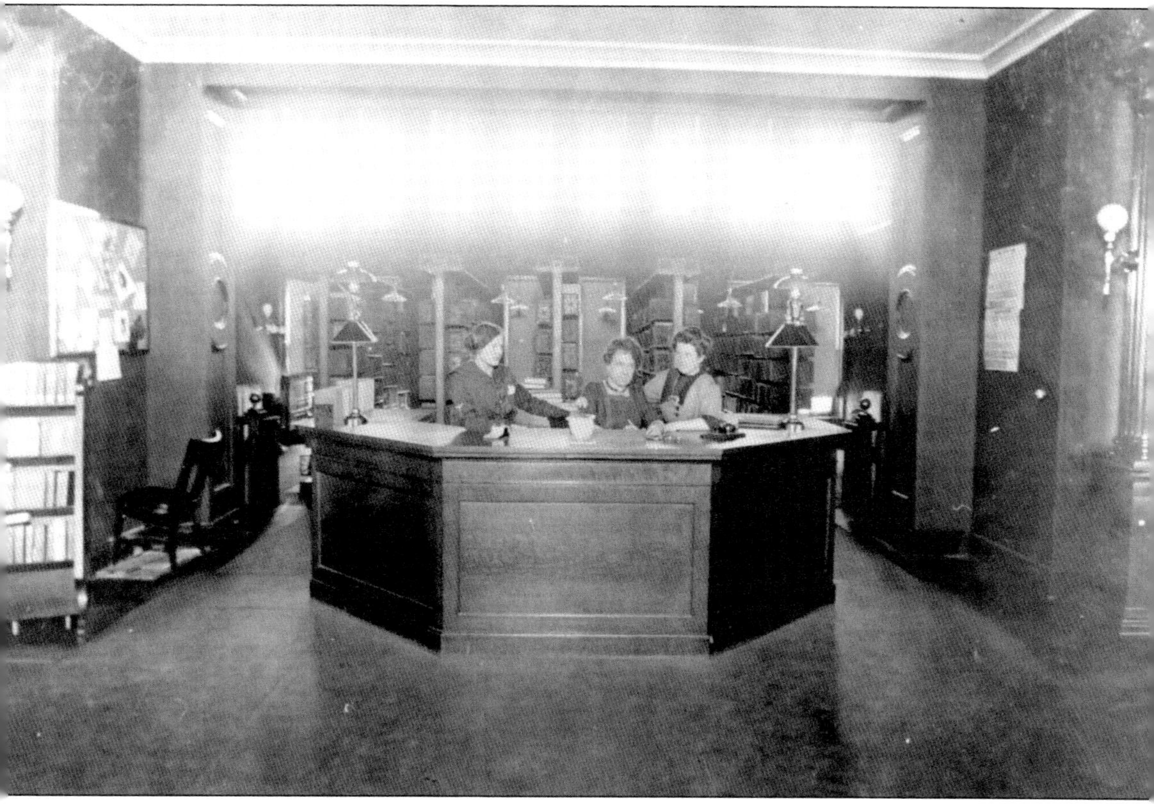

Considerably less radical than the Temperance Union in its approach to moral improvement, another women's organization called the Lakeside Club established Manistee's first public library. Before its founding, books could be checked out only by special permission from the Central School library, which lost significant holdings when the library housed in Union School burned in 1886. (The impact of Temperance fires on the inventory is unknown.) Organized in 1885, the goal of the Lakeside Club was to foster an "intellectual and social culture" in which women could actively participate. Any lady over 16 could join for an application fee of 50¢. Early meetings included literary readings and debates over such topics as heredity and coeducation of the sexes. The Public Library opened June 1, 1905. Staff members Theresa Cahill (left), Lulah Muenscher (center), and Ethel Peterson pose by the library's front desk in 1912. The same desk can be seen in the library today, but the second level of stacks in the current building had not yet been added. (Courtesy of the Manistee County Public Library.)

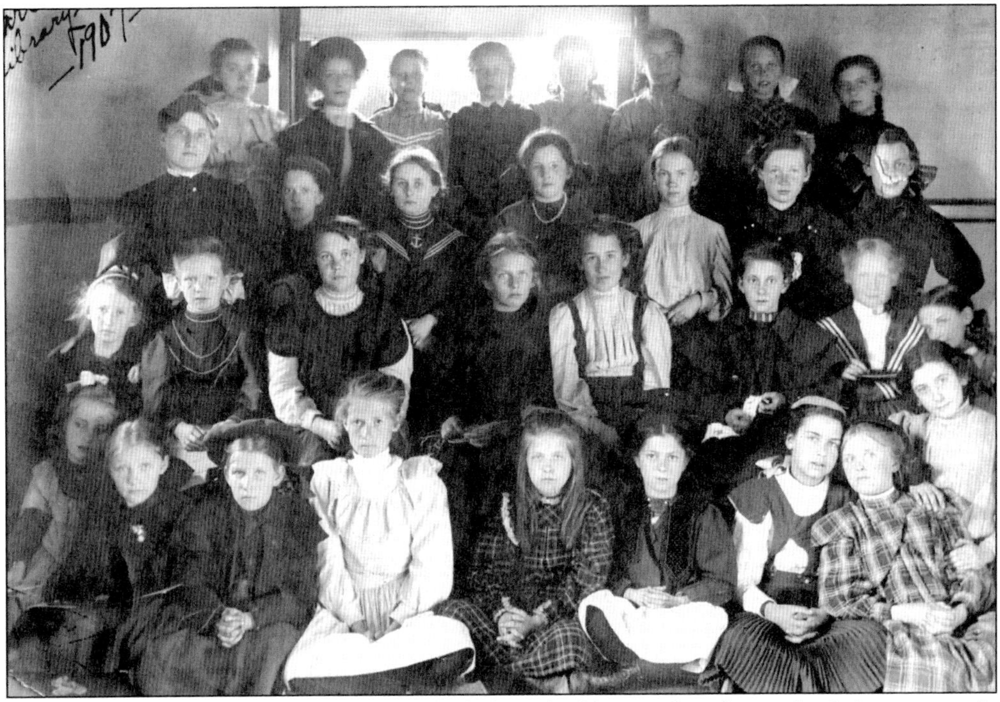

Besides providing an intellectual culture for ladies, the library's founders wished also to provide an educational environment for children. Shown above is a 1907 meeting of the girl's section of the children's Library Club. The library initially had two reading rooms planned for children: one for girls and one for boys. In 1907, membership included 27 girls and 77 boys. A group of adults formed their own reading group shortly after the library opened. In 1912, a special reading room was created for children in the library basement, separate from the adult section. If the coats and hats worn by the intently reading children in the photograph below are any indication, the room must have been quite chilly. (Courtesy of the Manistee County Public Library.)

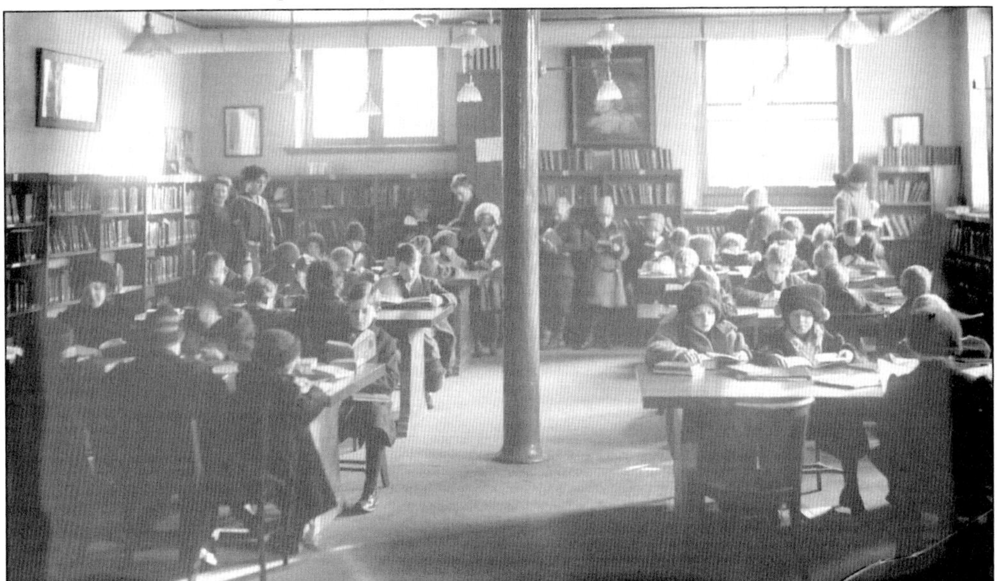

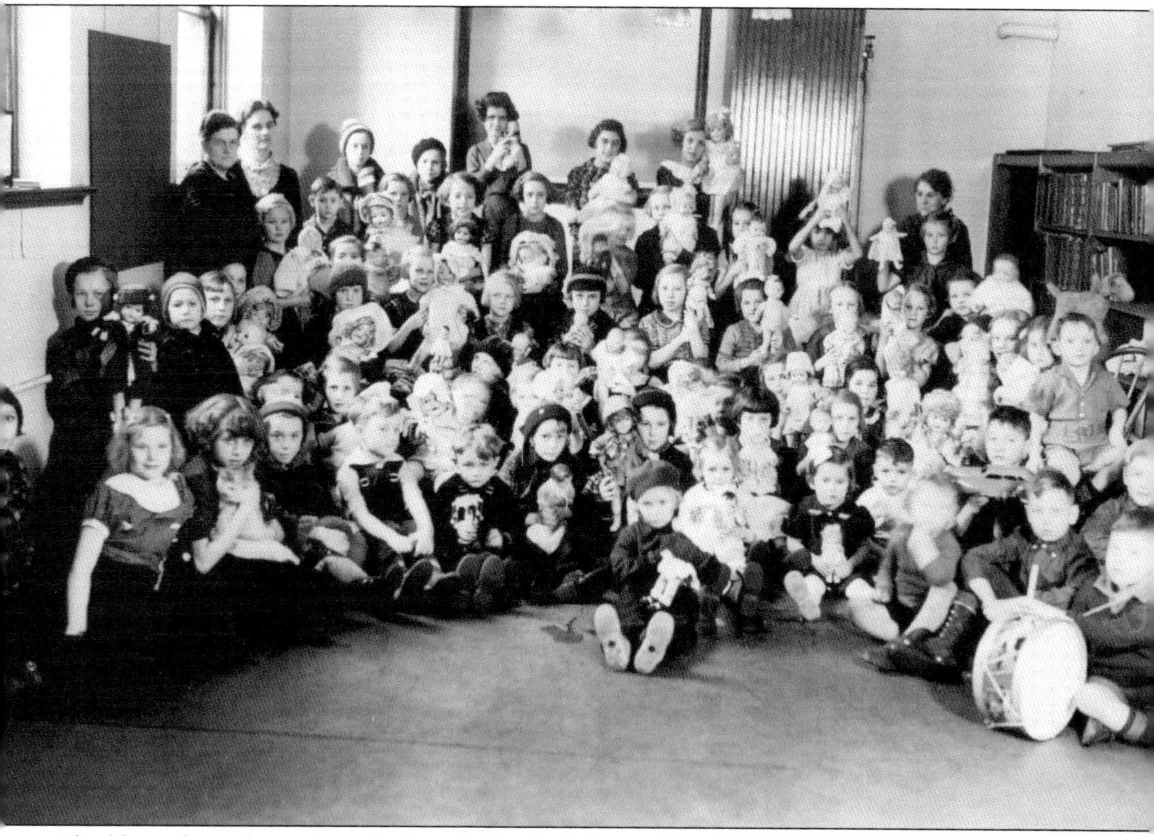

The library hosted a variety of other children's clubs, and kept special children's hours, usually Saturday and Sunday. Shown here is a meeting of the library Doll Club. Little boys were apparently also welcome along with the girls, and other toys seem to have been acceptable besides dolls. The women standing behind the group of children are identified as Amanda Froberg (left), Theresa Hansen (center), and Lucile Dahlrig. (Courtesy of the Manistee Country Public Library.)

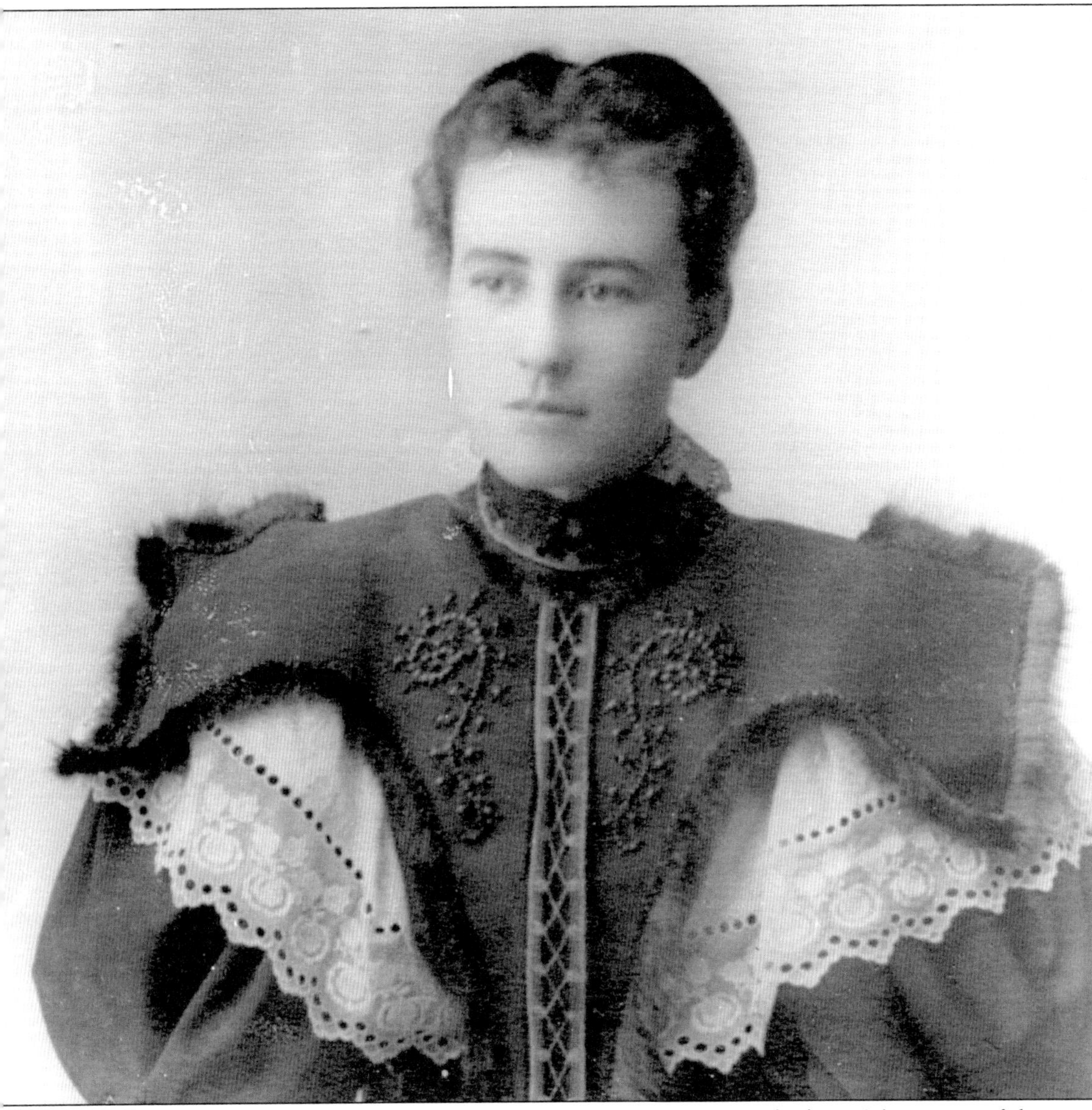

One of the most interesting characteristics of Manistee women in the late 19th century, if this 1896 Hanselman portrait of Agnes Kenny is any indication, is that high-mindedness did not necessarily conflict with high fashion. Daughter of the successful Thomas Kenny and secretary of the library board of the Lakeside Club, Agnes Kenny graduated from the University of Michigan with a degree in English at a time when college was not an option for most young women. After teaching high school for awhile and serving as a faculty member of the Milwaukee State Normal College, she turned her interest to finances and acquired a position in the investment department of the First National Bank of Milwaukee. Although the outfit she wears here, with its dense fabric, beaded fur-trimmed epaulets, and enormous leg-of-mutton sleeves, might appear excessive to contemporary eyes, this fashionable "walking suit" was at the time considered highly appropriate attire for a teacher. (Courtesy of the Manistee Historical Museum.)

In the 1992 portrait on the right, young Carrie Secor displays the hourglass figure so prized in late-Victorian fashion, accomplished through a combination of leg-of-mutton sleeves, flaring skirts, and rigid corseting. The costume worn by T. J. Ramsdell's daughter Winnogene, as she poses below near the front of her father's theater, displays the longer, narrower Edwardian line that came into fashion in approximately 1909. Achieving this look required donning long, straight, corsets that were made of steel strips and went nearly to the knees. (Courtesy of the Manistee Historical Museum.)

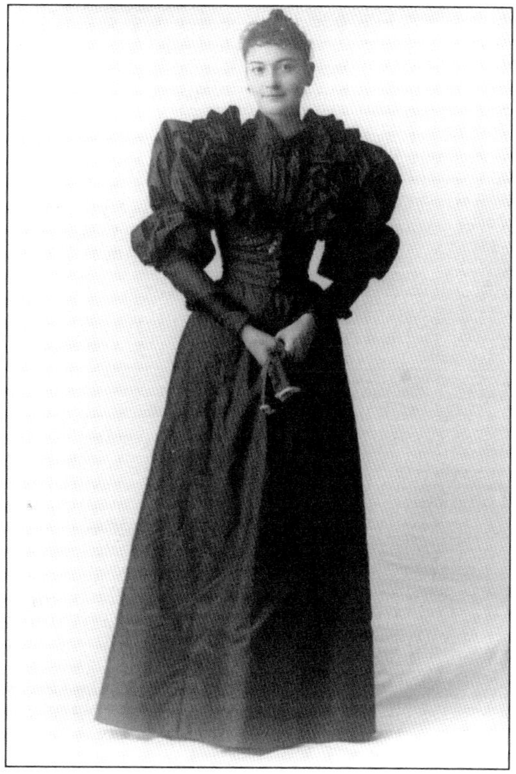

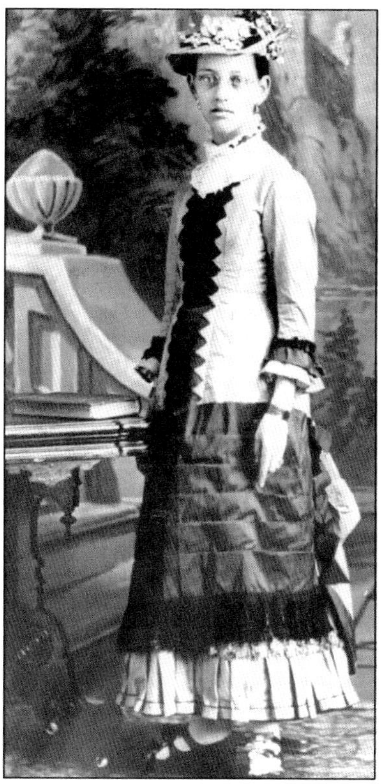

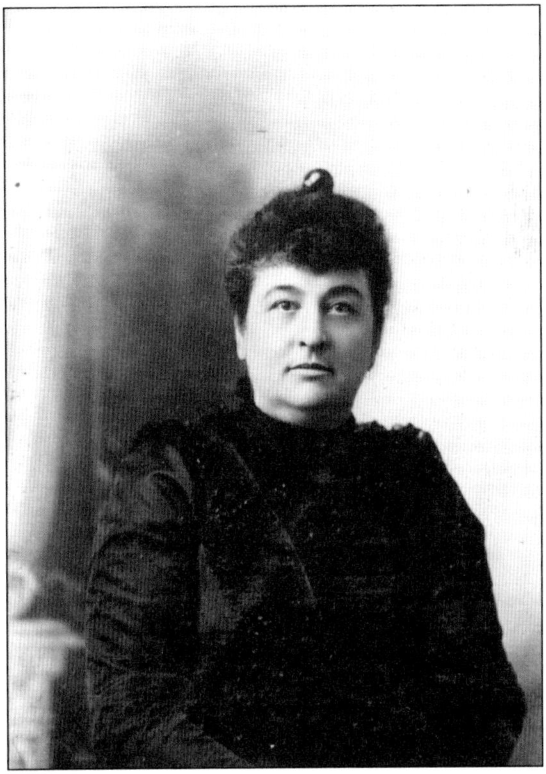

Carrie Filer (left), wife of D. Warren Filer, was noted for her generous contributions to local charities. In 1876, the couple began building a home on Cedar Street, finishing in 1878. Three stories tall, the home (below) was topped with a three-story tower. Venetian glass chandeliers lit the rooms, and mantelpieces of imported Italian marble decorated the fireplaces. Their bathroom featured two stained-glass windows and was rumored to be equipped with solid-gold plumbing and accessories. When Carrie died in 1909, she bequeathed her luxurious home to the care of elderly women. The Carrie Filer Home for Aged Women, which opened in 1910, remained in operation until 1959. Applicants were charged a fee of $300, but women lacking these funds were still accepted and cared for until death at no cost. (Courtesy of the Manistee Historical Museum.)

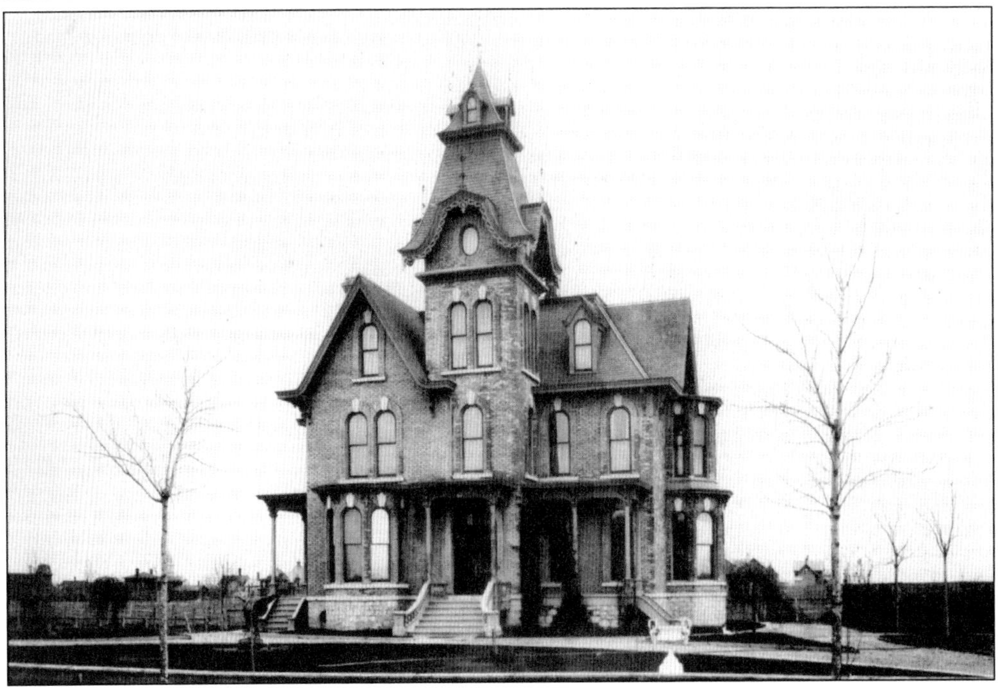

Women's career choices were limited and they earned considerably less than men, but their work was essential. Teaching offered a good career for bright young women both in the city and elsewhere in Manistee County. Emma Danforth, shown in the 1890 photograph to the right, began teaching in a log schoolhouse east of Brethren at age 16. She was the mother of Donald Crouch, the Brethren high school teacher famously credited by James Earl Jones for inspiring him to become an actor. Below, in a photograph taken around 1933, are Manistee County teachers representing several Manistee County districts. They are, from left to right, Anna Stone Kiszelek, Hazel Belcher Hanson, Grace Ringel Radtke, and Julia Jaitner. (Right, courtesy of the Brethren Historical Museum; below, courtesy of Mary Ann Kaczmarek.)

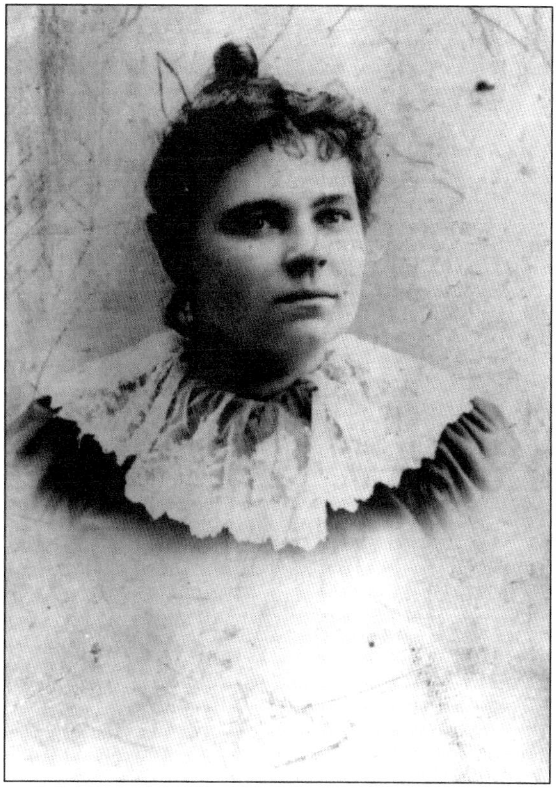

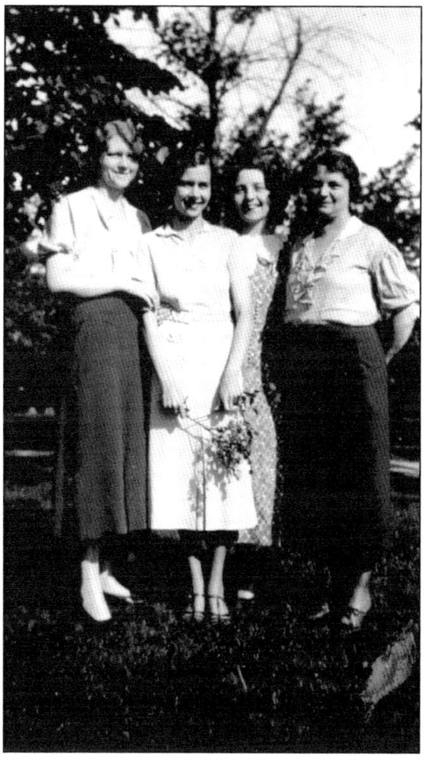

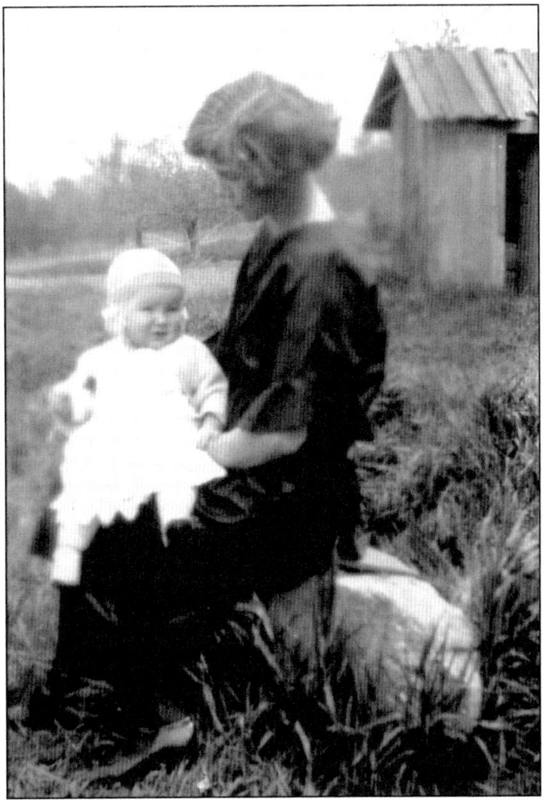

Up until the 1930s, American middle- or upper-class women rarely worked. Working-class women and those recently immigrated often worked hard as domestics, shop girls, or factory workers. On the homesteads and farms of Manistee County, however, women and girls worked alongside the men, taking on any number of tasks on top of their traditional roles as wives, mothers, and housekeepers. During the logging era, the men often spent the entire winter in logging camps, while their wives took full responsibility for running the farms as well as their homes. In the 1923 picture at left, young mother Anna Meister Christenson of Chief, Michigan, holds her baby daughter Lorraine in the family's yard. Below, Norma Krause confidently leads a team of horses and wagon across her family's Marilla farmyard. (Courtesy of Carol Schimke.)

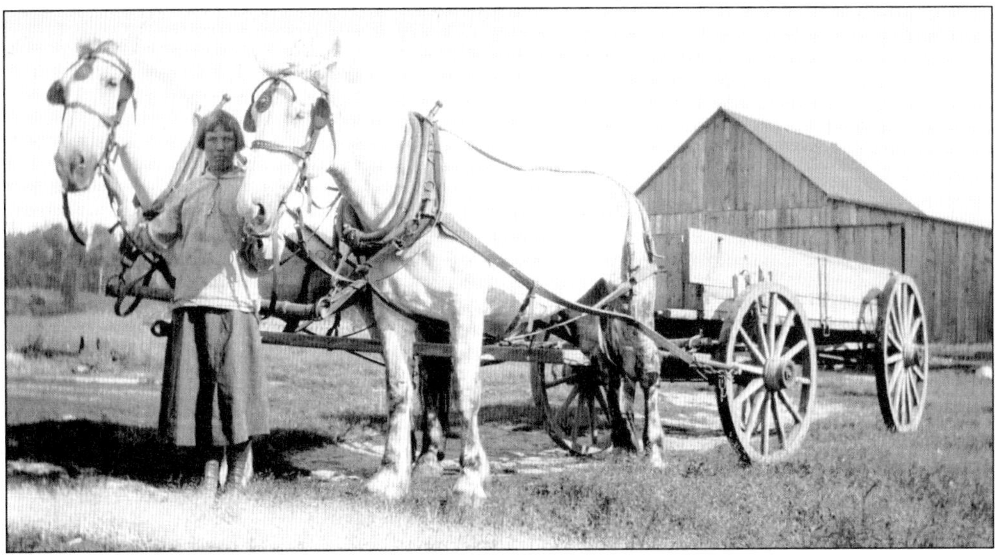

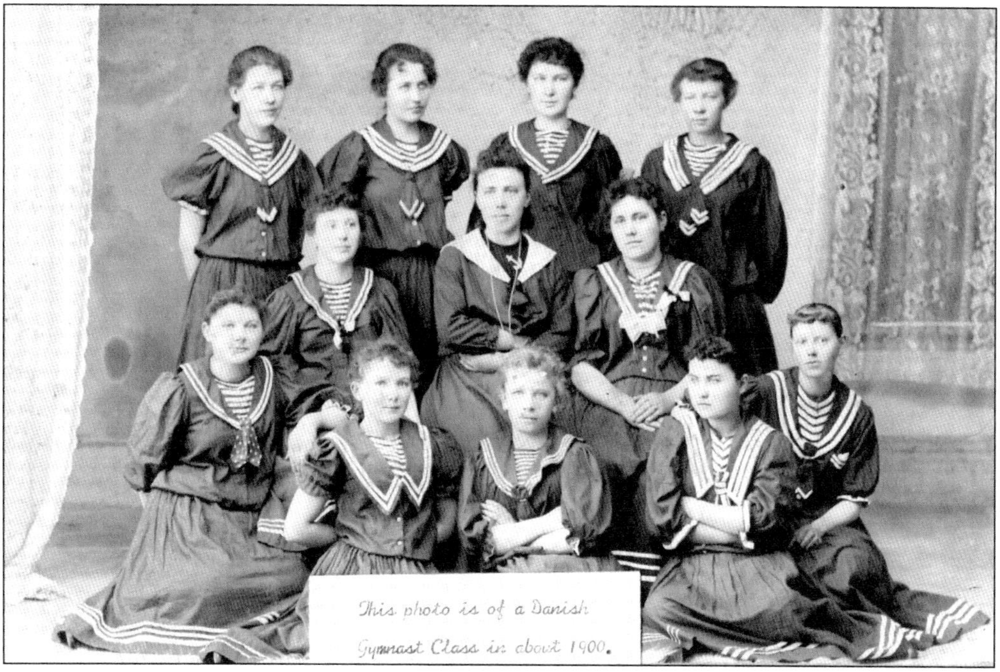

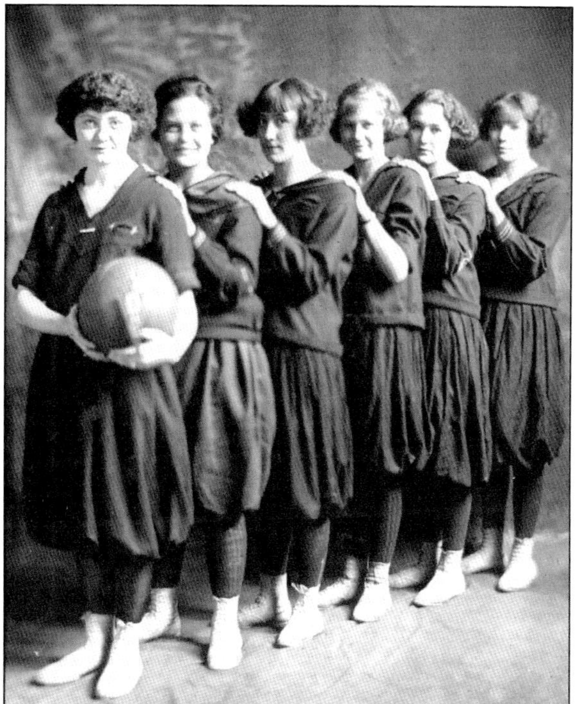

The late 19th and early 20th centuries saw a rise of participation in girls' athletics. Regular programs of physical education for American girls began sometime in the mid-1800s, an aspect of the same pursuit of physical and moral hygiene that gave rise to feminism and temperance campaigns. At the start of the 20th century, girls' athletics were introduced in American schools as a development of modern notions of progress. Gymnastics, however, was a European import and had been an integral part of Danish culture throughout the 18th century. The Danish Girls' Gymnastics Team poses above, around 1900. Its members are unfortunately unidentified. To the right, the Onekama High School girls' basketball team gathers for a photograph in 1923. (Above, courtesy of Our Saviour's Historical Museum; right, courtesy of Carol Schimke.)

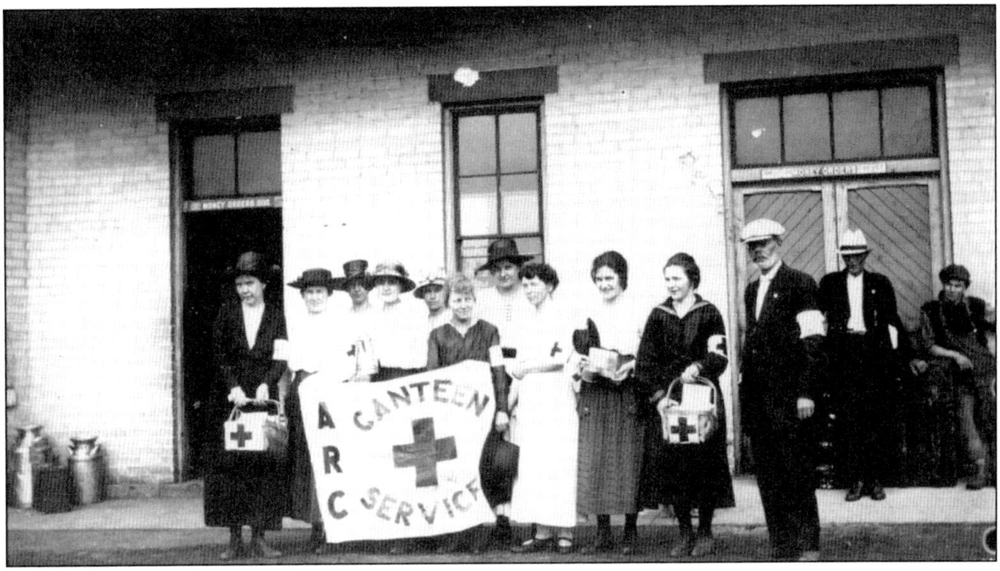

In wartime, Manistee County women volunteered in patriotic efforts. The Kaleva Red Cross Canteen Service (above) was organized by Dr. Coates. After the 1918 Armistice, Kaleva Canteen volunteers would meet every train full of returning soldiers with hot meals and coffee. During World War II, women took on men's jobs. The mostly female group below proudly poses with tools outside a sawmill in the village of Chief. Pictured here, from left to right, are the following: (first row) Sally Siegfried, Norma Soper, and Marian Whittum; (second row) Mr. and Mrs. Wyse, Sophie Christenson Rhodes, Everton and Rose Anderson, Anna Meister Christenson, Lawrence Whittum, Iva Schmuker Watson, Marvin Schimke, Charlotte Gauthier O'Hagan, Art Soper, unidentified, and Lester and Miriam Wyse. (Above, courtesy of the Kaleva Historical Society; below, courtesy of Carol Schimke.)

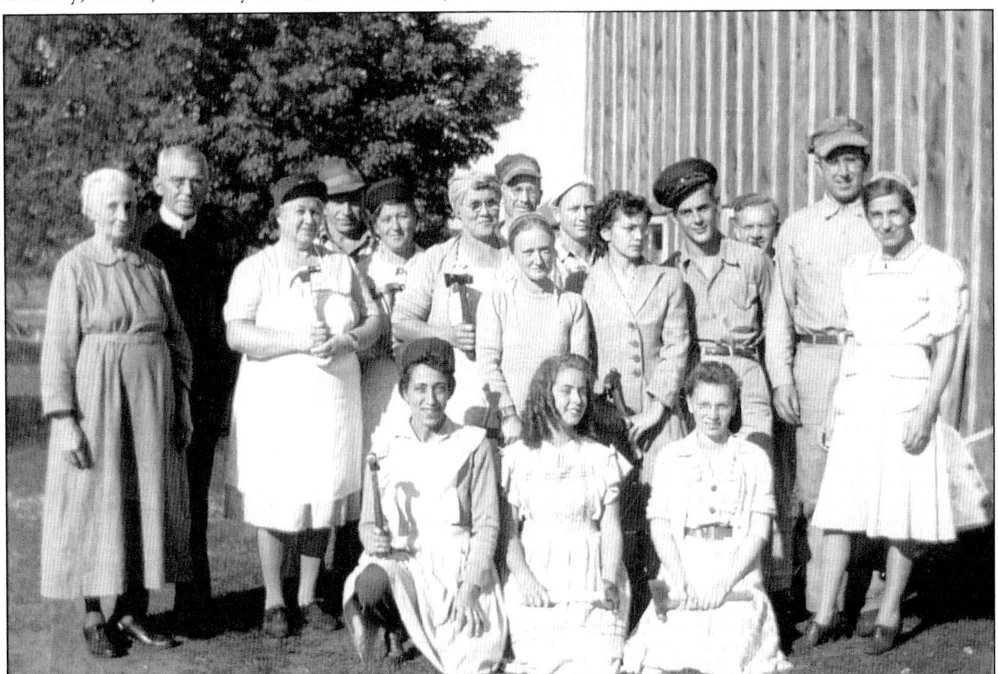

Six

The Rest of the World

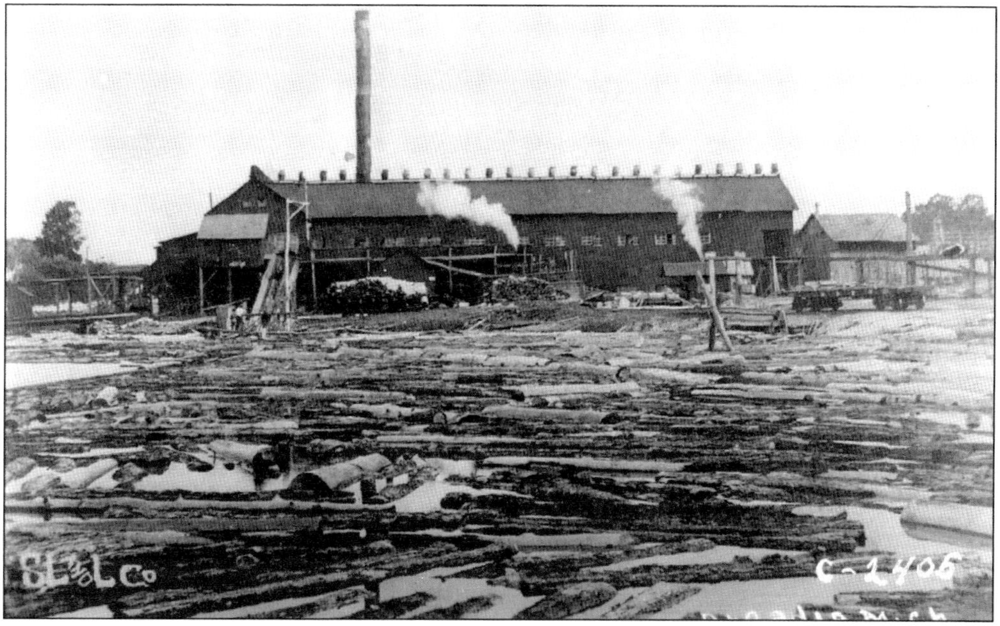

Although the first townships of Manistee County were founded in the 1850s, at approximately the same time as the city was developing, they remained for the most part, quite independent. Settled by sturdy homesteaders and immigrants who preferred rural life, they are best characterized by their self-sufficiency. Arcadia, some 20 miles north up the coast from Manistee, was one such settlement, until Henry Starke, a Milwaukee industrialist who had helped build Manistee Harbor, built the village of Arcadia and a sawmill in 1880 on what was then called Bar Lake—apparently as a hobby for his retirement to the northern forest where he used to enjoy his Sunday walk. To facilitate shipping directly from Arcadia Harbor, he had built a 1,300-foot bridge pier. Later, when this proved impractical, he dredged the harbor, so that ships could actually enter. When the original mill burned down, Henry rebuilt another, and the business became the Starke Land and Lumber Company, shown here. The barrels visible on the roof collected rainwater, as a fire prevention system. (Courtesy of the Arcadia Area Historical Society.)

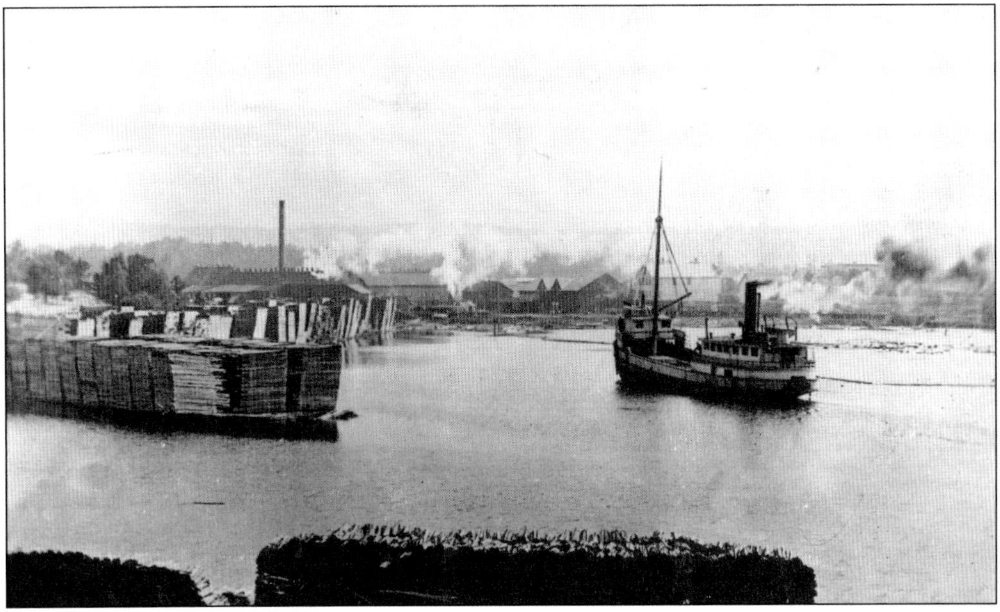

Built in Milwaukee in 1888 from timber cut in the local mill, the *Arcadia* was a steam barge that hauled lumber for the Starke Land and Lumber Company. The *Arcadia* shipped massive stacks of individual boards to Wisconsin and Illinois, until it was sold in 1906. This view, which includes the sawmill, looks northeast from the north end of Bar Lake.

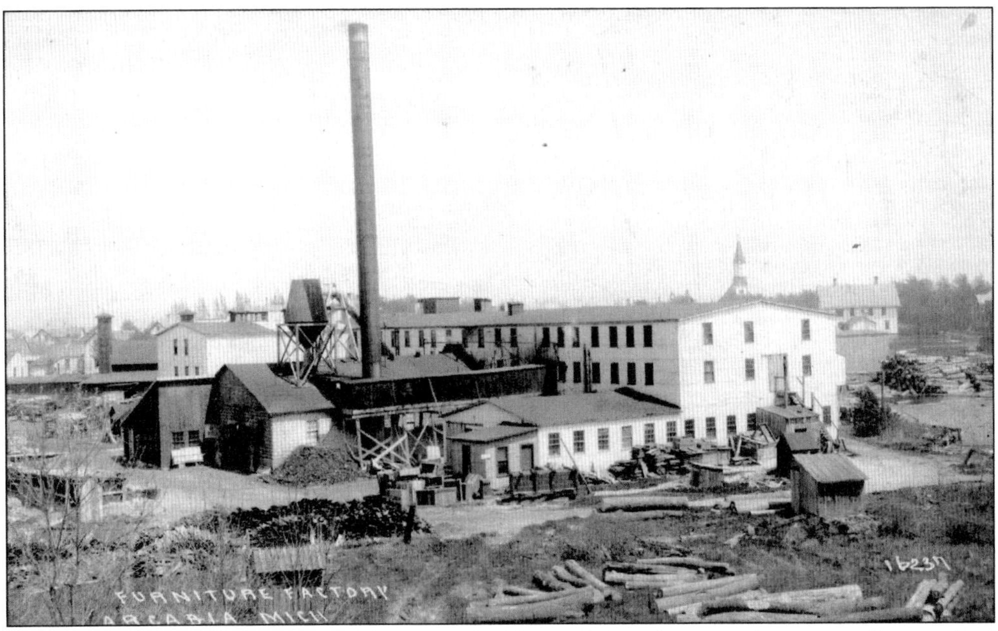

In 1906, the sawmill burned to the ground. Although by this time Manistee County had been almost completely denuded of pine lumber, good hardwood remained on Henry Starke's land. Henry's adopted son Charles strategically decided to replace the mill with a furniture firm. The Arcadia Furniture Company produced bedroom furniture from native hard maple for several decades, maintaining a vital economy when the city of Manistee was faltering. (Courtesy of the Arcadia Area Historical Society.)

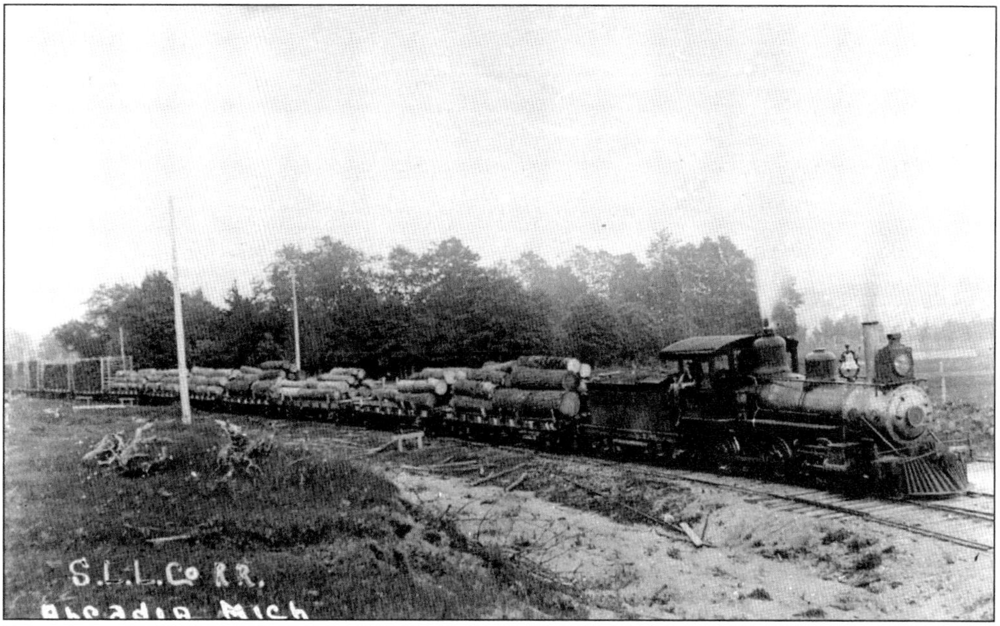

Like most northern Michigan lumbermen, Henry Starke built a narrow-gauge railway in 1881 to transport lumber to his mills. Foreseeing, as most did, the end of the lumber boom, Starke began construction of a more versatile standard-gauge railroad, which would eventually reach Copemish 21 miles away. (Courtesy of the Arcadia Area Historical Society.)

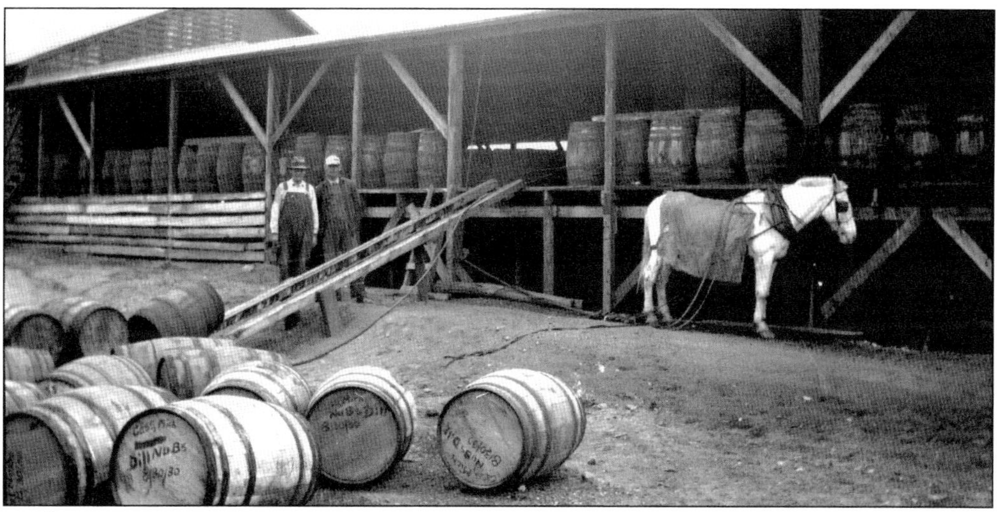

Starke's conversion of his narrow-gauge to the starndard-gauge Arcadia and Betsey created a sustainable local economy. Not only did it transport Starke lumber and passengers, but also produce from local farms. Stopping along the way at small processing factories, like the pickle house shown here, the train would pick up produce brought in by farmers on wagons for transport to junction towns like Henry and Copemish. There, the local lines would meet larger commercial trains for transport to distant markets. (Courtesy of Carol Schimke.)

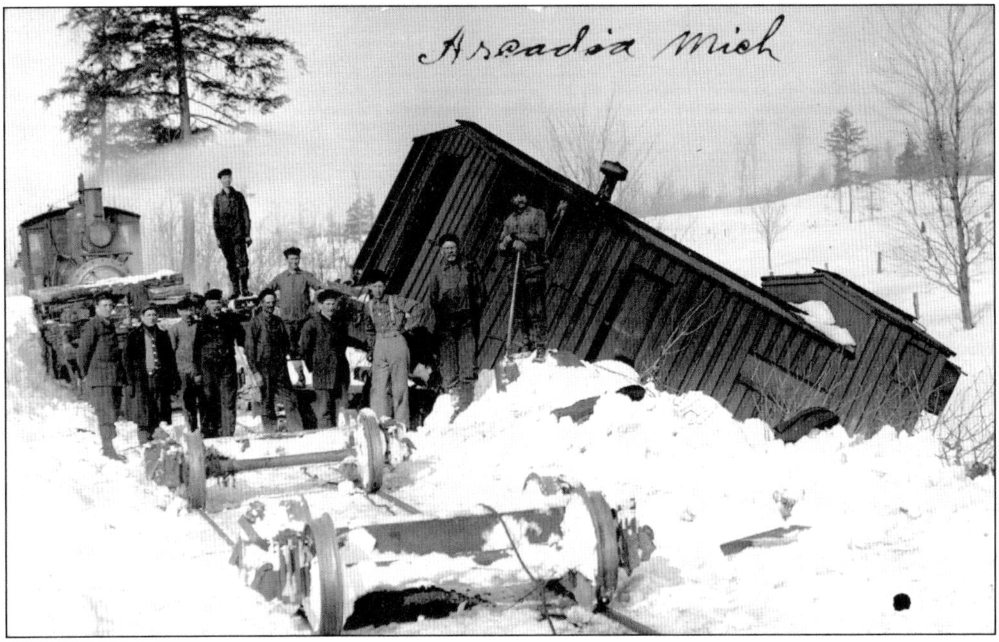

Early rail transport though northern Michigan winters was a treacherous prospect at best, and train wrecks were not unusual. In fact, the Arcadia and Betsey experienced its fair share. The photograph above, taken sometime in the early 1900s, possibly just outside of Henry, gives a good view of a typical transportation problem. When the snow was particularly deep and such wrecks were a concern, schoolboys or Starke Land and Lumber factory workers would be released to help shovel, as seen below. At times, a steam-powered crane would be deployed to right the freight cars. (Courtesy of the Arcadia Area Historical Society.)

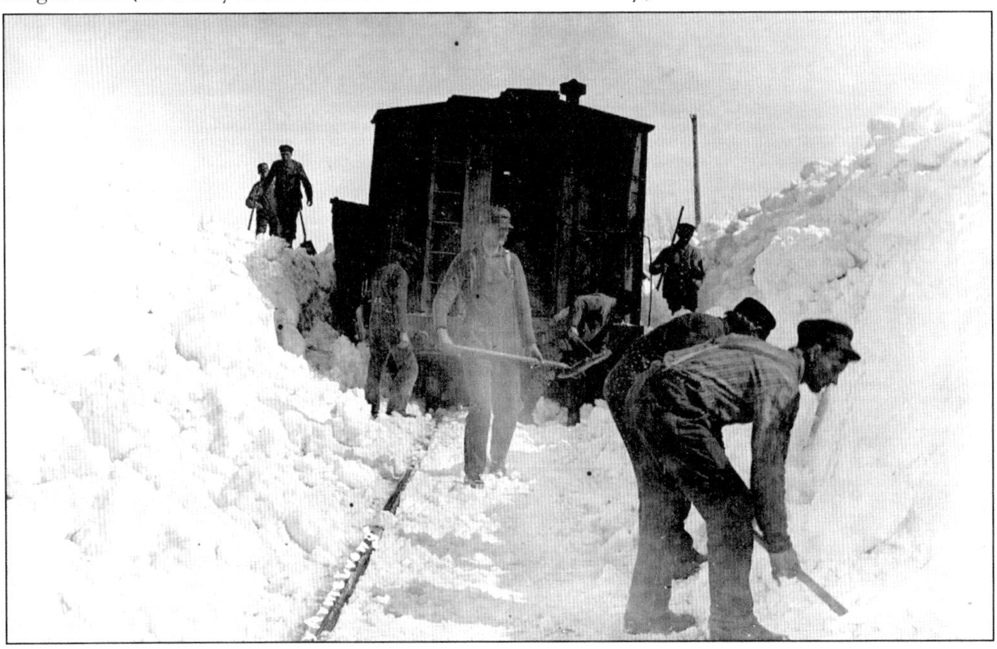

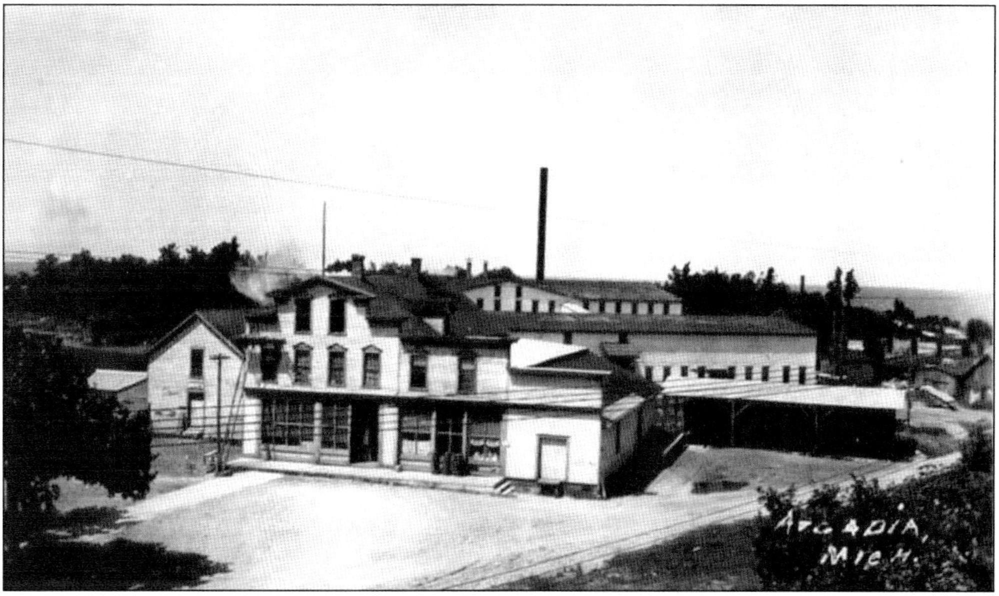

The Arcadia Furniture Company Store was located at the west end of Lake Street on First Street. Like most such stores, it sold necessities to factory workers. Once the plant closed, the store had several other incarnations. Eventually it became a Thanksgiving turkey processing factory. One of the few company buildings that remained standing, it finally burned in the 1950s, with two million turkeys inside.

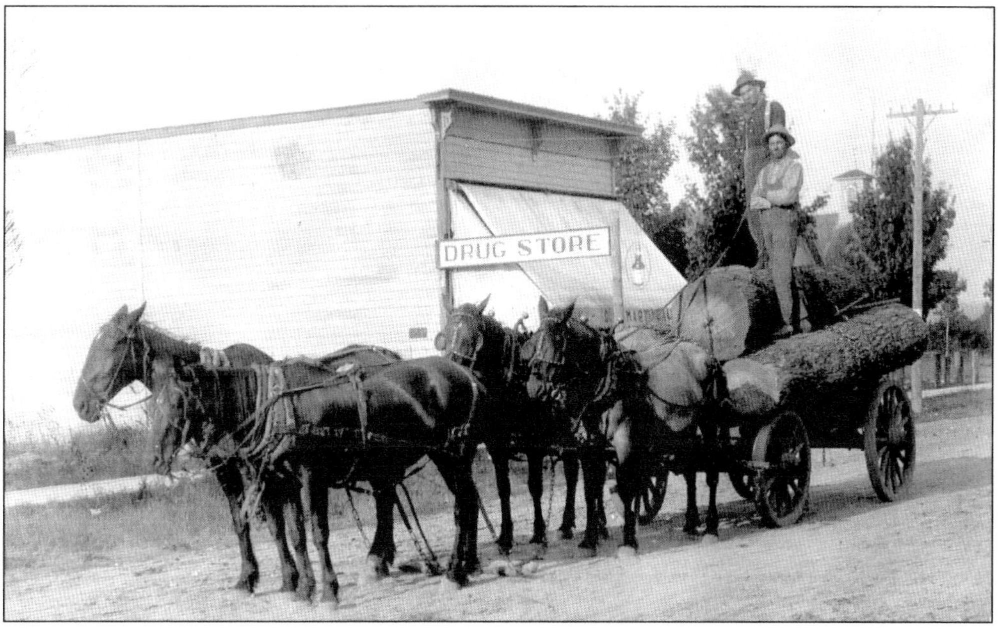

A wagonload of logs passes in front of the first Martineau's Drug Store on Fourth Street, facing Lake Street. Visible in the upper right corner is one of Arcadia's twin schools—so called because a mill town a few miles north of Arcadia called Burnham closed when its lumber ran out; most of its buildings, including the school, were moved to Arcadia. The Burnham school was then placed next to the one already established in Arcadia. (Courtesy of the Arcadia Area Historical Society.)

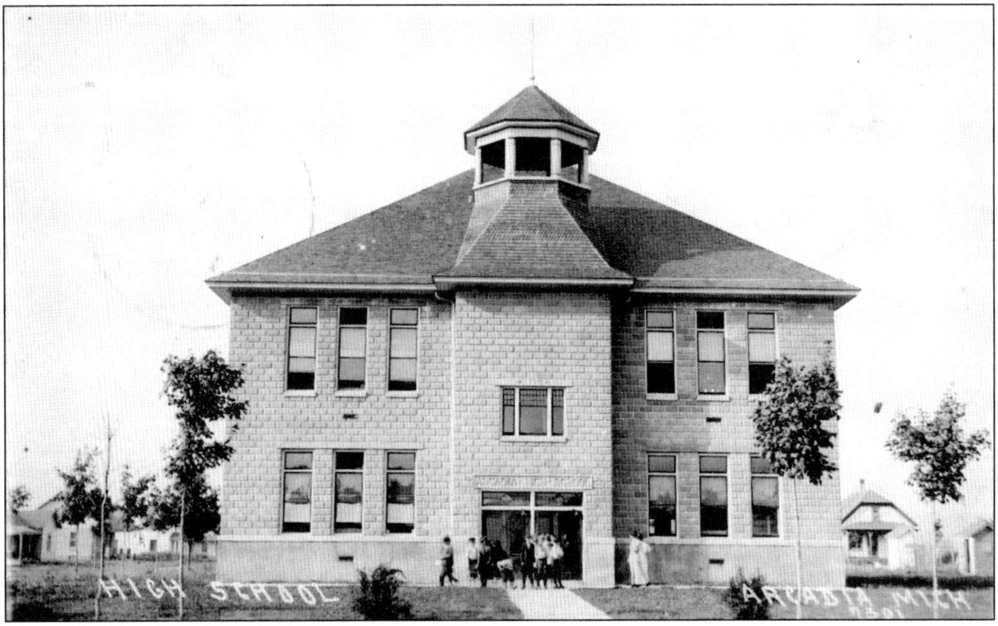

As transportation was severely limited in the early days, children in rural northern Michigan were educated at first in small, local one-room schools. Those near Arcadia were consolidated into Arcadia High School in 1910. Elementary grades were on the first floor, while high school students used the second-floor classrooms.

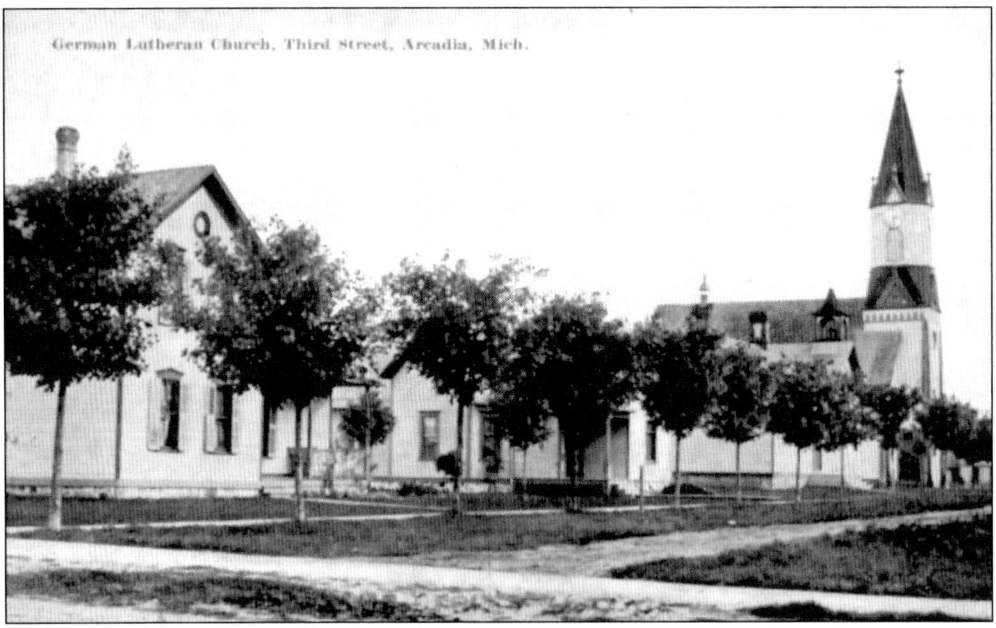

Like many of Manistee's early settlers, those who came to the village of Arcadia were largely German Lutheran. Although the congregation was founded in 1881, the church was not dedicated until 1888. The Trinity Lutheran complex consisted of, from left to right, the parsonage, teacherage, school, and church, featuring a Nels Johnson Century Clock. Services were mostly in German, as were the parochial school classes. After the eighth grade, Lutheran students tested to pass into public school. (Courtesy of the Arcadia Area Historical Society.)

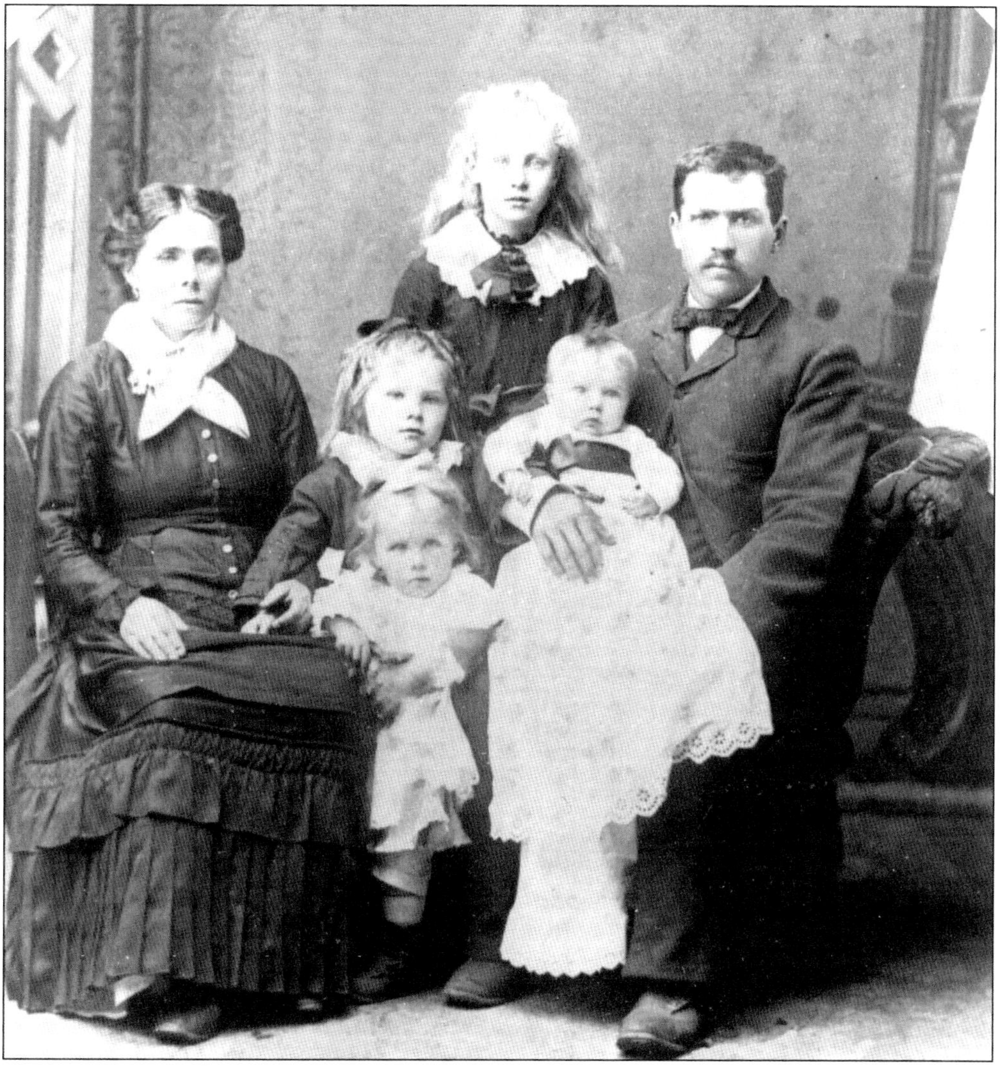

Some Europeans who immigrated to America in the 1870s and 1880s chose the country life. By this time, much of north and central Manistee County had been cleared by logging operations, and early homesteaders had established several townships. The Polish were not the only ones who resisted Otto Bismarck's quest for empire. Dan Meister, like many young men from the former Prussian provinces, fled to the United States to avoid forced conscription. In 1875, he left Germany with his wife, Ottilie "Tillie," and two daughters, Ida and Emma. The Meisters arrived in Manistee in 1883, settled in Bear Lake Township on Eight Mile Road, raised their children, and made a living as farmers. The family members pictured here, from left to right, are Tillie, Emma with Emilia "Mamie" in front of her, Ida, and Dan with baby Albert on his lap. (Courtesy of Carol Schimke.)

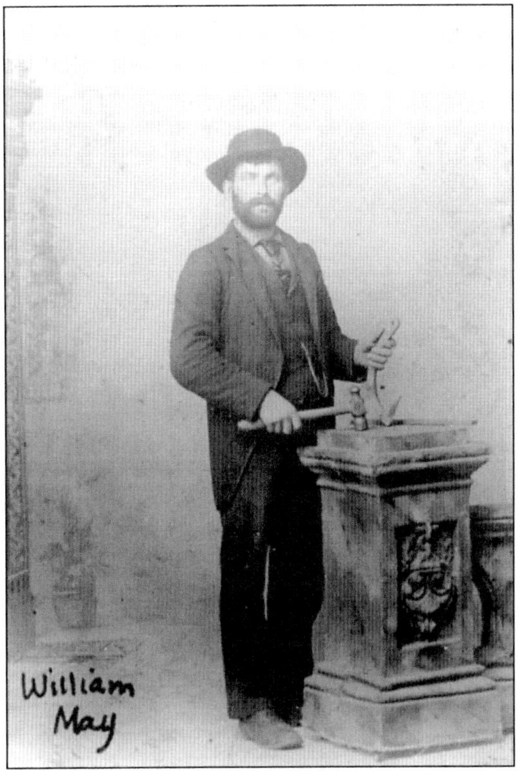

Other new arrivals became valuable community members because they brought skilled trades from the Old Country. William May, pictured at left, possibly in Germany, was both a blacksmith and carpenter who lived just outside of Onekama on Eight Mile Road. On November 23, 1895, he married Dan and Tillie Meister's oldest girl, Ida. Their wedding portrait is below. (Courtesy of Carol Schimke.)

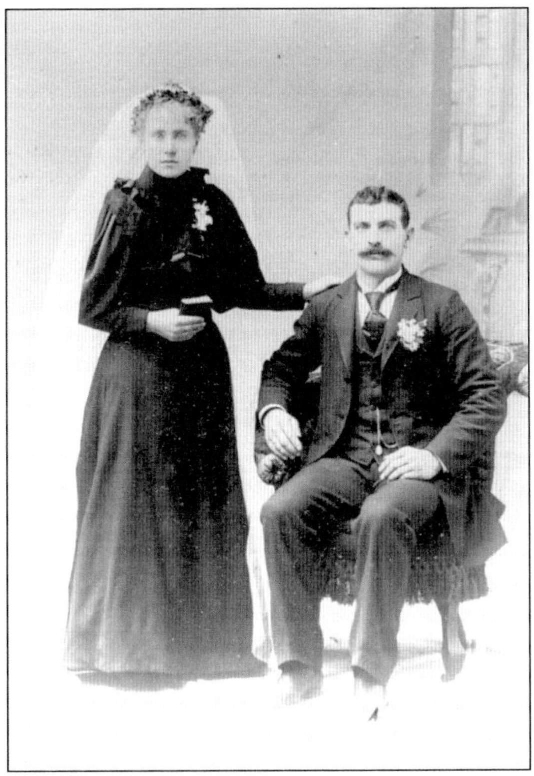

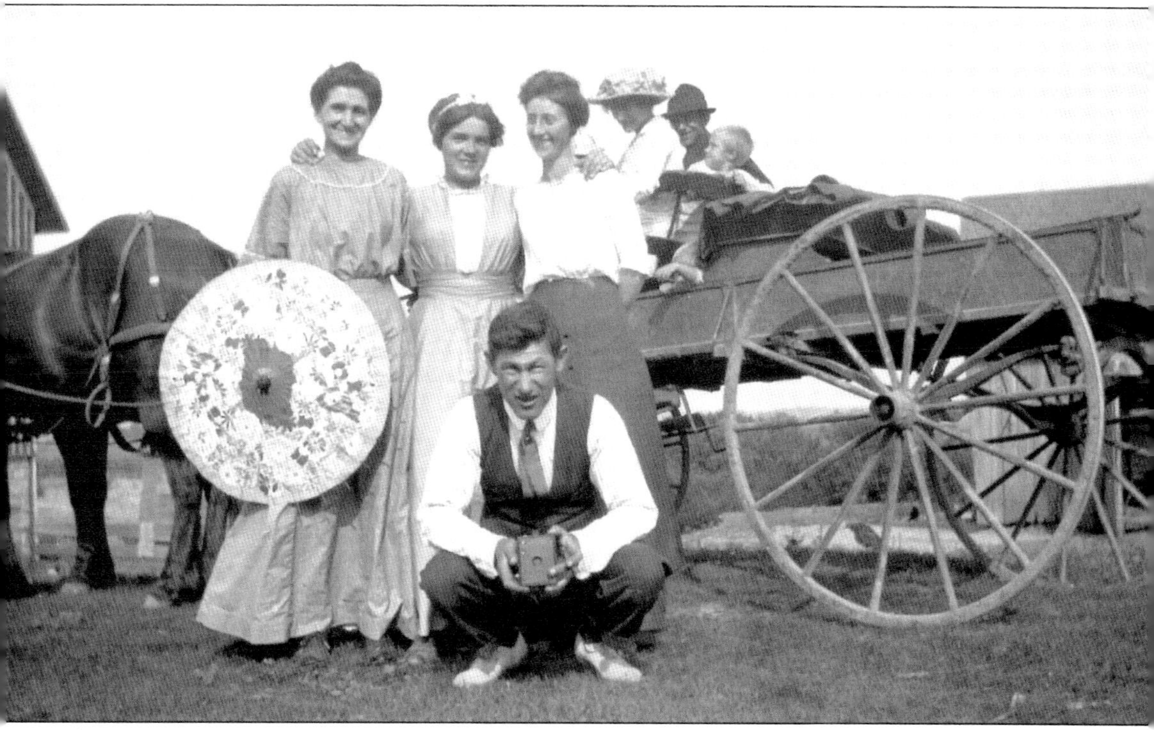

Elsie Meister, second from the left, married a man named Albert Krause. She was an especially accomplished seamstress, often sewing dresses for her nieces. The man with the camera is Alvin Johnson, a neighbor who lived just north of downtown Chief. His camera is most likely a No. 2 Brownie box, first manufactured by Eastman Kodak Company in 1907. Sold for a list price of $2 and widely distributed, the Brownie created a revolution in photography. For the first time, rather than seeking out a professional for a potentially costly formal studio portrait, ordinary people could easily make snapshots of family life and events of interest to them. Many of the graceful images of rural family life in this chapter were likely shot with a Brownie. (Courtesy of Carol Schimke.)

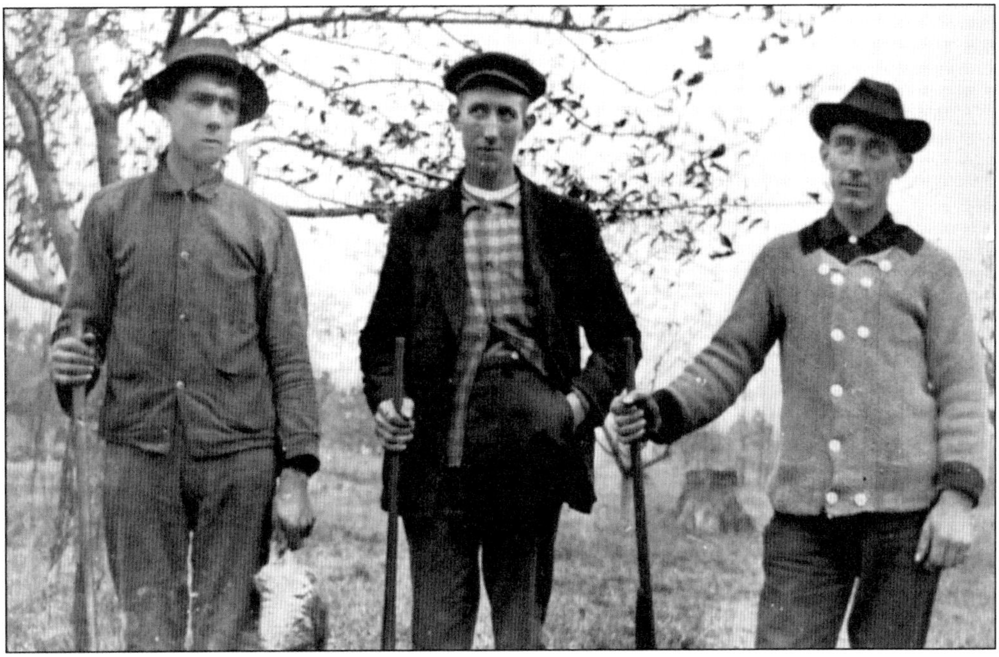

Farmers in rural Manistee County at the beginning of the 20th century were almost completely self-sufficient. They grew their own vegetables and raised enough hogs, cattle, and chickens to supply the family meals. What could not be raised was caught. Some expeditions, like hunting, were typically male endeavors. Albert Meister (left), friend and neighbor Fred Krause (center), and Fred's brother Albert pose above after a successful hunt in 1910. Fishing, on the other hand, was a family sport. Below, the Meister family and friends show a particularly good catch around 1919. Pictured here, from left to right, are Otto Meister, his sister Anna, Tillie (who often wore elaborate hats), George, Dan, Albert Krause, and Arthur May. (Courtesy of Carol Schimke.)

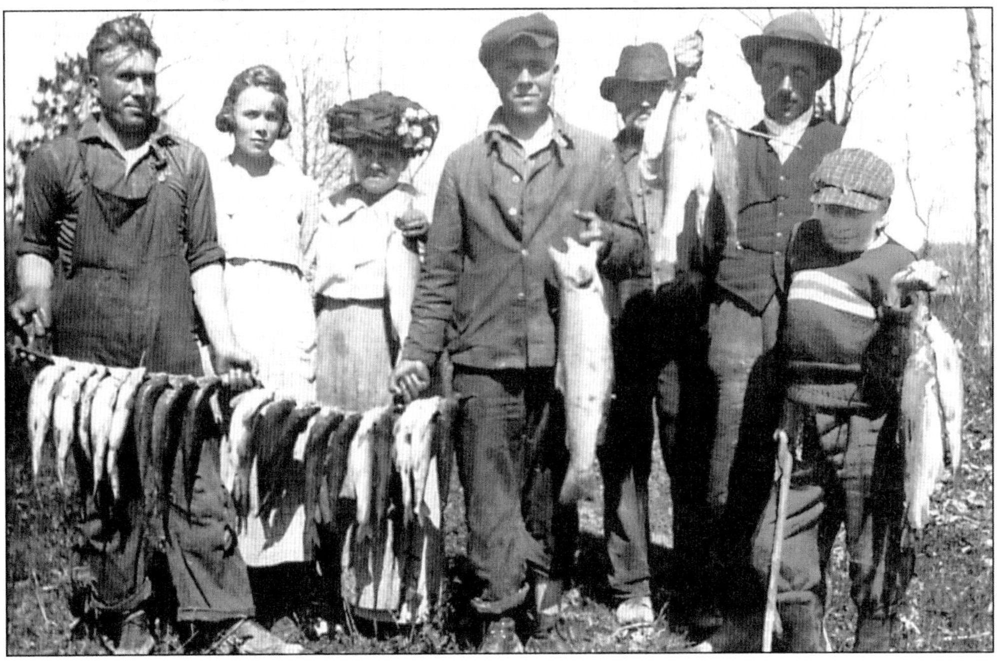

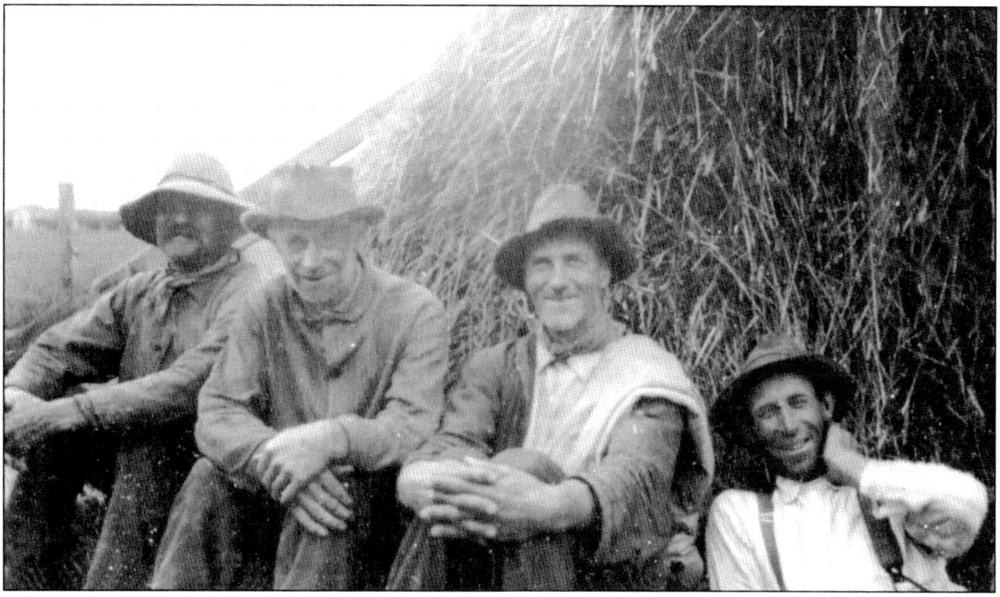

Since they were responsible for feeding their livestock as well as their families, most farmers grew their own hay. The work was difficult and the weather unpredictable. Neighbors usually helped each other get the hay in. From left to right, Dan Meister is shown here with neighbors Andy Mann, Charlie Briske (who lived across Eight Mile Road), and an unidentified man. (Courtesy of Carol Schimke.)

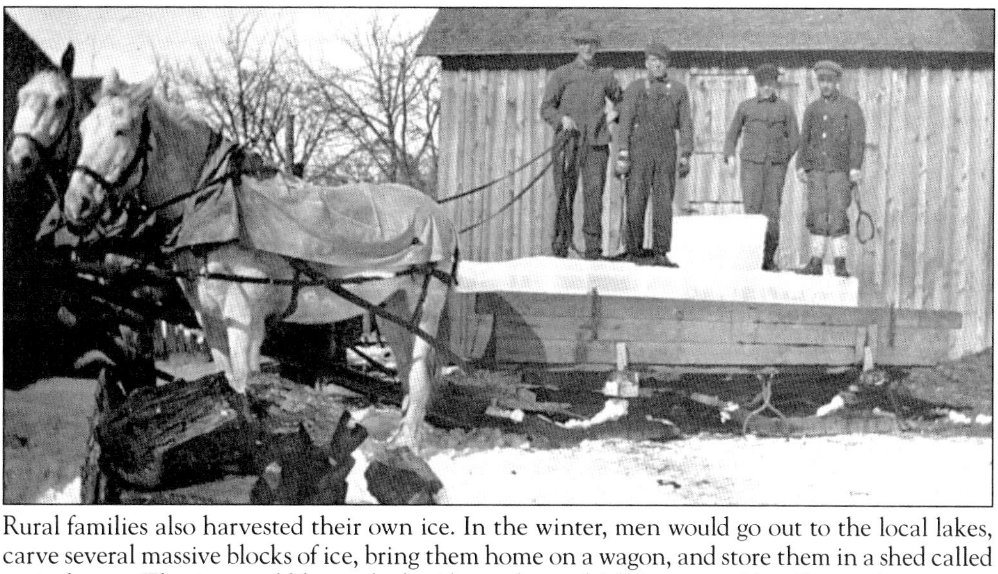

Rural families also harvested their own ice. In the winter, men would go out to the local lakes, carve several massive blocks of ice, bring them home on a wagon, and store them in a shed called an icehouse. The ice would be packed with sawdust, which kept it cold well into the summer months. Brothers Otto (left) and George (right) Meister pose between two unidentified men, pausing from their work in the winter of 1920. (Courtesy of Carol Schimke.)

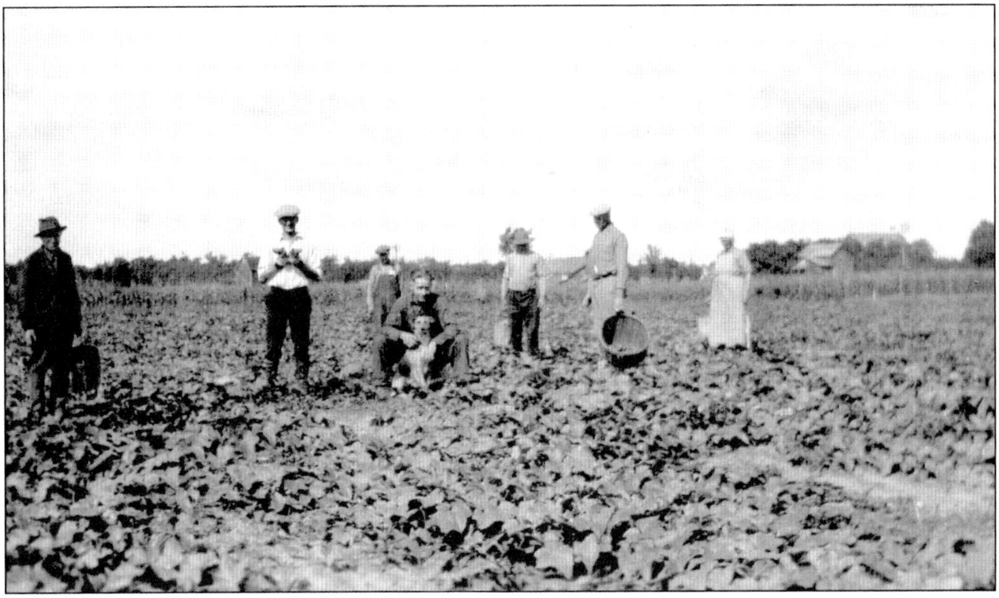

The arrival of standard-gauge rail in Manistee's agricultural regions meant that local farmers could gain an income selling their produce. Pickles are still an essential cash crop in Bear Lake and Brown Townships, and their sales sustained the region during the Depression. Pictured above, from left to right, are Ove Christenson, possibly Albert Krause holding the pickles, Ove's sons Emil Christenson and Edvard Christenson, unidentified, Bill Christenson, and Emma Ronning Christenson, Ove's wife. In the scene below, the Schimkes pick apples in the family orchard by Pierport, near Herkelrath Road. Seen here, from left to right, are Otto Schimke, Julius Pirsig, Otto's daughter Ella, and Clara Lange Schimke. Frank Schimke stands in front. (Courtesy of Carol Schimke.)

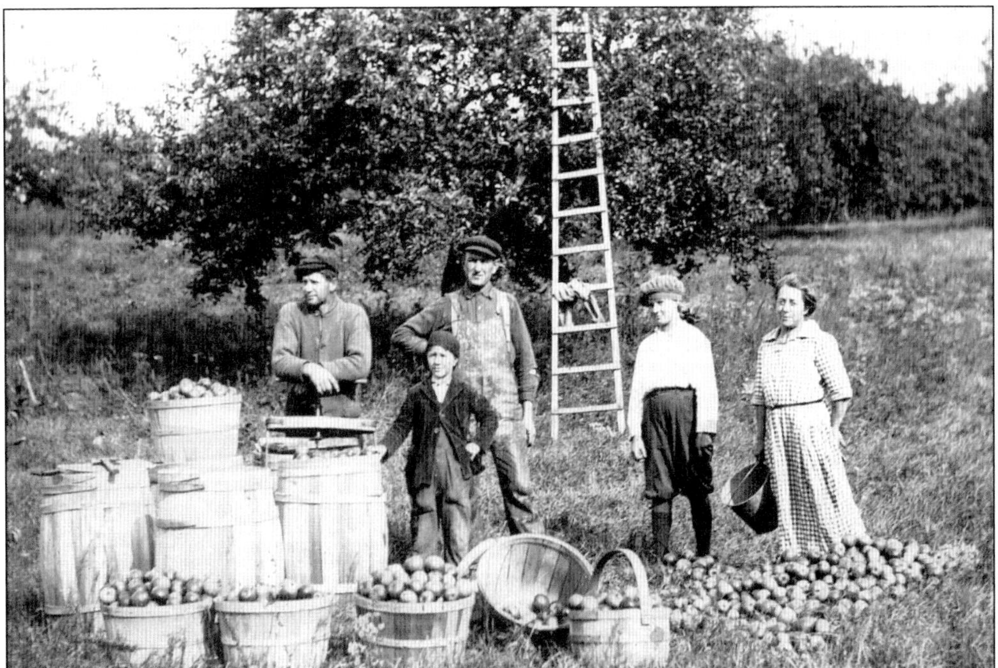

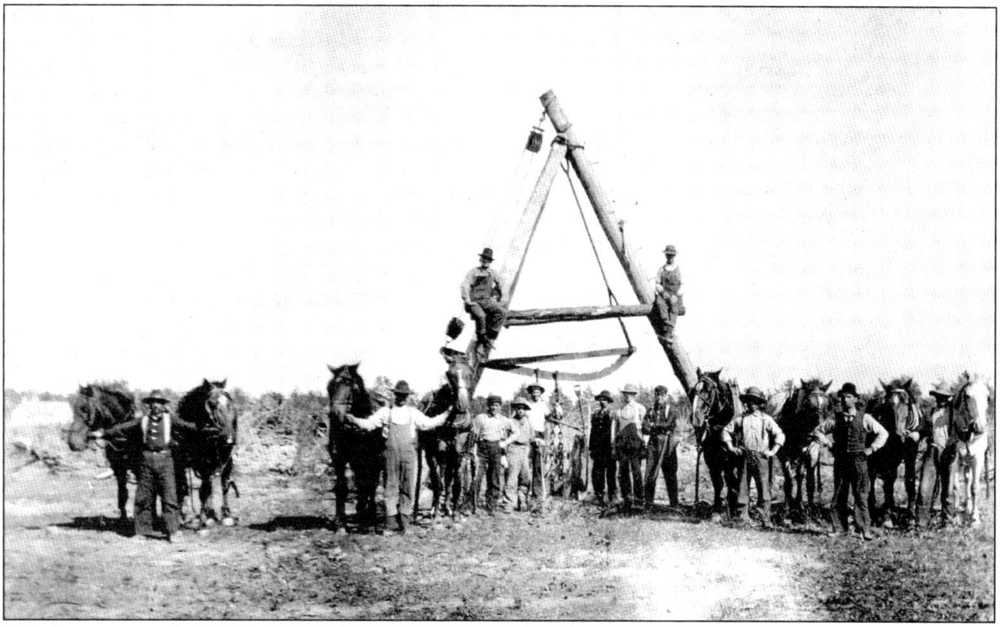

Like logging, early-20th-century farming combined traditional and developing technologies. The object above is a stump puller similar to a model patented in 1880 by John G. Trump of Vassar, Michigan. This device, handy in a logging area, replaced the previous method of oxen and brute force. The harnessed horses walked in a circle around the stump, using physics to multiply force, thus pulling the stump from the ground. Just as steam power revolutionized logging, it also caused enormous changes in farming. Steam-powered farm implements, such as the c. 1910 thresher below, made that work enormously easier. As this equipment was very expensive, one farmer would often buy a machine and contract use of it to other farmers. (Above, courtesy of Rose Siuda Miller; below, courtesy of Maxine Tompke Harrigan.)

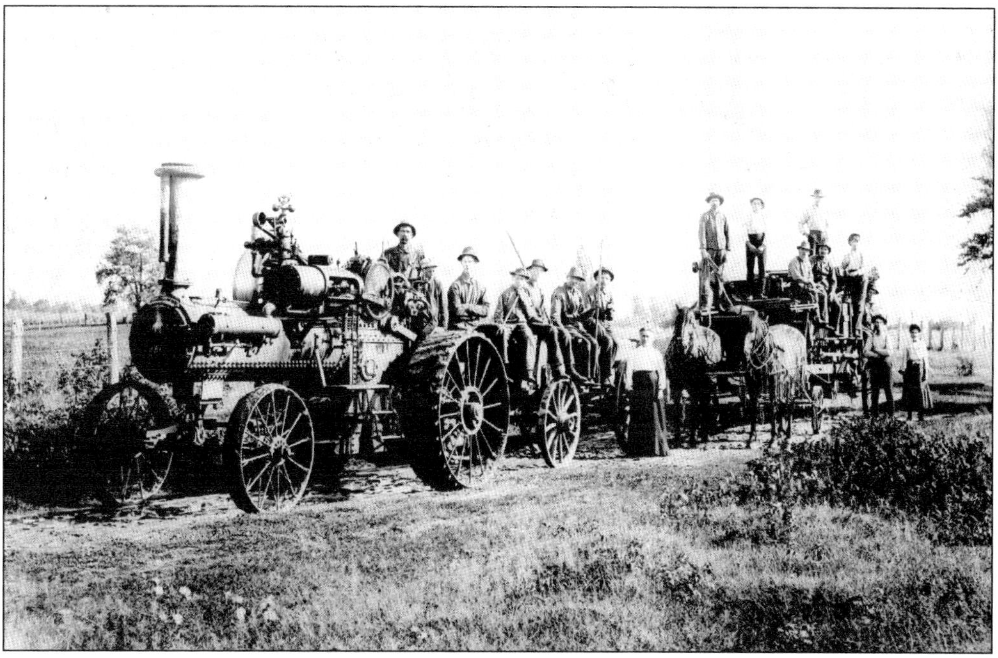

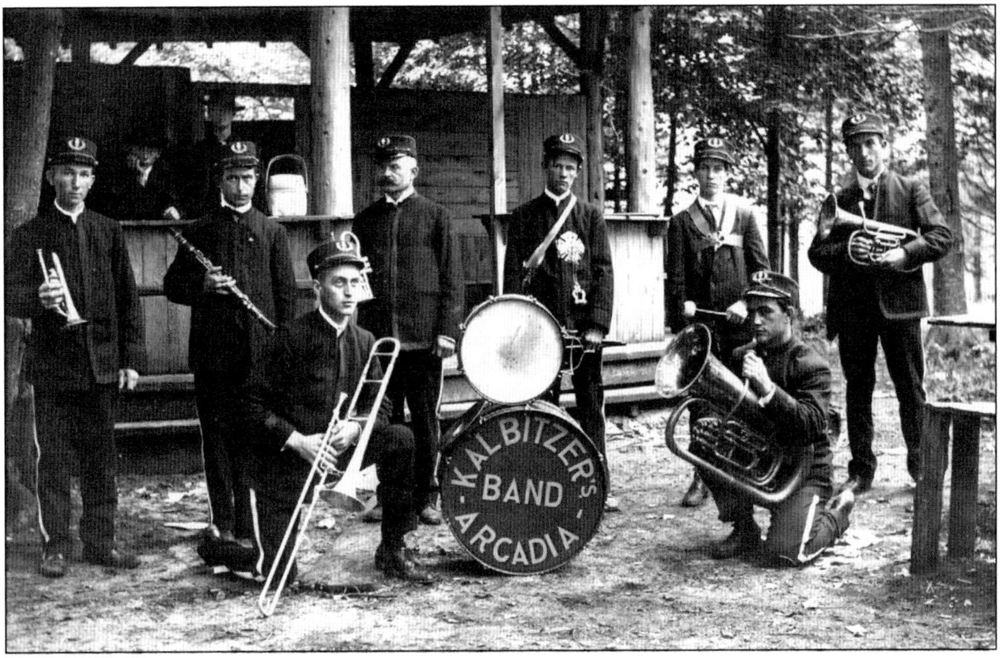

Before the days of radio, entertainment in the country and small towns was usually self-provided. Shown above is Kalbitzer's Band of Arcadia. Arcadia's first musical group was Saxon's Band, starting sometime in 1895. In 1903, a merchant named Fred Kalbitzer organized a band. After practice sessions in Kalbitzer's pig barn, the group played regular concerts in what is now Finch Park, as well as at town picnics, dances, and church events. Ed Johnson, Kalbitzer's son-in-law, took over the band in 1909. The man on the far left is Bill Larsen; the others are unidentified. Below, Onekama Marine Band members wear full regalia at a Fourth of July concert at Bear Lake in 1911. (Above, courtesy of the Arcadia Area Historical Society; below, courtesy of Carol Schimke.)

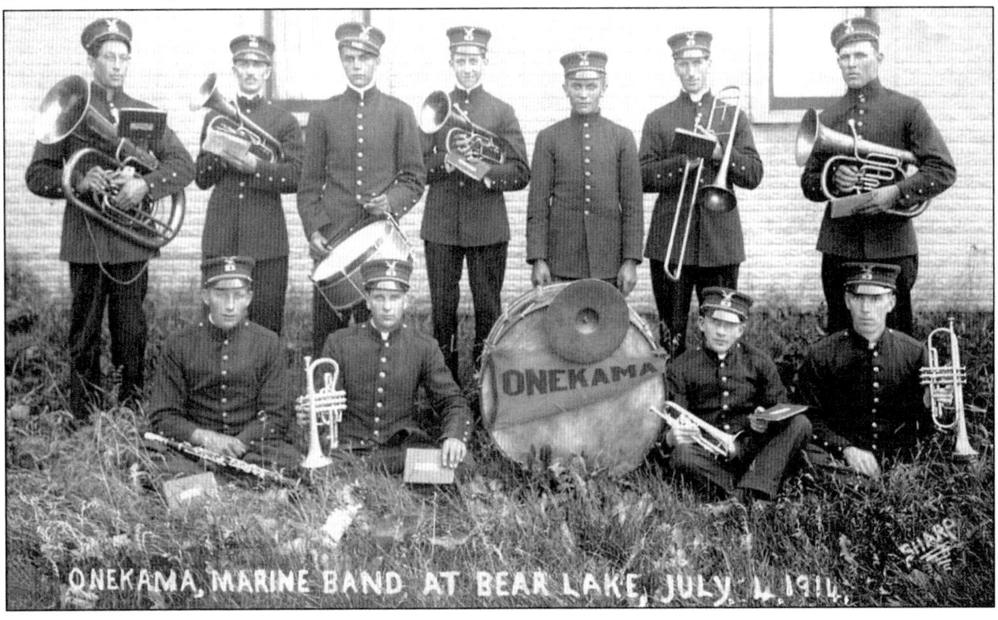

During this time, people even made their own music. Families would play and sing together in the evenings or on holidays. In the photograph to the right, likely taken in 1912, Otto Meister practices the accordion, accompanied by his younger brother George on violin. Although they almost certainly did not think so at the time, the scene below seems to modern eyes considerably less innocuous. It was apparently not uncommon for children and adults in small towns to don blackface and perform minstrel shows. Pictured here, from left to right, are Ruth Johnson, Esther Johnson, ? McCurdy, possibly Anna Christenson, Mrs. Lutz, Mrs. Vic Johnson, ? John, schoolteacher Evelyn Patterson, and possibly Ailie Meister. These parents of Johnson School students would often travel to other schools in order to perform. (Courtesy of Carol Schimke.)

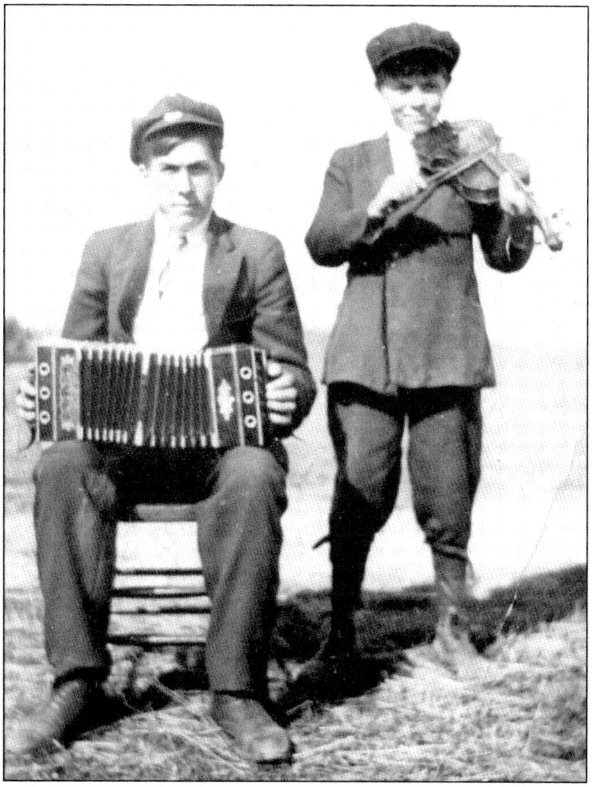

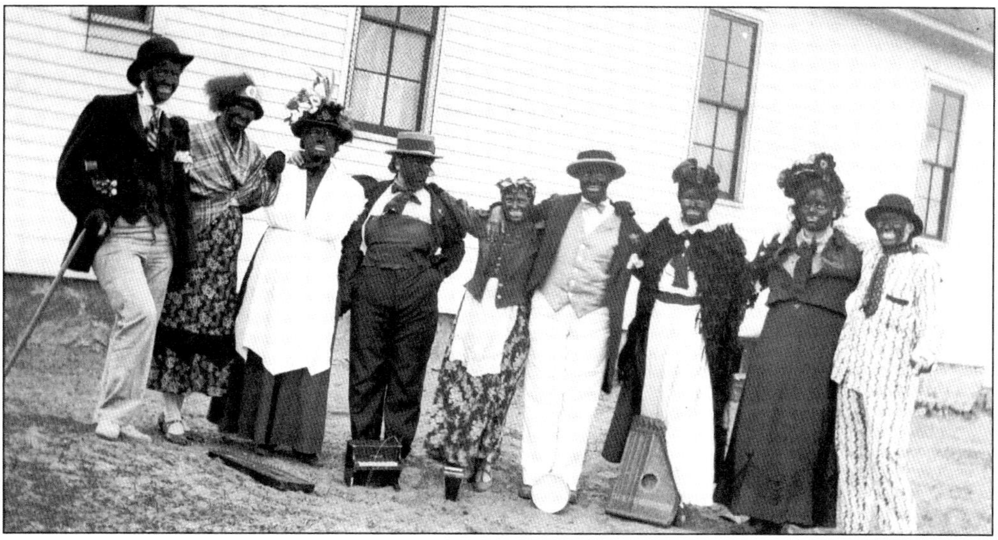

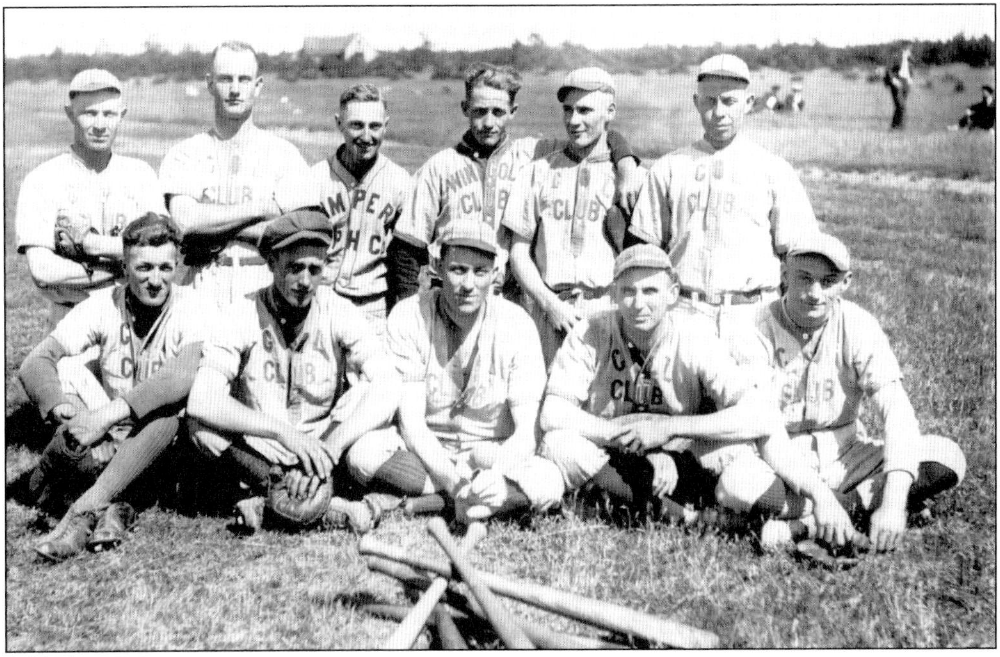

Every American town had at least one baseball team. Around 1922, the Chief Lake Club included the following members, from left to right: (first row) Alvin Johnson, John Thomas, Rube McCurdy, Morris McCarthy, and possibly Frank Jalinski; (second row) Randall McCurdy, Bill Archer, ? Keppler, Edward Christenson, Frank Thomas, and Bill Christenson.

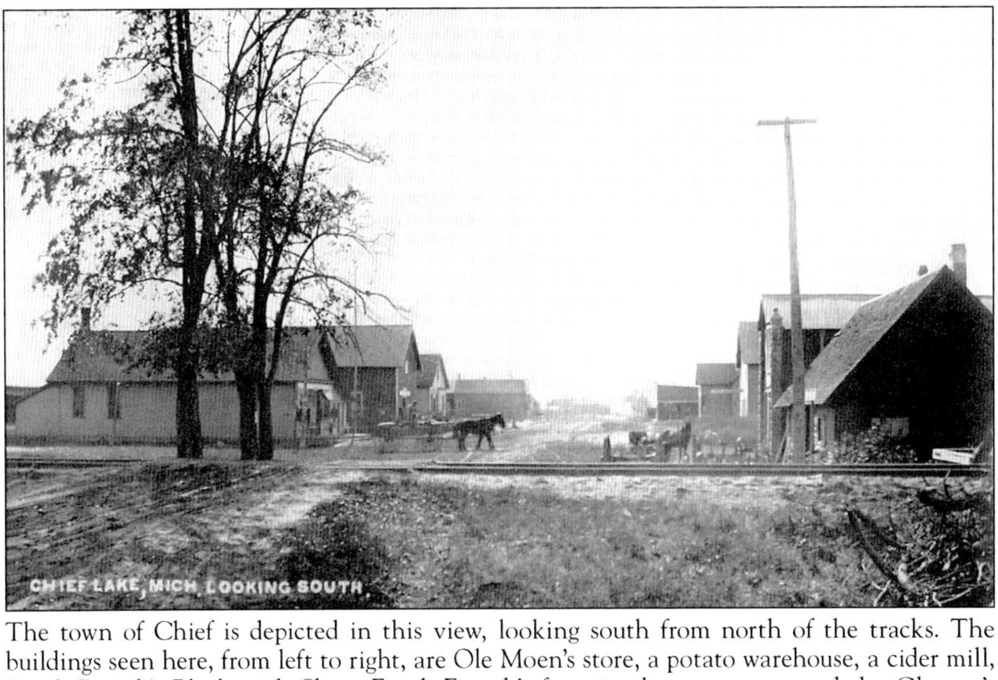

The town of Chief is depicted in this view, looking south from north of the tracks. The buildings seen here, from left to right, are Ole Moen's store, a potato warehouse, a cider mill, Frank French's Blacksmith Shop, Frank French's farm implements store, and the Gleaner's Hall, which had a dance hall upstairs. Philip and Drusilla Breen owned the adjacent house. (Courtesy of Carol Schimke.)

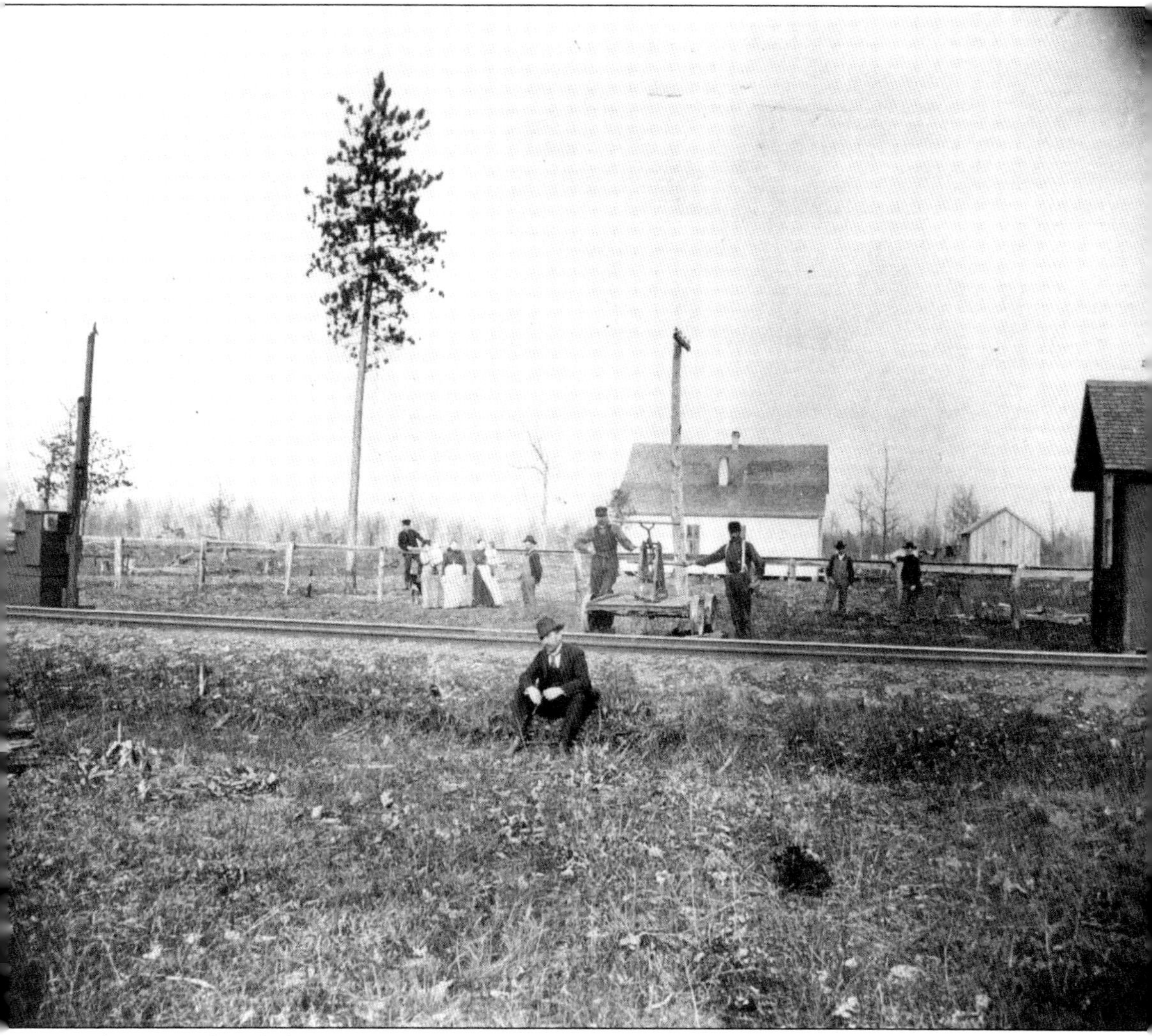

Brethren was founded on a uniquely American combination of speculation and faith. By the beginning of the 20th century, nothing remained of the once-vast Michigan pine forest but stumps. Lumbermen, left with useless land and non-profitable land, needed a solution. Samuel S. Thorpe, a district agent of the Michigan Land Association, found one. He wrote a letter to members of the German Baptist Brethren, a hardworking religious community then settled in Indiana and Ohio. Thorpe's letter contained vivid descriptions of the fertile soil and the gentle climate that awaited the Brethren in northern Michigan. When the colony arrived, they found circumstances not precisely as advertised. Nonetheless, they persevered, and through faith and hard work, remade the scorched earth into farms that would sustain them. This is how Brethren looked before its founding in 1901. The town was almost named Lone Pine, after the single pine visible on the left. The man sitting in front of the tracks may be Sam Thorpe. The white building right of center is Mary Ann Leckrone's original rooming house. (Courtesy of the Brethren Historical Museum.)

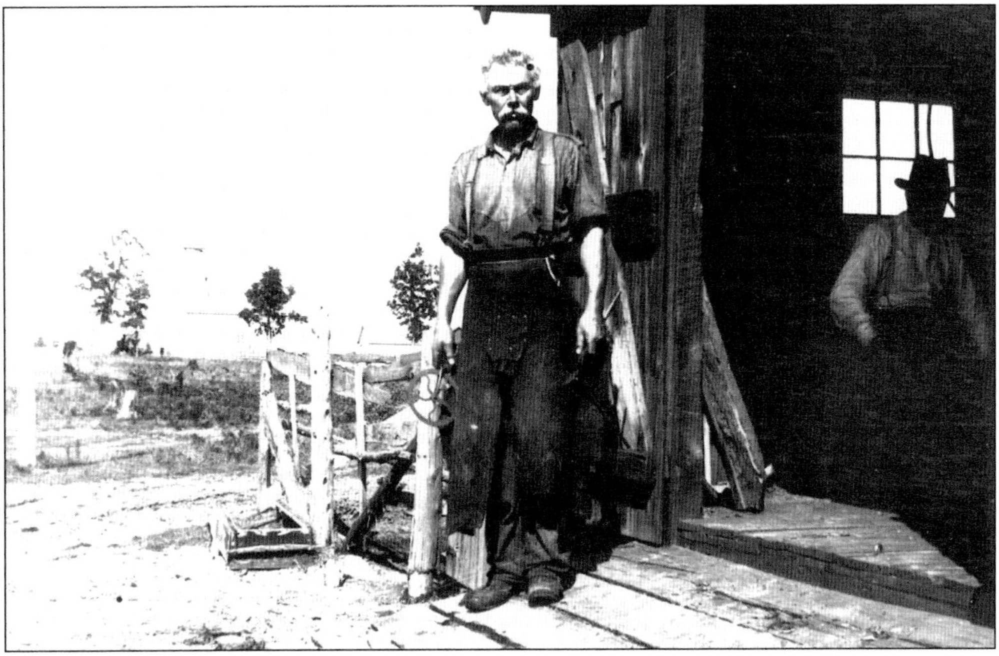

John Payne Sr. stands in front of his blacksmith shop. A legendary character, he also sponsored the first automotive repair performed in Brethren when John Miller's brand-new Model T Ford broke down. A mechanic had to come all the way from Traverse City, and Payne offered his shop as a makeshift garage.

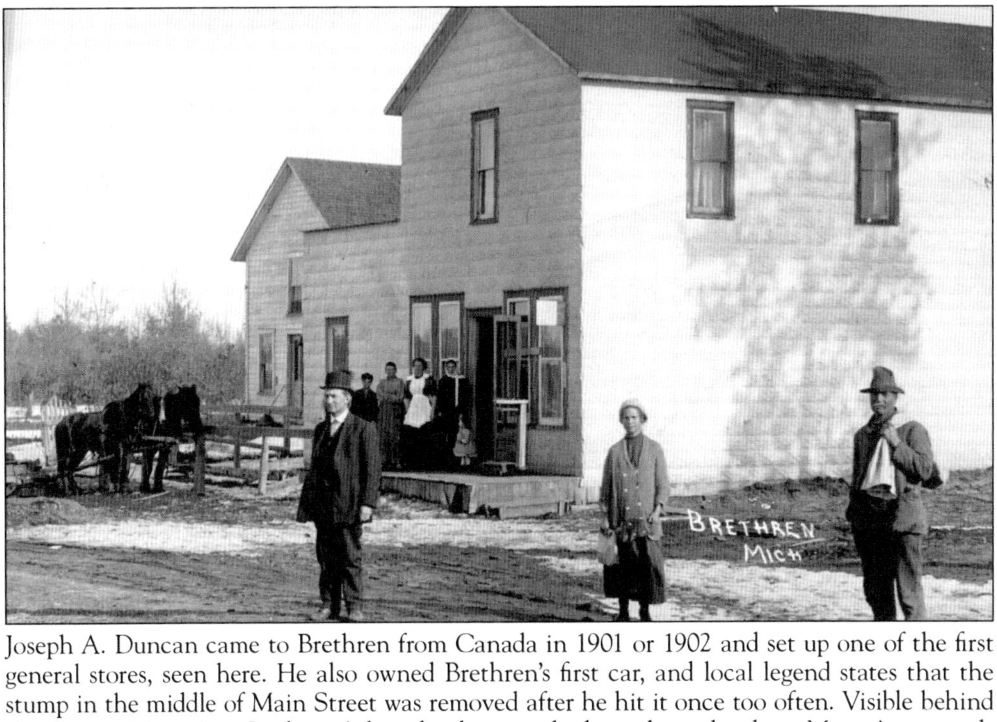

Joseph A. Duncan came to Brethren from Canada in 1901 or 1902 and set up one of the first general stores, seen here. He also owned Brethren's first car, and local legend states that the stump in the middle of Main Street was removed after he hit it once too often. Visible behind the store is Mary Ann Leckrone's boardinghouse, which predates the shop. Mary Ann stands second from the left on Duncan's porch. (Courtesy of the Brethren Historical Association.)

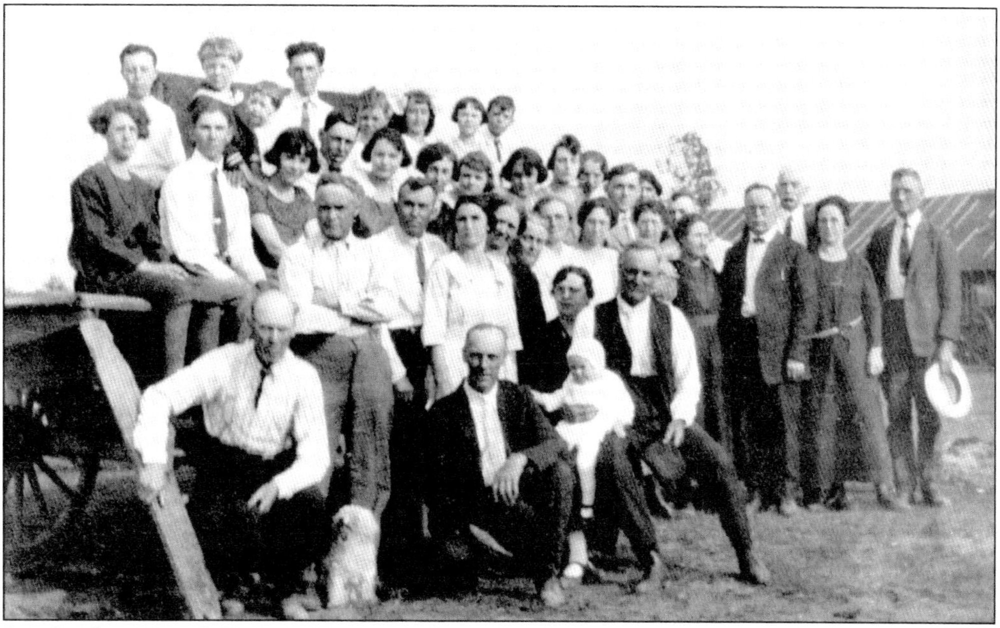

Besides the original German Baptist Brethren, the town had several Methodist families, such as the Bakers, Hindmans, Roses, Shields, and Millers, pictured here around 1921. In order to build their church, these families transported an empty church building from Cross Village on U.S. 131, just south of the straits of Mackinac, and reassembled it in Brethren. Virgil Rose (back row, second from the left) is still living.

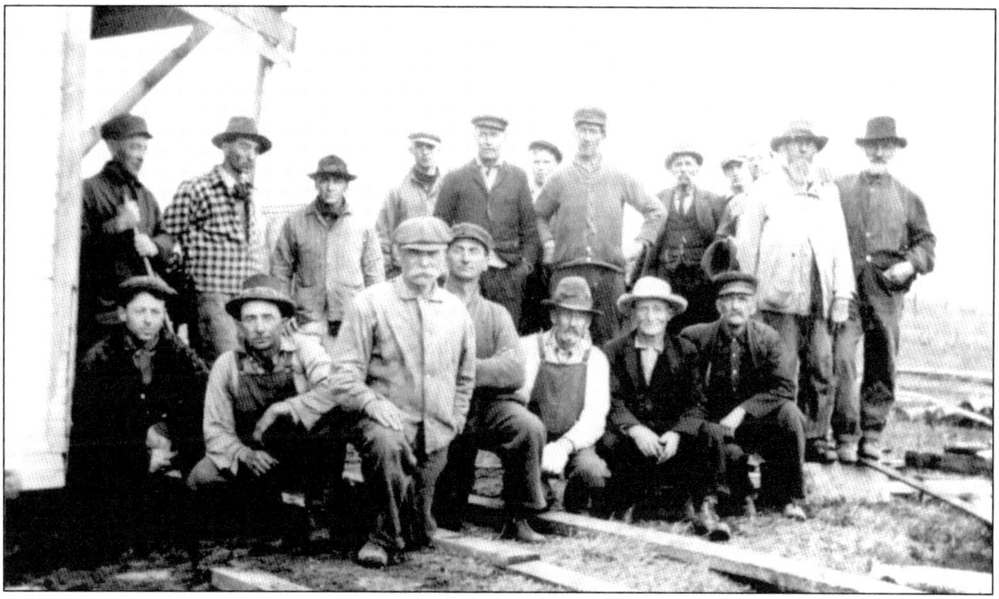

Relocating entire buildings was a surprisingly common practice. Assisted by others, the Leckrone boys have just moved their mother's rooming house a block north across Coates Highway with log rollers and stump pullers. George Leckrone kneels in the first row, second from the left. Will Leckrone stands second from the left, while Dan is fourth from the left, behind the mustached man. The rest are unidentified friends and neighbors. (Courtesy of the Brethren Historical Association.)

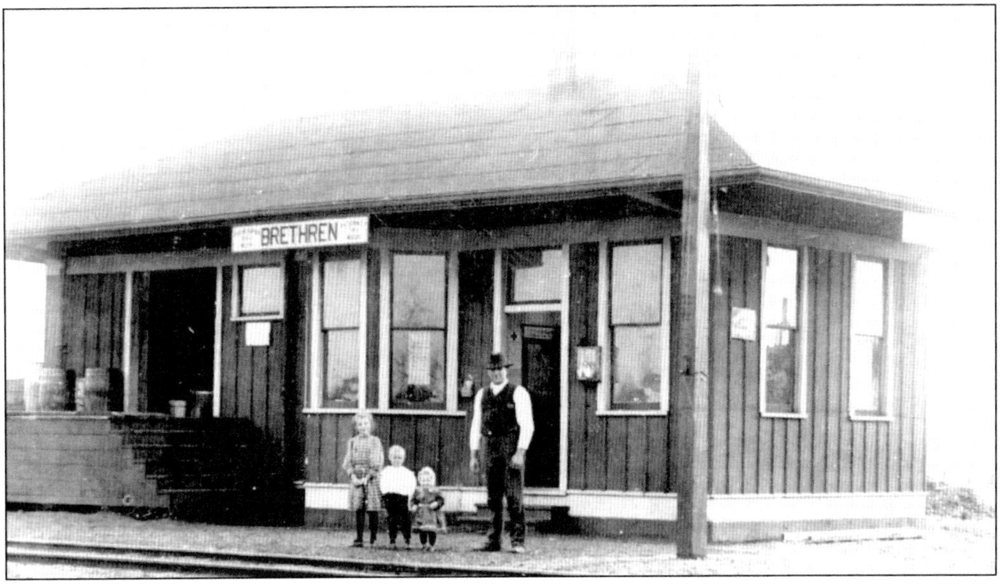

George Deardorff stands at the Brethren train station with his children, from left to right, Ruby, Ray, and baby Marie. Besides being the stationmaster, he also served as the town postmaster. An early settler from Indiana, he arrived in 1901, before the town had even been named Brethren.

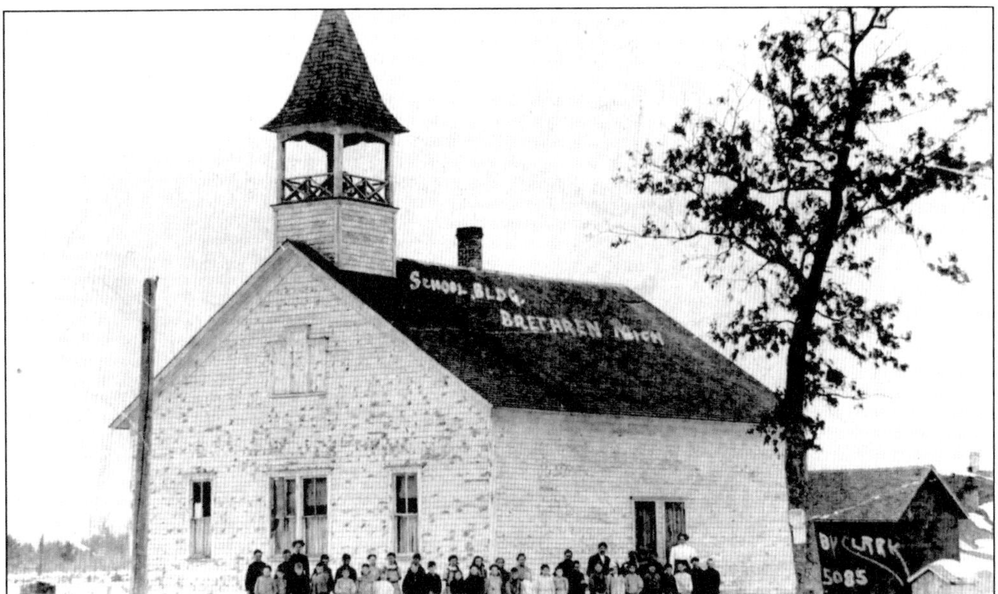

The original one-room Brethren School was remodeled as a two-room schoolhouse around 1915 in order to accommodate the growing population. Young children up to the fifth grade entered on the north side, and high school students—grades 6 through 10—came in on the south. The entire building was heated from an iron stove in the center. Donald Crouch, the teacher who inspired Brethren native and actor James Earl Jones, was the first high school teacher there. (Courtesy of the Brethren Historical Association.)

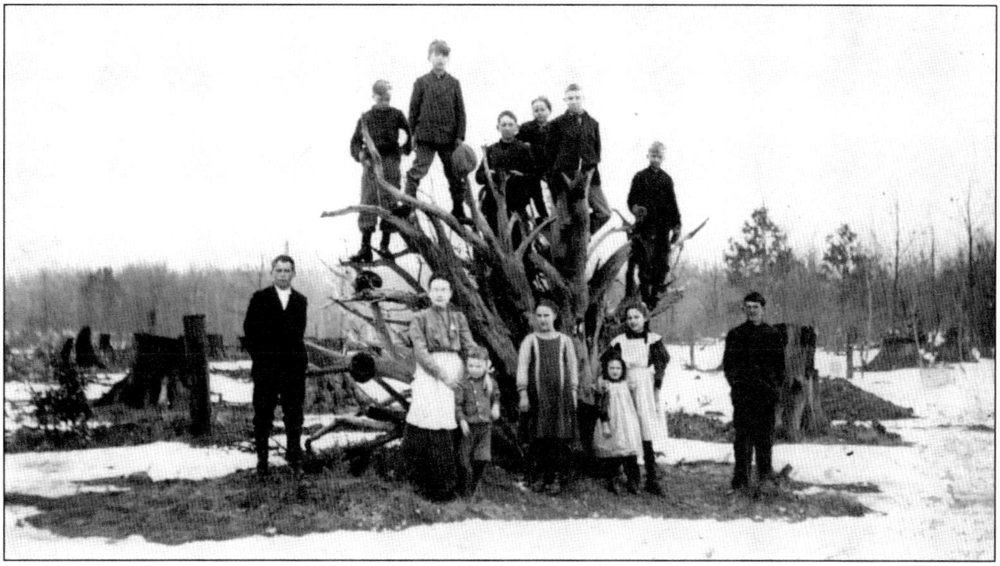

Stumps were such a common landscape feature in 1900s Manistee County that they regularly served as a scenic backdrop for casual portraits, like this one of Oak Grove students and their teacher. Alice Taylor, the teacher, is second from the left in the first row. The next two children are unidentified. The smallest girl, fifth from the left, is Gladys Danner, who, as of 2006, is 100 years old. Next to Gladys on her right is her sister Ruth. The others are unidentified. (Courtesy of the Brethren Historical Museum.)

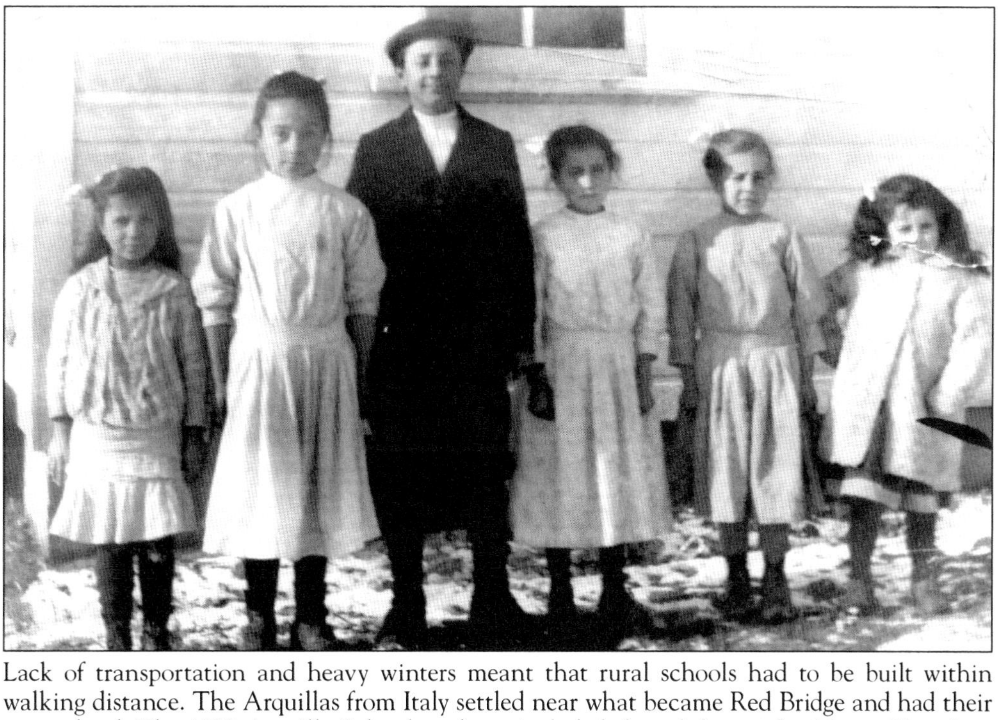

Lack of transportation and heavy winters meant that rural schools had to be built within walking distance. The Arquillas from Italy settled near what became Red Bridge and had their own school. The 1913 Arquilla School students included, from left to right, Elvira, Eliza, Jim, Mary, Kate, and Lucia. When the school burned the following year, the family attended the tiny Red Bridge School. (Courtesy of the Brethren Historical Association.)

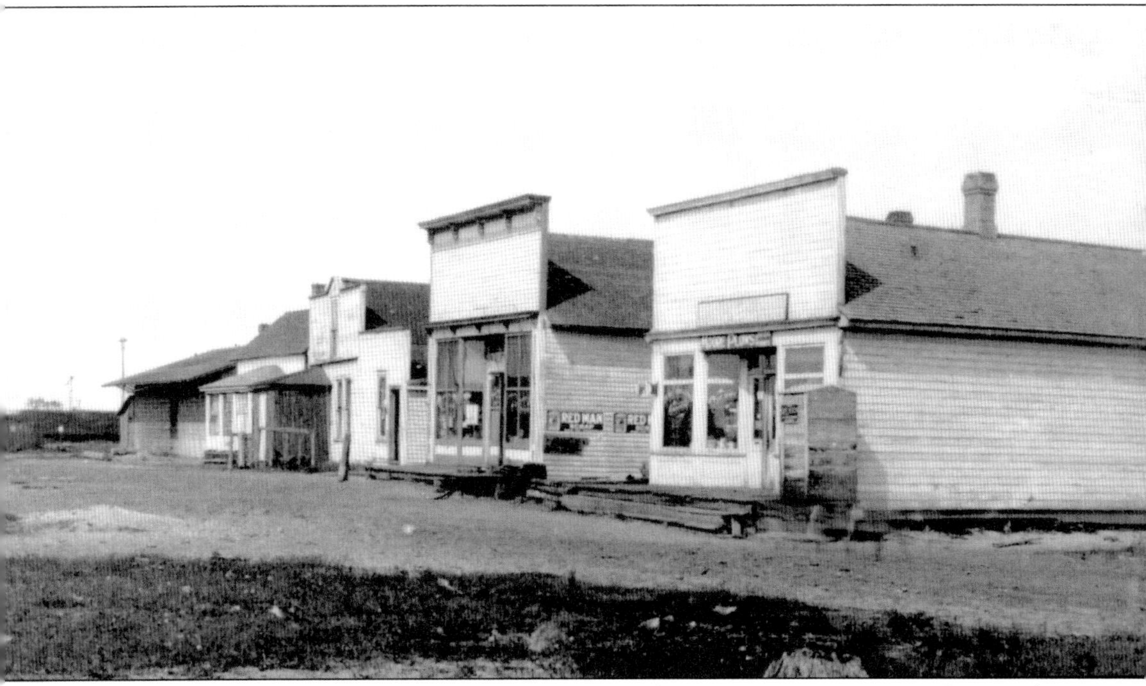

Like Brethren, Kaleva was settled by devout settlers drawn to Manistee County by speculative promises of fertile farmland. Perhaps the thin soil and harsh winters they found when they arrived were no real deterrent because the basis of faith for both the German Baptist Brethren and the Lutheran Finns of Kaleva is that the reward for hard work on earth is salvation in Heaven. The village of Kaleva is named after the Finnish epic *The Kalevala*. Written in the 19th century from a collection of stories in the oral tradition, Finns read it as a model for an ideal Finnish nation. Fortified with these ideals, along with a national sense of *sisu*, or perseverance and courage, Kaleva's new arrivals built their village accordingly. This is Kaleva's main street in the early 1900s, shortly after it was first built. The buildings, from left to right, are "Till" Milk's livery stable, Milk's house, Kurt Hilliard's ice cream parlor, I. N. Hilliard's store, and Andy Kullgren's store. Most of these structures burned in 1913. (Courtesy of the Kaleva Historical Society.)

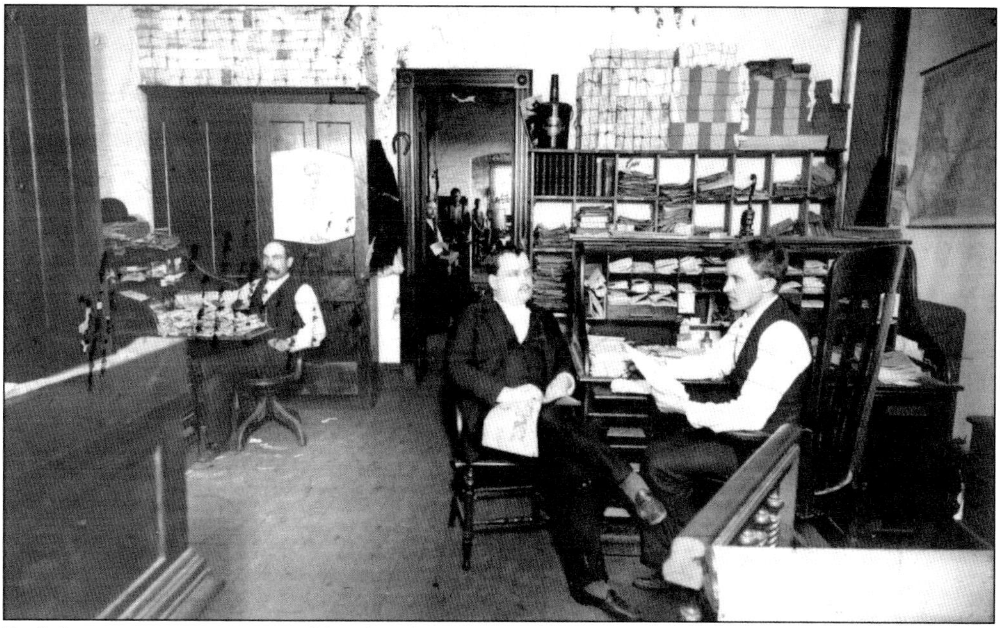

Built by enterprising men and hardworking farmers, Kaleva also had an active intellectual life. Founded in 1902 by the town intelligentsia, the newspaper *Siirtolainen* (Immigrant) continued publication until 1933. Some of the paper's founders are pictured in this shot of the interior office. On the left is Alex Ketonen, the financial manager and owner of several buildings in town. The others are unidentified.

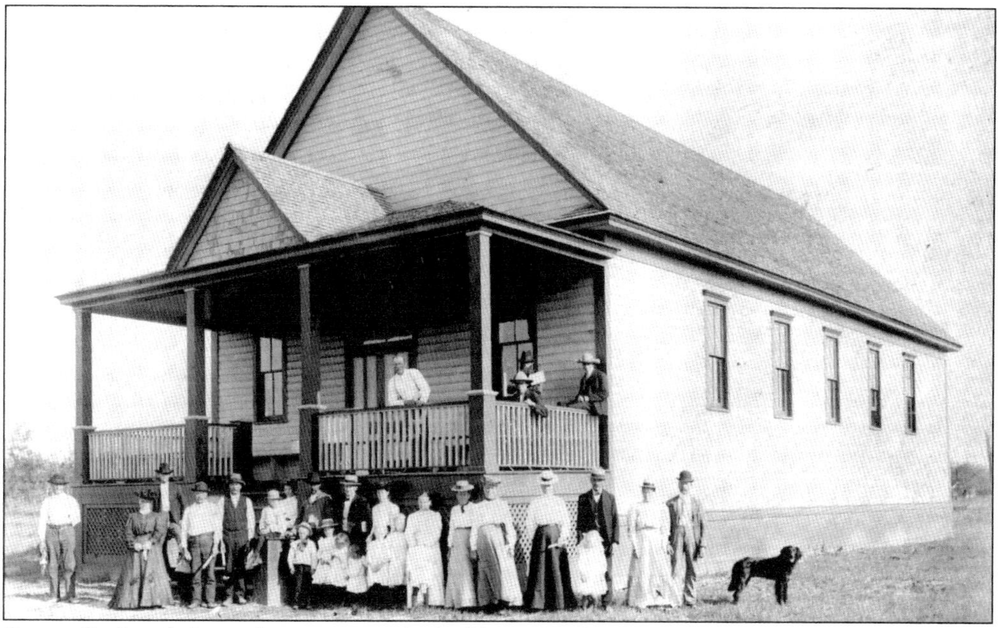

Originally founded in order to prevent the building of a saloon in town, the Kalevatar Temperance Society quickly formed the nexus of a lively social center. Shown here, it served as a community center from 1902 until 1933. Church services were also held here until 1913, as were township meetings, school board meetings, and even medicine shows. Identified among the group in the first row are Jakob Sippola and his wife. (Courtesy of the Kaleva Historical Society.)

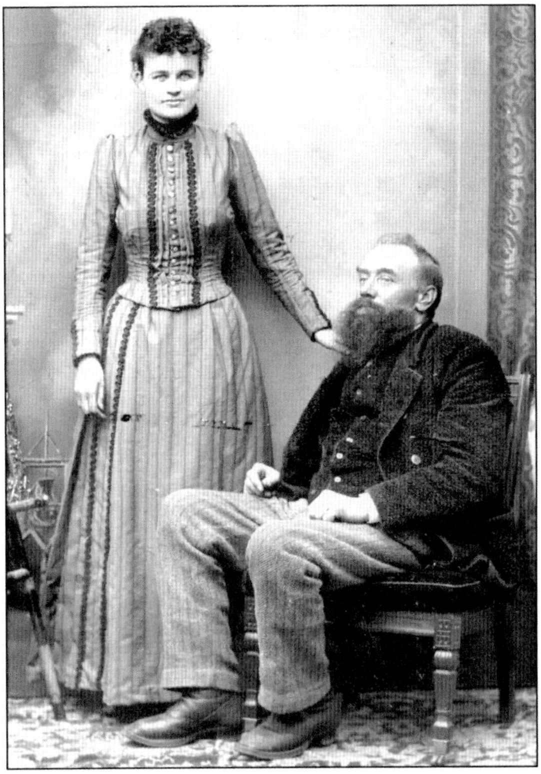

Frank Shimmel, Kaleva's first postmaster, came to Michigan from New York in 1844 with his family. He settled in Kaleva before the Finns arrived, when it was still called Manistee Crossing for the railroad lines that met there. A prosperous man, Shimmel also owned extensive acreage east of Kaleva. This portrait of Frank and his wife was taken in 1891.

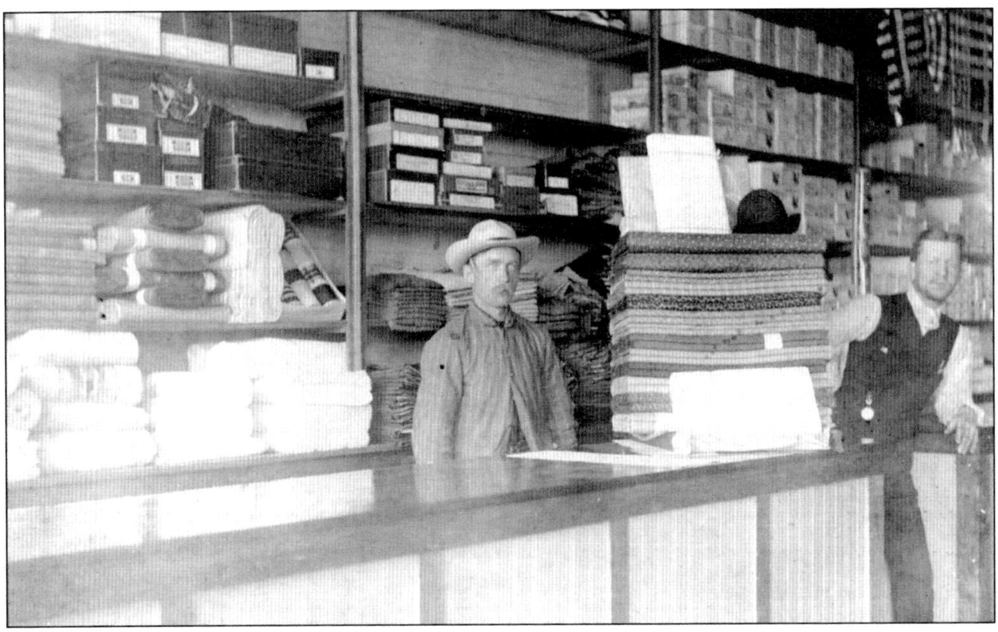

The interior of the Union Store of Kaleva is depicted around 1913. Founded in 1907 by a group of Finnish farmers, it was organized as a mutual stockholding venture for whomever in the community wished to buy shares. The finnish invented cooperatives, and this Union Store brought this innovative business model to America. It served the community until 1954. (Courtesy of the Kaleva Historical Society.)

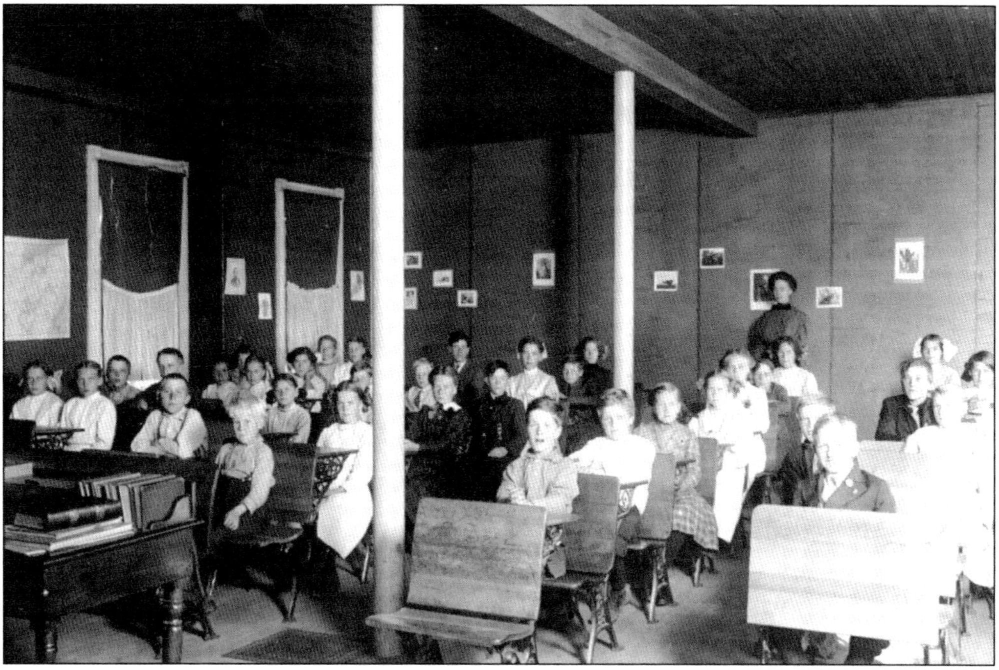

Grades four through eight from Kaleva's one-room school gather for a photograph around 1909. Most of these children would probably have spoken Finnish at home, but lessons were in English.

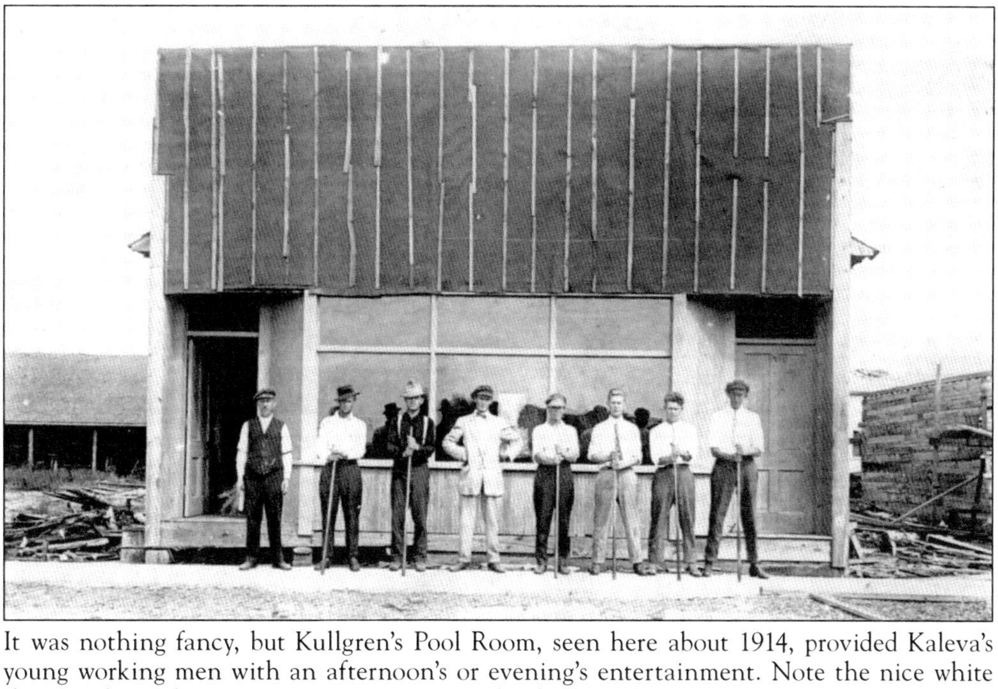

It was nothing fancy, but Kullgren's Pool Room, seen here about 1914, provided Kaleva's young working men with an afternoon's or evening's entertainment. Note the nice white shirts and ties the young men are wearing. Clearly they played a gentleman's game even in this remote village.

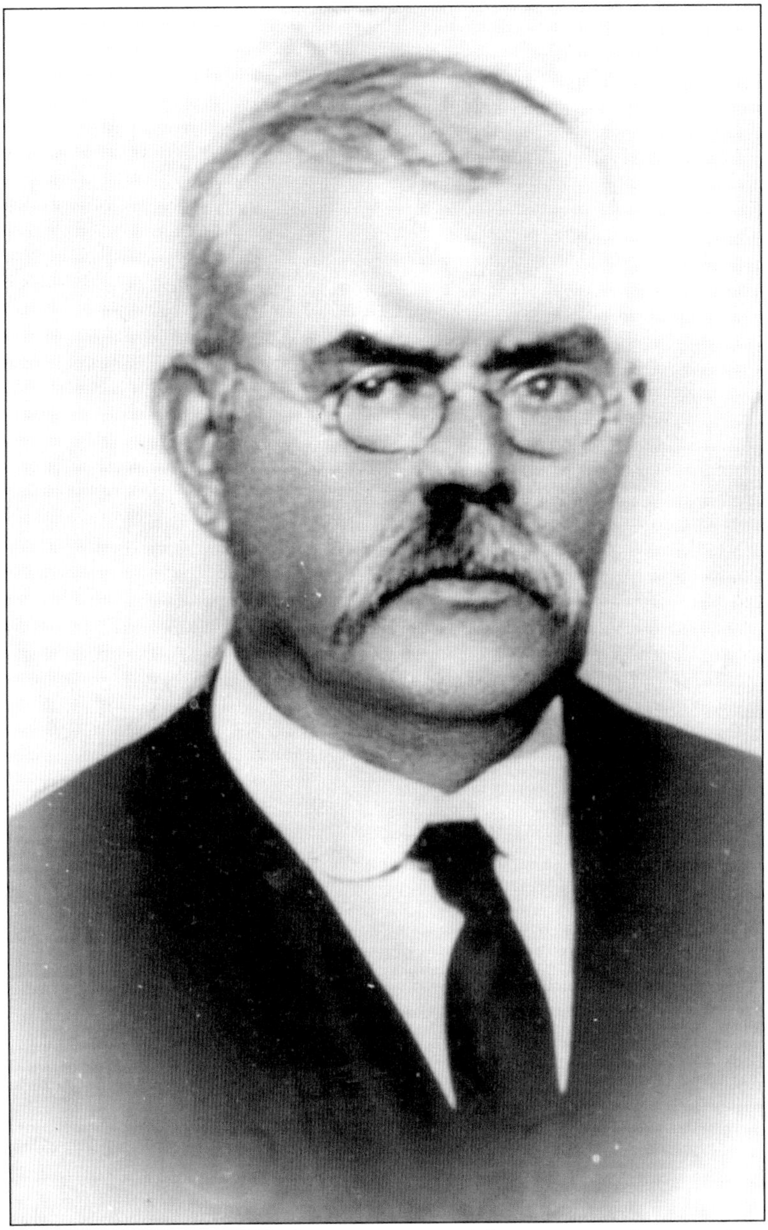

Born in Milwaukee in 1870, Dr. W. E. Coates was one of the most prominent and active citizens in bringing better health care and modern sanitary conditions to rural Manistee County. Before attaining his medical degree at the University of Illinois, Coates taught school in Arcadia, Browntown, and District Seven and served a term as principal at one of the rural high schools. Upon his return to Manistee, he established a practice at 407 River Street. Like many enlightened medical men of the 19th century, he was a fierce proponent of good sanitation, helping to found one of the nation's first municipal departments of dairy inspection. He later moved to Onekama, where he established the Onekama Heights Sanitarium Association, whose mission was to foster better care of tuberculosis patients. About 1912, Coates moved to Kaleva as its resident physician. As he was also an outspoken advocate of improved roads, Coates Highway is named for him. (Courtesy of the Manistee County Historical Museum.)

Seven

All the Sights to See

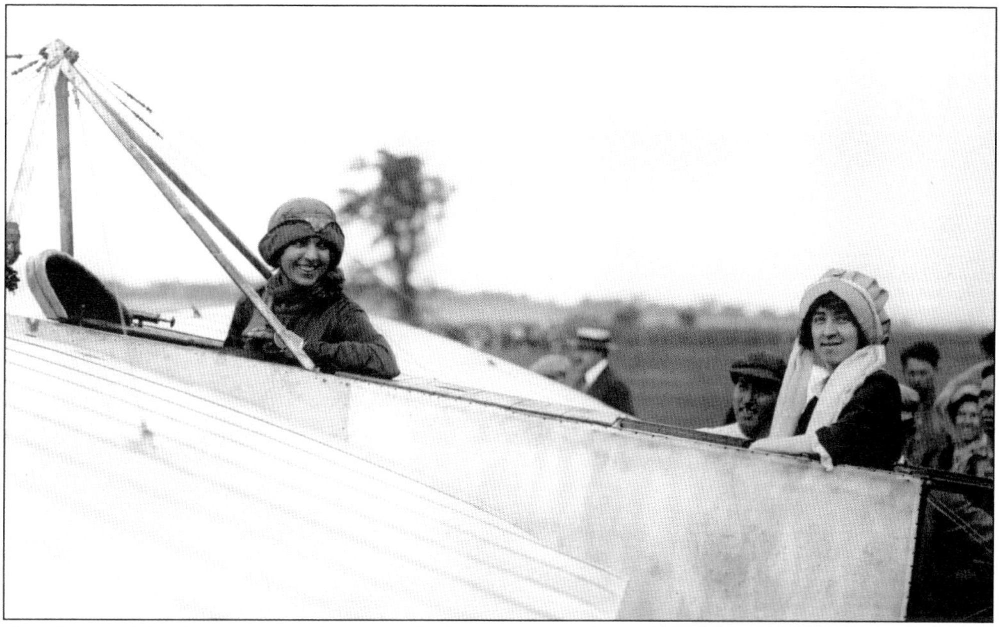

The dawn of the 20th century brought the height of the Gilded Age. The industrial boom of the previous decades brought all manner of glorious excess. For the first time in history, a significant number of people were financially comfortable enough to spend money on entertainment. This was the era of spectacles: carnivals, amusement parks, and grand media exhibitions. Born in Arcadia to a family of homesteaders, Harriet Quimby (left), America's first licensed female aviator, delighted crowds with her purple satin flight suit and her amazing stunts—especially when she flew across the English Channel in the spring of 1912 in a Bleriot monoplane. She died as spectacularly as she lived. At an aviation meet on July 1, 1912, near Quincy, Massachusetts, she and her passenger fell from her plane, dropping for hundreds of feet in front of hundreds of people and reporters. This photograph was taken on the day of that crash. The woman in the back seat, Gertrude Stevenson, is a reporter who was to have been her passenger. (Courtesy of the Arcadia Area Historical Society.)

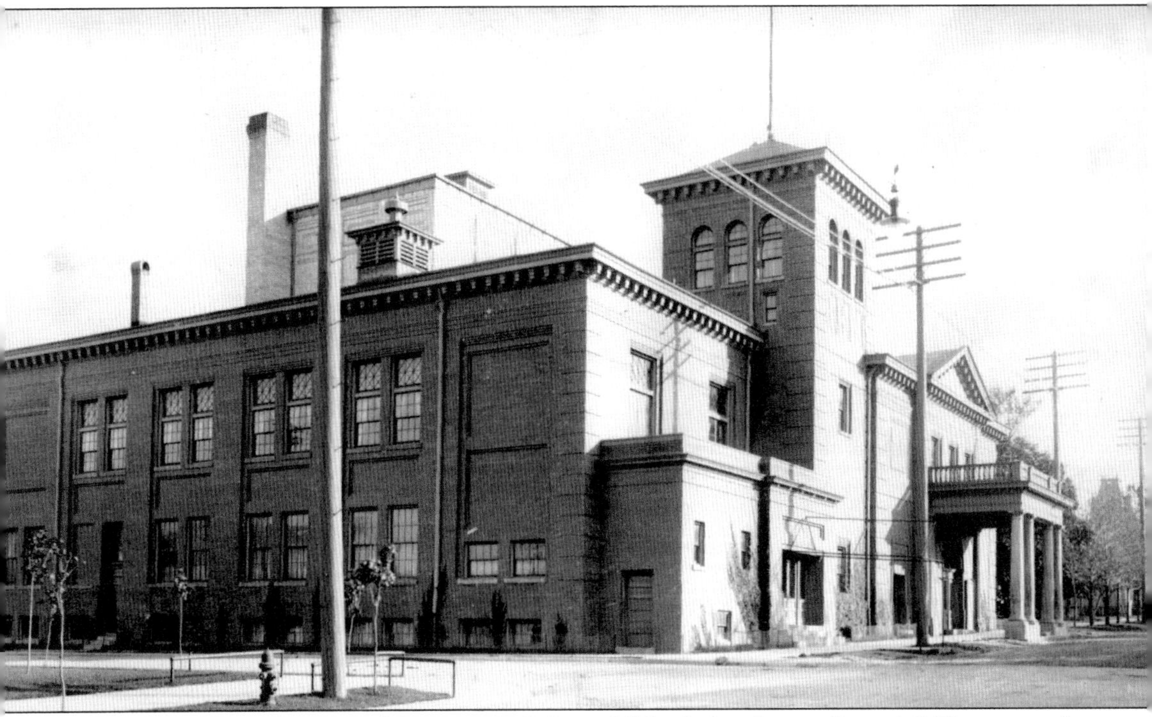

In keeping with the spirit of the times, T. J. Ramsdell built the glorious Ramsdell Theater on the corner of First and Maple Streets in 1903. Designed by Chicago architect Solon S. Beman, the theater took two years to complete. The famous Walter Burridge painted the scenery and the drop curtain, and T. J.'s son Frederic Ramsdell painted the exquisite scenes inside the lobby and around the dome. Opening night was September 4, 1903, with a performance of the Broadway smash *A Chinese Honeymoon*. The Shubert's New York Casino Theatre company came to Manistee for the performance, transporting scenery by chartered train at great expense. Main floor ticket prices were $5 and $10. The theater building is said to be haunted; some insist the ghost is Ramsdell himself, though current executive director Ron Steinberg thinks Ramsdell's youngest daughter may be there as well. (Courtesy of the Manistee Historical Society.)

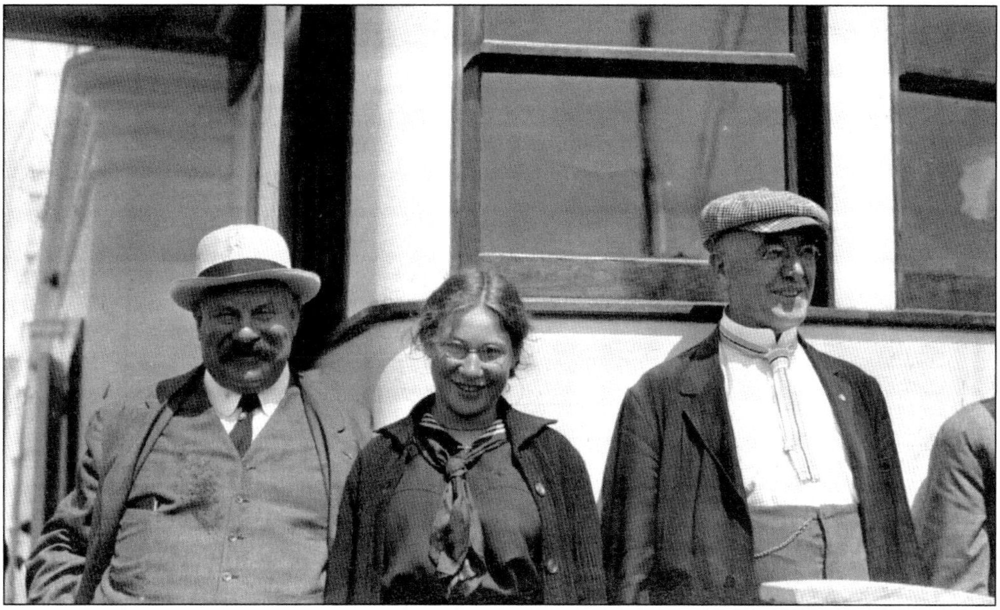

Gustav "Gus" Kitzinger, originally from Milwaukee, organized the Manistee Ludington and Milwaukee Transportation Company in 1903. Shortly thereafter, he purchased several steamers that became known as the Pere Marquette Line steamers and took up residence on Fifth and Maple Streets in Manistee. He is pictured here with his daughter Harriet. The man on the right is unidentified. (Courtesy of Clarence Nowak.)

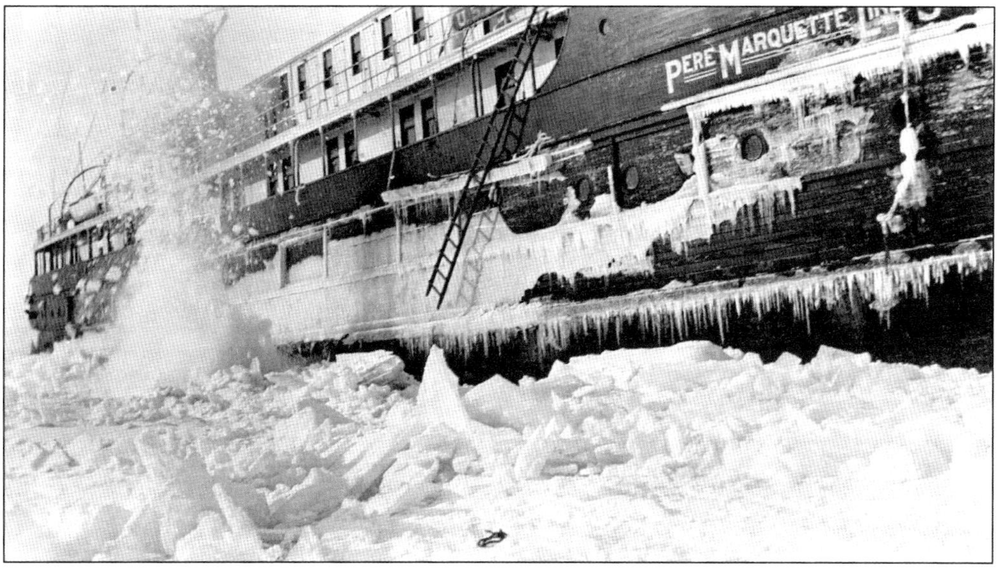

Previously, most ships that crossed the Great Lakes had been freighters. But the Pere Marquette passenger lines brought waves of tourists across. Most people had come to Manistee in the previous century to work, but this new leisure class traveled strictly to see the sights, enjoy the mineral baths, visit the beach resorts, and buy picture postcards. As demonstrated in this dramatic view of the Pere Marquette No. 3 about to be crushed by Lake Michigan ice in the early 1920s, the ships were capable of crossing the lake all year long, but winter crossing was dangerous. (Courtesy of Sandee Jones.)

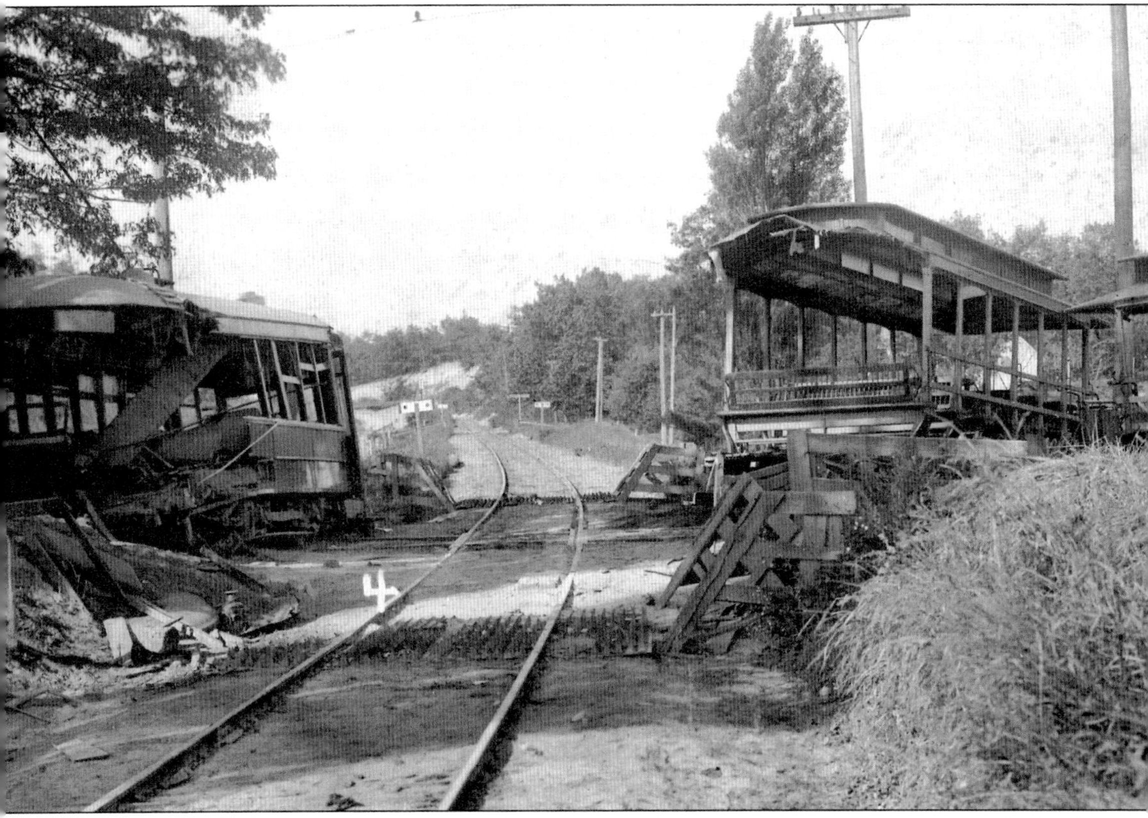

The coming of streetcars and trolley lines to most American towns at the start of the 20th century was another major step in the evolution of the tourist industry. Although railroads made it possible to travel between towns or states, visiting across town or places in the country where trains did not run required horses, boats, or a great deal of walking. Trolley lines, however, allowed leisure travel, and once-remote waterfront portions of Manistee County such as Orchard Beach and Red Park became popular resorts, both for city residents and out-of-towners. As this image clearly shows, the logistics had not yet entirely been ironed out. At Peanut Junction, just north of the city of Manistee, the tracks for the Orchard Beach trolley crossed a set of railroad tracks. Schedules were apparently not well-coordinated, and on July 4, 1917, the inevitable ensued. (Courtesy of Sandee Jones.)

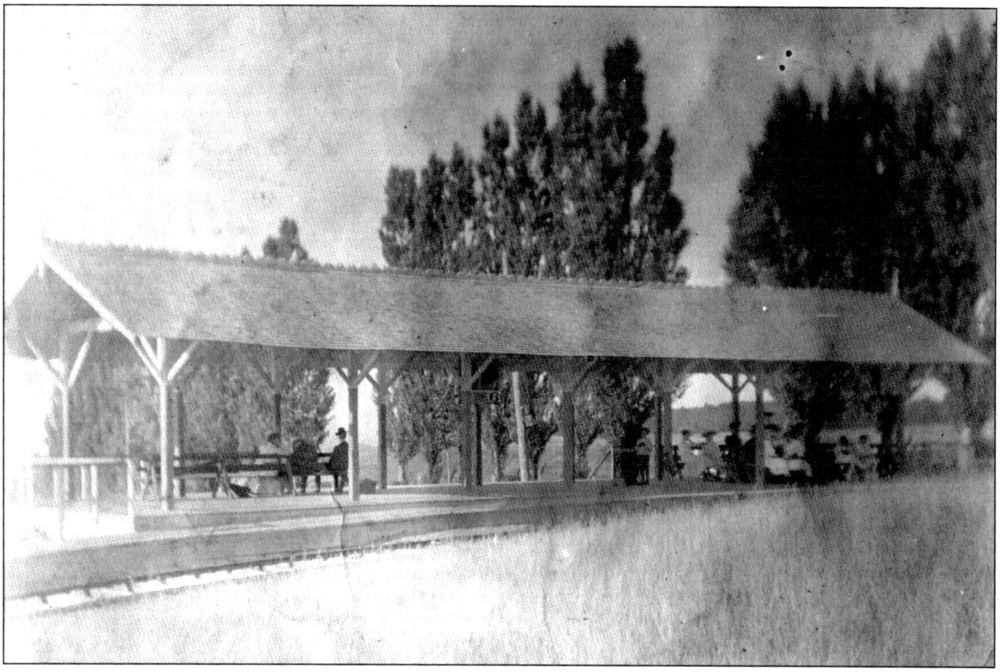

George A. Hart ran a "model farm," which was a kind of rural early theme park for the enjoyment of tourists. Around 1900, Hart sold his farm to a local streetcar line: the Manistee, Filer City, and Eastlake Railway Company. The railway turned the farm into a beach park and installed streetcar lines to it. Despite occasional mishaps, Orchard Beach became a favorite summer destination for locals.

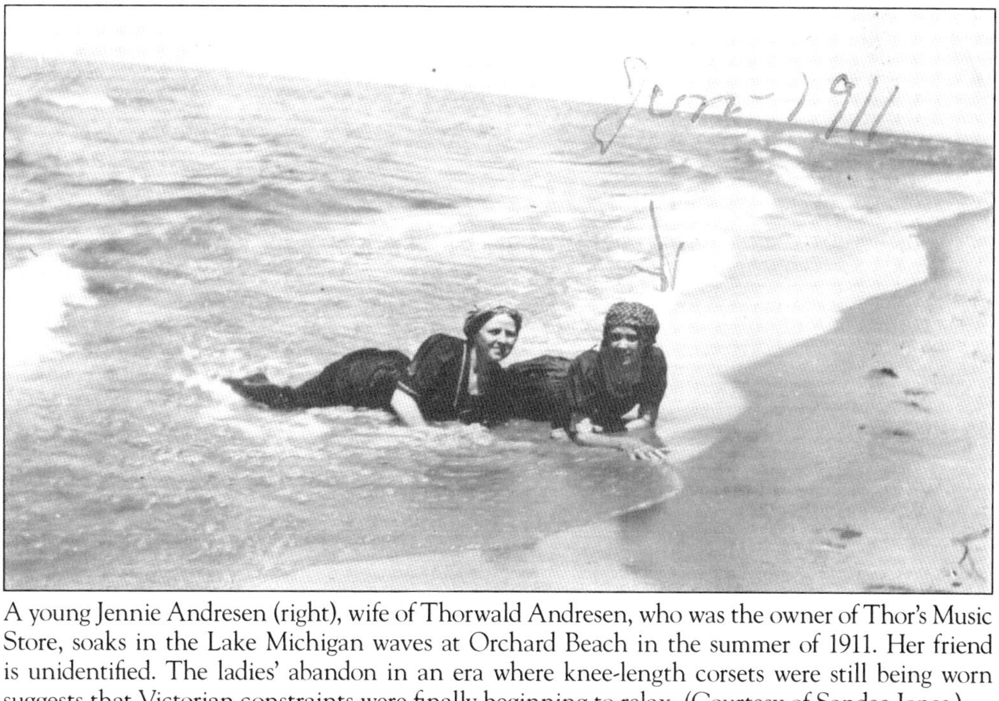

A young Jennie Andresen (right), wife of Thorwald Andresen, who was the owner of Thor's Music Store, soaks in the Lake Michigan waves at Orchard Beach in the summer of 1911. Her friend is unidentified. The ladies' abandon in an era where knee-length corsets were still being worn suggests that Victorian constraints were finally beginning to relax. (Courtesy of Sandee Jones.)

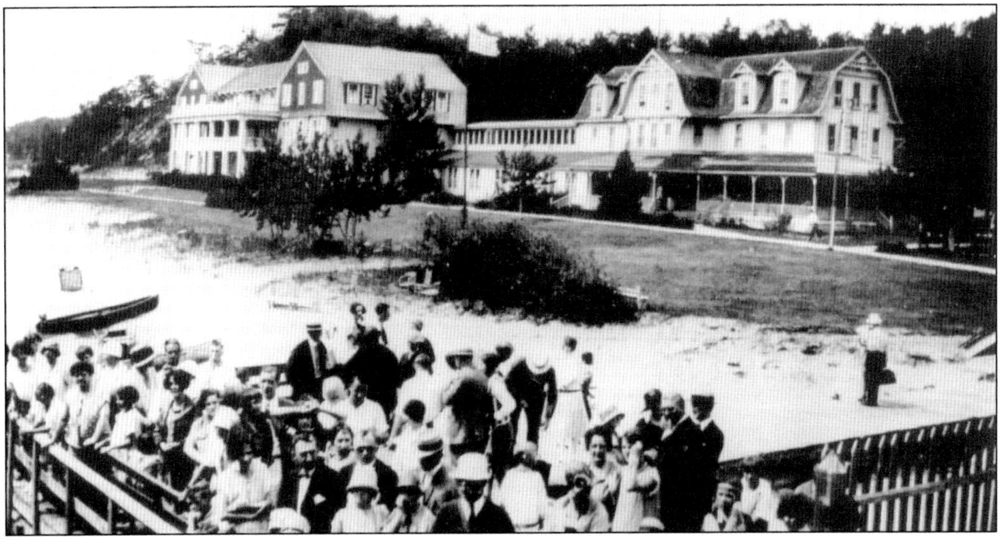

Tourism offered a way for Manistee County to sustain itself after the lumber industry was thoroughly exhausted. In 1897, the Michigan state legislature enabled the formation of corporations in order to build resorts. The Portage Point Inn, built just west of Onekama in 1902 by the Portage Point Assembly, opened for guests on June 20, 1903. Crowds would come across the lake by steamer and disembark on the Portage Lake shore, as shown here. (Courtesy of the Portage Point Inn.)

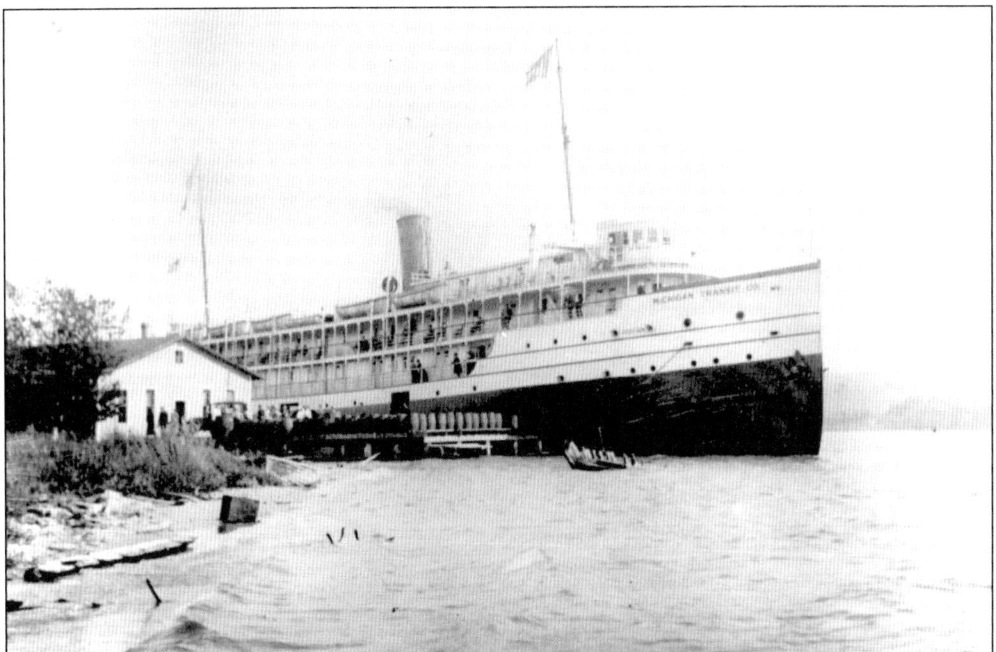

At first, Portage Point Inn guests could not travel directly by steamer, but had to transfer to small steamers at Manistee. By 1914, however, the inn was served both by the Northern Michigan Transportation Company and the Pere Marquette line. (Courtesy of the Portage Point Inn.)

Summer camps were another innovation in this era of leisure and tourism. Camp Tosebo on Portage Lake was founded by Noble Hill (right). An idealist who believed in progressive education, he ran the Todd Seminary for Boys in Woodstock, Illinois. Camp Tosebo was designed as a summer nature experience for students. Its name, "To-Se-Bo," is derived from the name of the school, and was intended to sound like a Native American word. The boys stayed in a row of tents (below) in the main area known as the Hill. (Courtesy of Dave Wallace.)

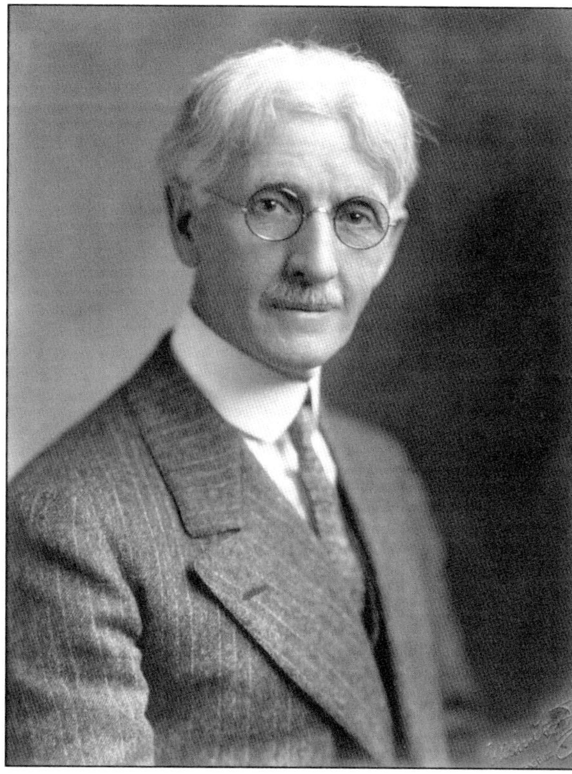

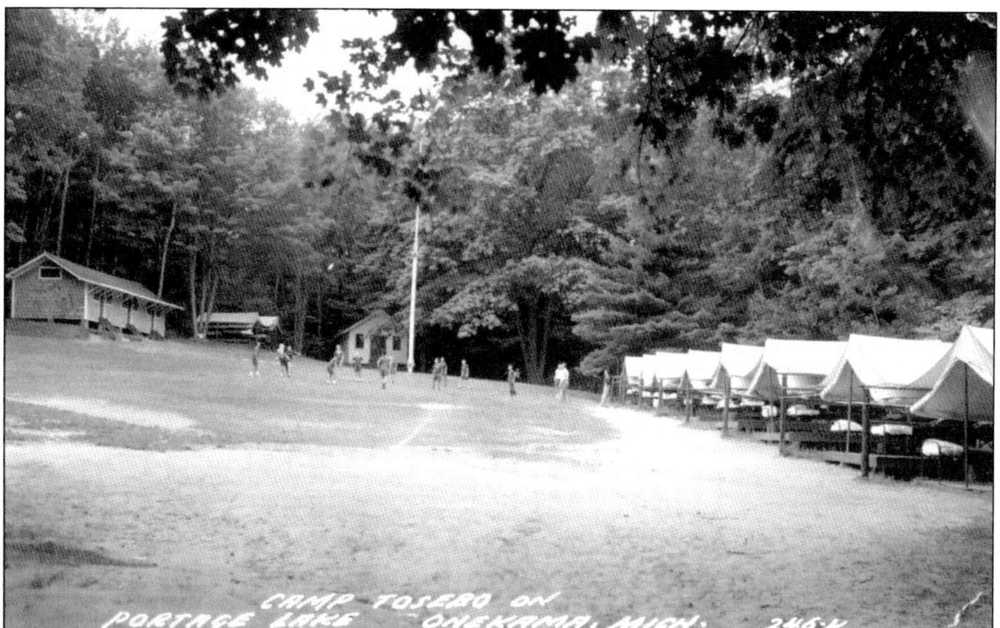

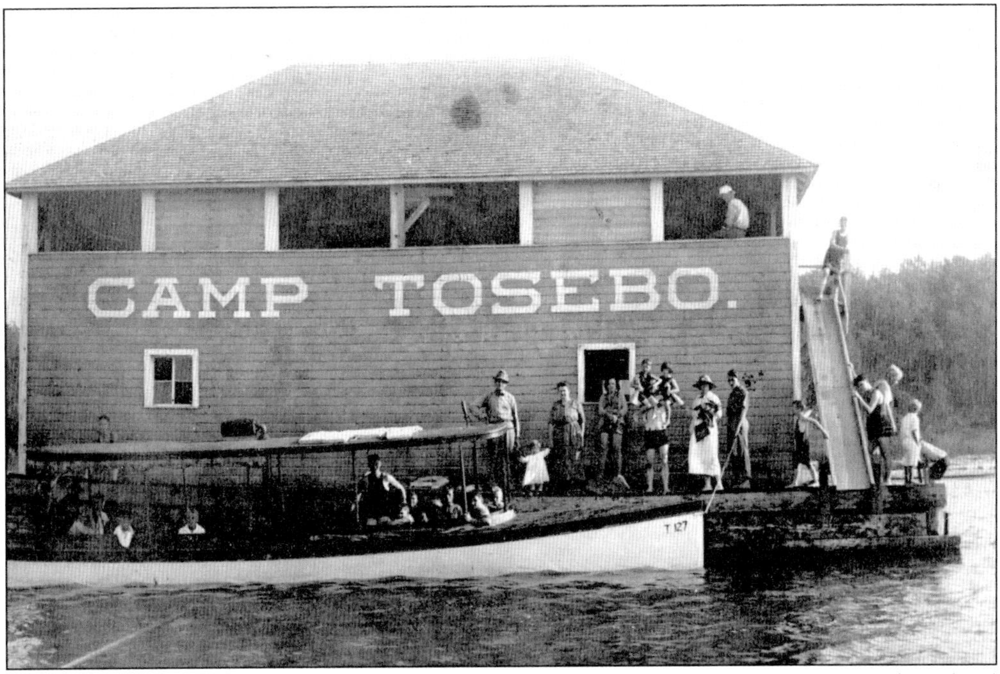

Students would come to the camp from Chicago by steamer and arrive directly on the school dock at this boathouse. The schooner, also named *Tosebo*, was usually stored inside the structure. It wrecked in 1917 from misuse, according to John Dexter, former Tosebo camper and counselor. (Courtesy of Dave Wallace.)

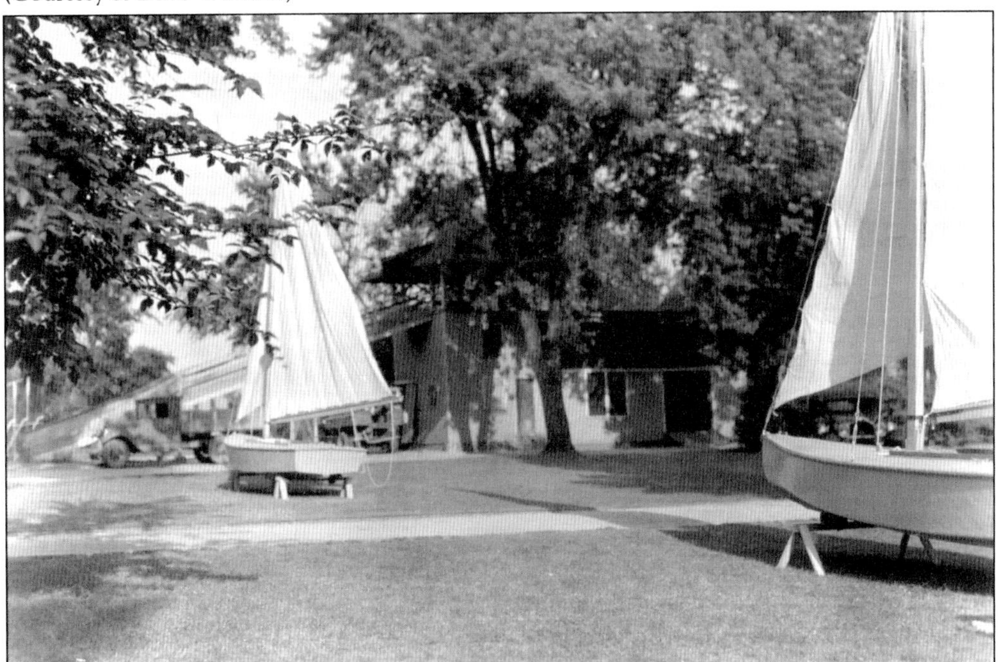

These small, single-masted boats, called catboats, were made by students in the Todd workshop, as part of the school curriculum. One boat was named *Nip*, and the other *Tuck*. (Courtesy of Dave Wallace.)

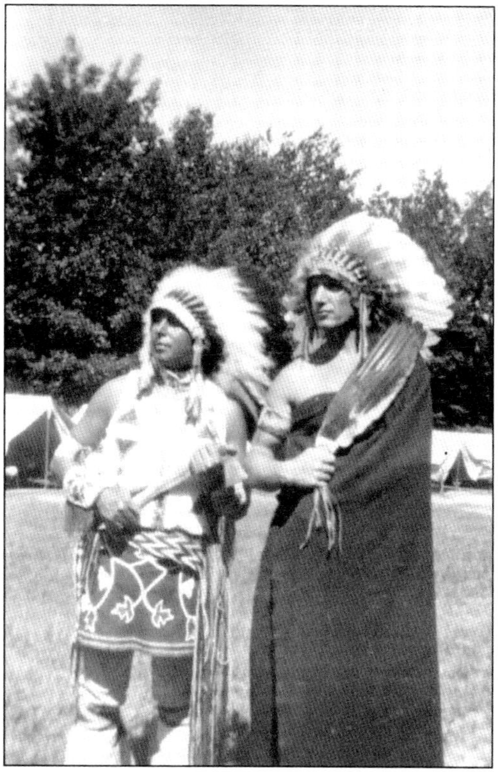

In keeping with the belief of the time that American Indians were closer to nature, Camp Tosebo had an American Indian theme and a Native American coach. In the photograph on the right, Chief Whirling Thunder (left), along with camp coach Tony "Coach" Roskie (right), gave campers instruction in ceremonies as well as athletics. Students were given Native American names, divided into tribes, and as shown below, dressed in tribal attire as part of camp activity. (Courtesy of Dave Wallace.)

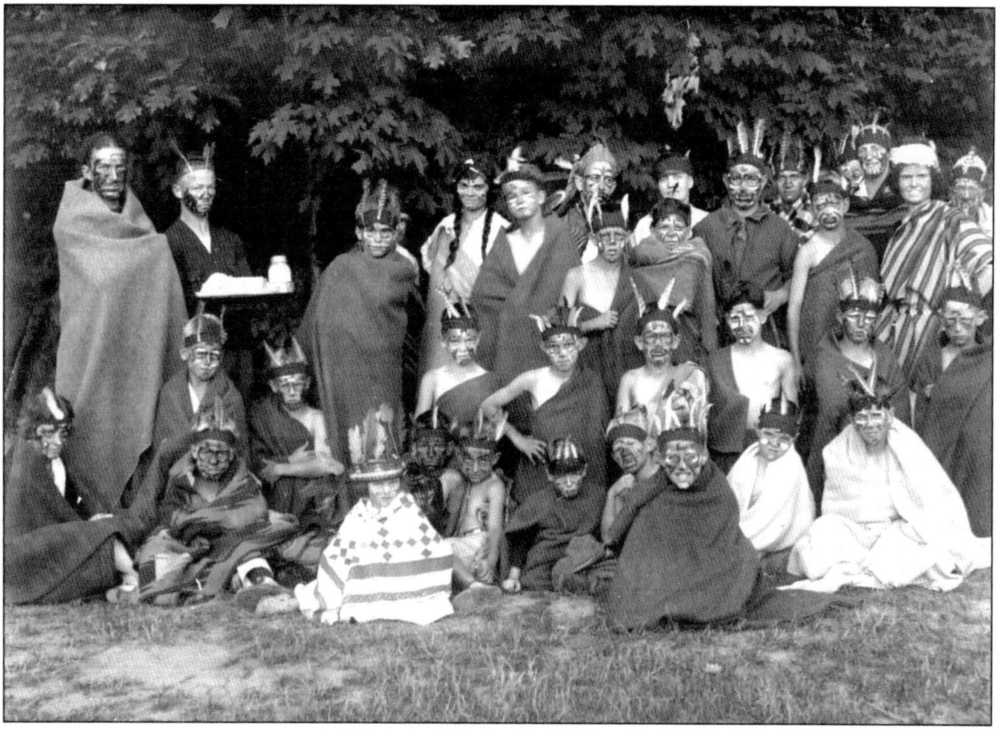

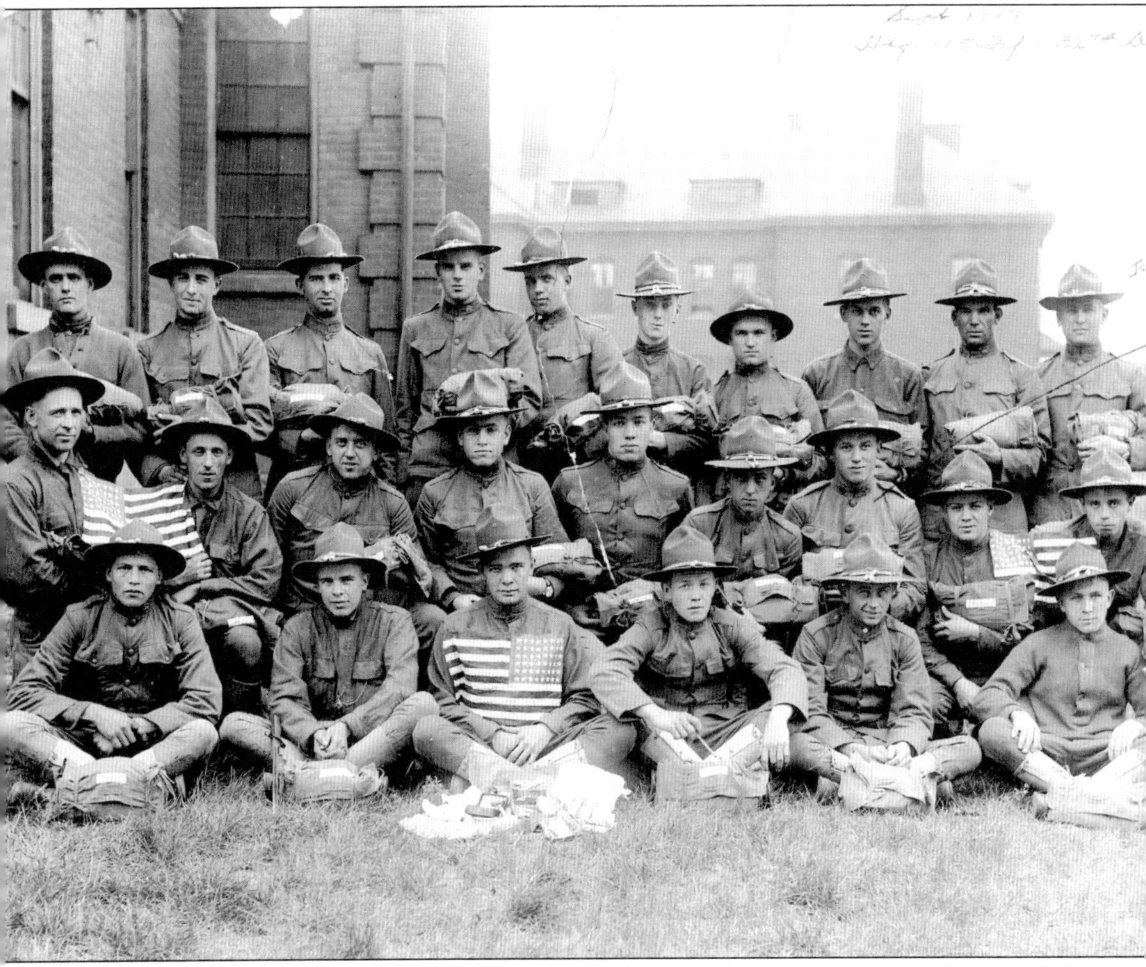

America's entry into World War I after a long-held policy of political neutrality dampened the Gilded Age festivities somewhat. Young men from all over Manistee County responded to the call to serve. The photograph above, dated September 1917, depicts Headquarter Company, 125th Infantry, 32nd Division, before departing for France with the American Expeditionary Force under "Black Jack" Pershing. Pictured here, from left to right, are the following: (first row) Francis Babnaw, Lester Walsh, Herman Fredricksen, Carl Hansen, Earl Kenny, and John King; (second row) Frank O'Conor, William Star, Steven Bucholtz, Walter Holingsworth, Clarence Wall, Joe Gorleski, John Eckoff, Max Schimke, and Glen Schindler; (third row) John Andersen, Axel Oleson, Alfa Hendricks, Weston Christenson, Arnold Peterson, Jack Conway, Ted King, Ed Belter, Martin Krukowski, and Ellis Merkley. (Courtesy of John C. Eckoff.)

Eight

The Long Road to Manistee

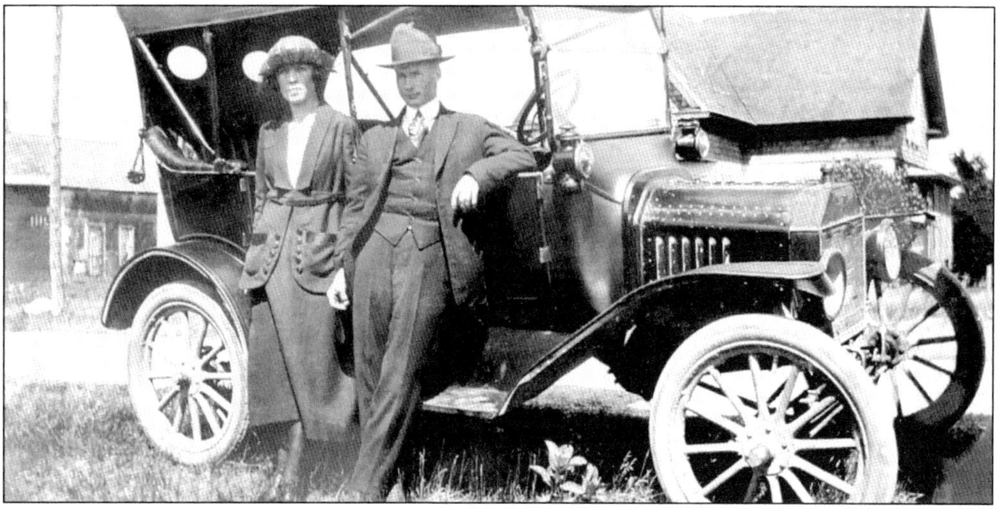

Soon after the first Model T rolled off the Ford Motor Company assembly line, Americans hit the roads: a wealthy few at first, for the grandiose display of it, but then more until the roads—at that time mostly dirt—were crowded with motorists, giddy with motion and wanting nothing so much as to drive anywhere as quickly as possible. The already frenetic tourist industry exploded, and the rapid construction of roads to take automobile tourists where they wanted to go, and of amusing things to see along the way, thoroughly transformed the American landscape in ways that even the railroad had not. Indeed, with motorists free to drive wherever they wished to go, rail travel was rapidly becoming obsolete. Automobiles were associated with modern stylishness. By the early 1920s, even most small towns had roads, significant automobile traffic, and gasoline pumps. Emil and Anna Christenson of Chief, beautifully dressed, stand beside their 1914 Model T. This photograph was taken across from the site of their future home in Chief, with Moen's building on the left. (Courtesy of Carol Schimke.)

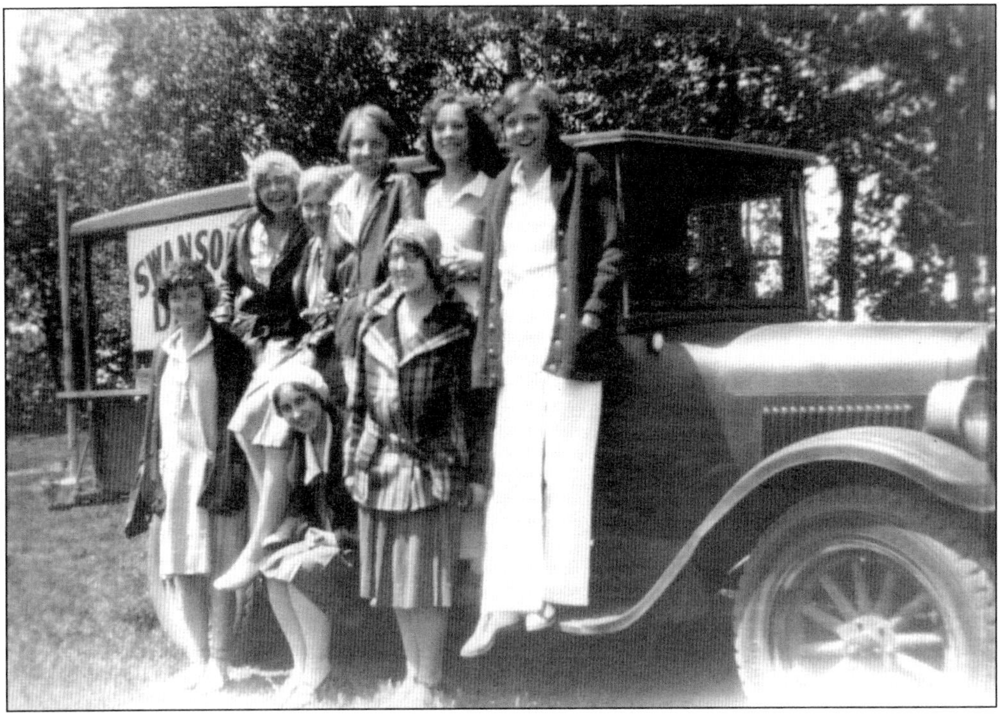

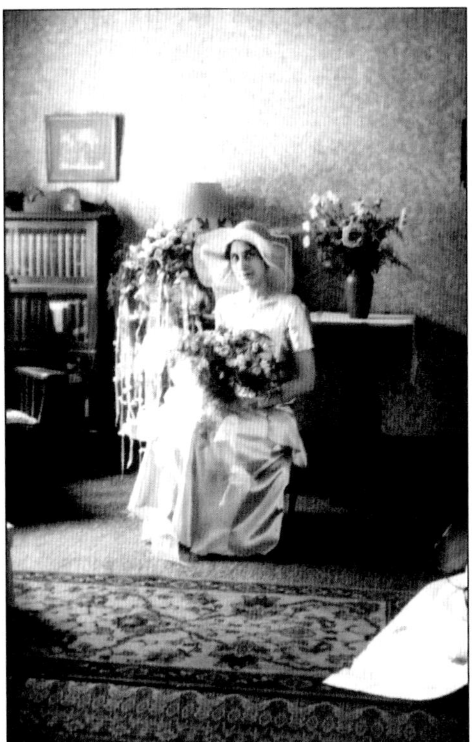

The ready availability of automobiles to most American families by the end of the 1920s revolutionized everyday life, particularly courtship. For the first time, young people could go out on dates outside of parental homes and beyond supervision. Cars came to be associated with fun and flirtatiousness—an association maintained well after the novelty had passed. Above is the Swanson Dairy Milkwagon, sometime in the 1930s. Owner Harold Swanson was a milkman in Manistee for many years, and his business was evidently a draw for young ladies. The girl sitting on the running board is Lucille Ferguson, his future wife. Lucille and Harold were married in Guardian Angels Parsonage by Father Steffes on June 19, 1934. Lucille's wedding portrait is to the left. (Courtesy of Mary Ann Kaczmerek.)

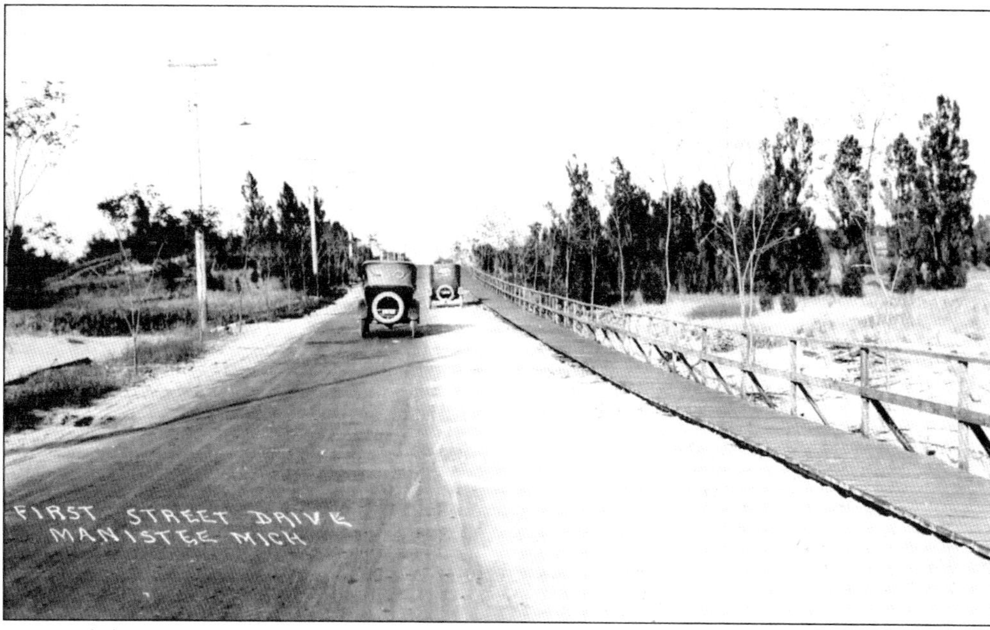

Many of the main roads in Manistee County were originally Native American trails. In the mid-1800s, most traffic was industrial, and the Manistee landscape, with mill smokestacks and salt wells jutting into the sky in every direction and tangles of logs and stumps, was a decidedly industrial one. By the 1920s, that landscape had softened, and the old roads became scenic drives, images of which were mass-produced on postcards as souvenirs for the tourists to virtually relive the experience at will. Shown here are two such postcards intended to entice automobile tourists. The one above depicts Manistee's First Street Drive, and the one below is Arcadia's Inspiration Point. (Above, courtesy of Jon Rose; below, courtesy of the Arcadia Historical Society.)

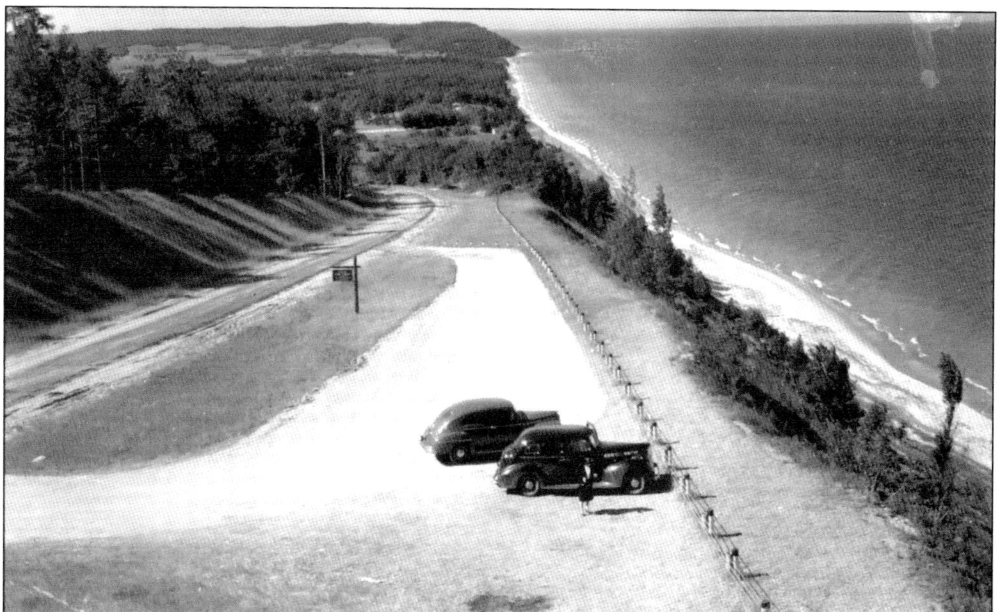

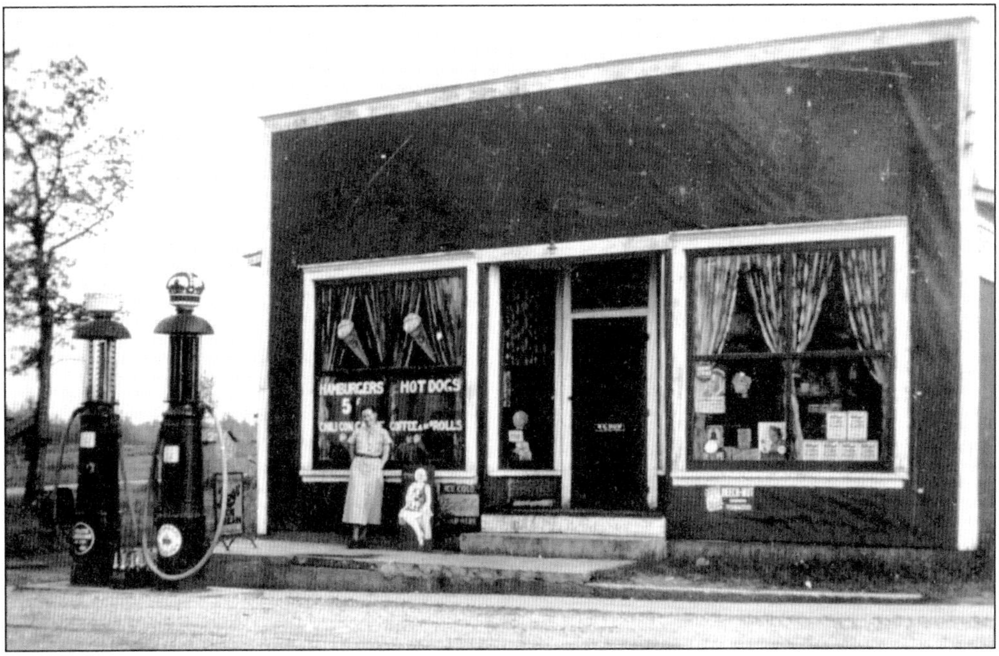

Even tiny Brethren had become a way stop. Maude Shields (née Tritten) stands here in front of the combination store, café, and gas station known locally as Mrs. Baker's Café and owned by the Baker and Shields families. The pumps dispensed standard Red Crown gas. (Courtesy of the Brethren Historical Museum.)

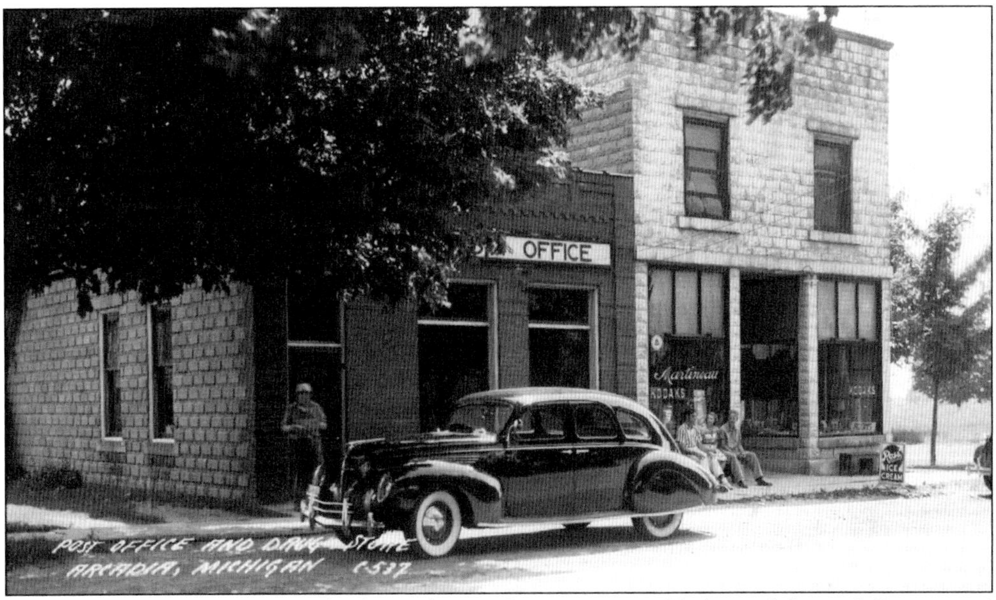

Martineau's Drug Store was rebuilt on the southeast corner of Lake and Second Streets and remodeled into a modern communication and transit center. Besides being a drugstore and soda fountain, it served as a post office, Greyhound Bus stop, Western Union office, and call center, as it had the only telephone in town. When information came in from the front during World War II, the Martineaus were the first to know and would spread the news to others. (Courtesy of the Arcadia Area Historical Society.)

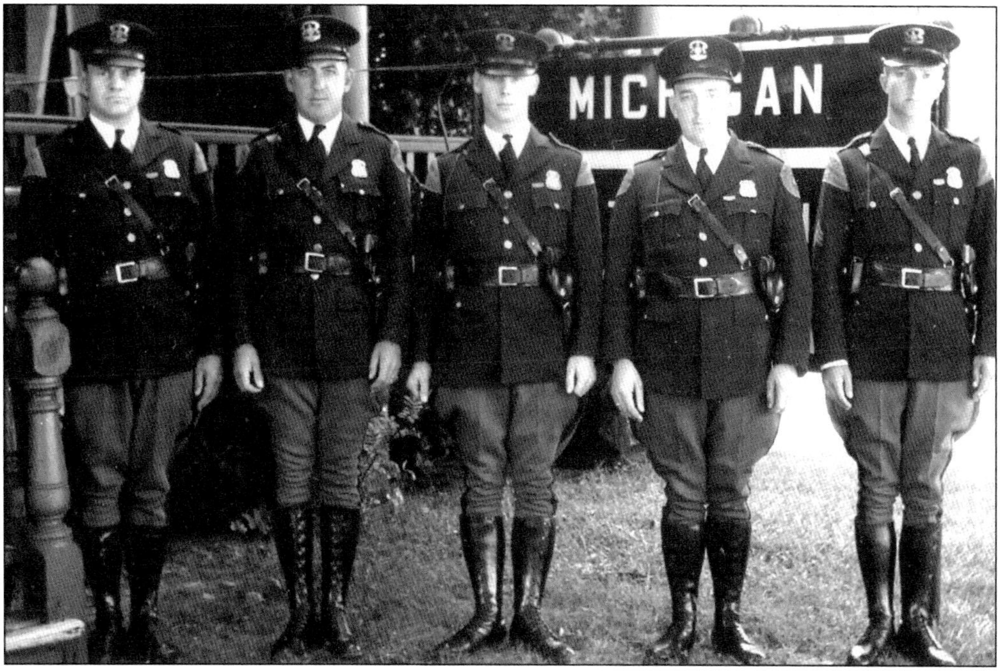

The growth of mass media in the early 20th century sometimes caused unusual local occurrences to become mass entertainment. Two events in Manistee drew national attention. One was the Kaleva Bank robbery on January 3, 1933. When four armed bandits held up the Kaleva Bank, police updated each other via two-way radio for the first time, making national news. Manistee County residents eagerly listened in over their own radios. Above, the Michigan State Police officers who apprehended the robbers pose for a photograph. Pictured from left to right are Ken Cook, Melvin McFall, Gerhard Carlson, Floyd Peters, and Sgt. Colburn Mungor. The other major event was the death of the world's tallest man, Robert Wadlow, at the 1940 National Forest Festival. Below, his giant coffin is transported on a flatbed truck out of Manistee for burial in Alton, Illinois. (Courtesy of Mary Ann Kaczmarek.)

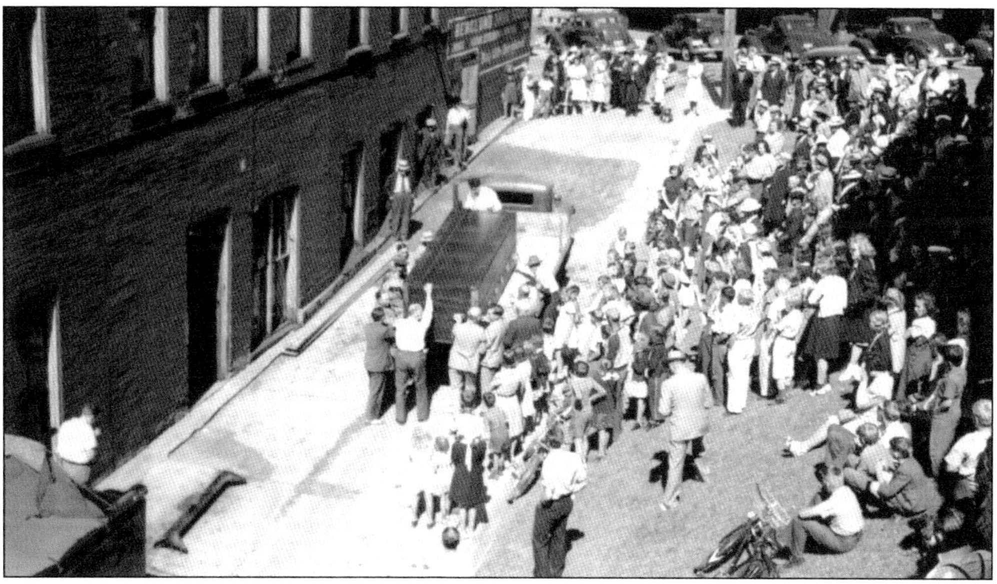

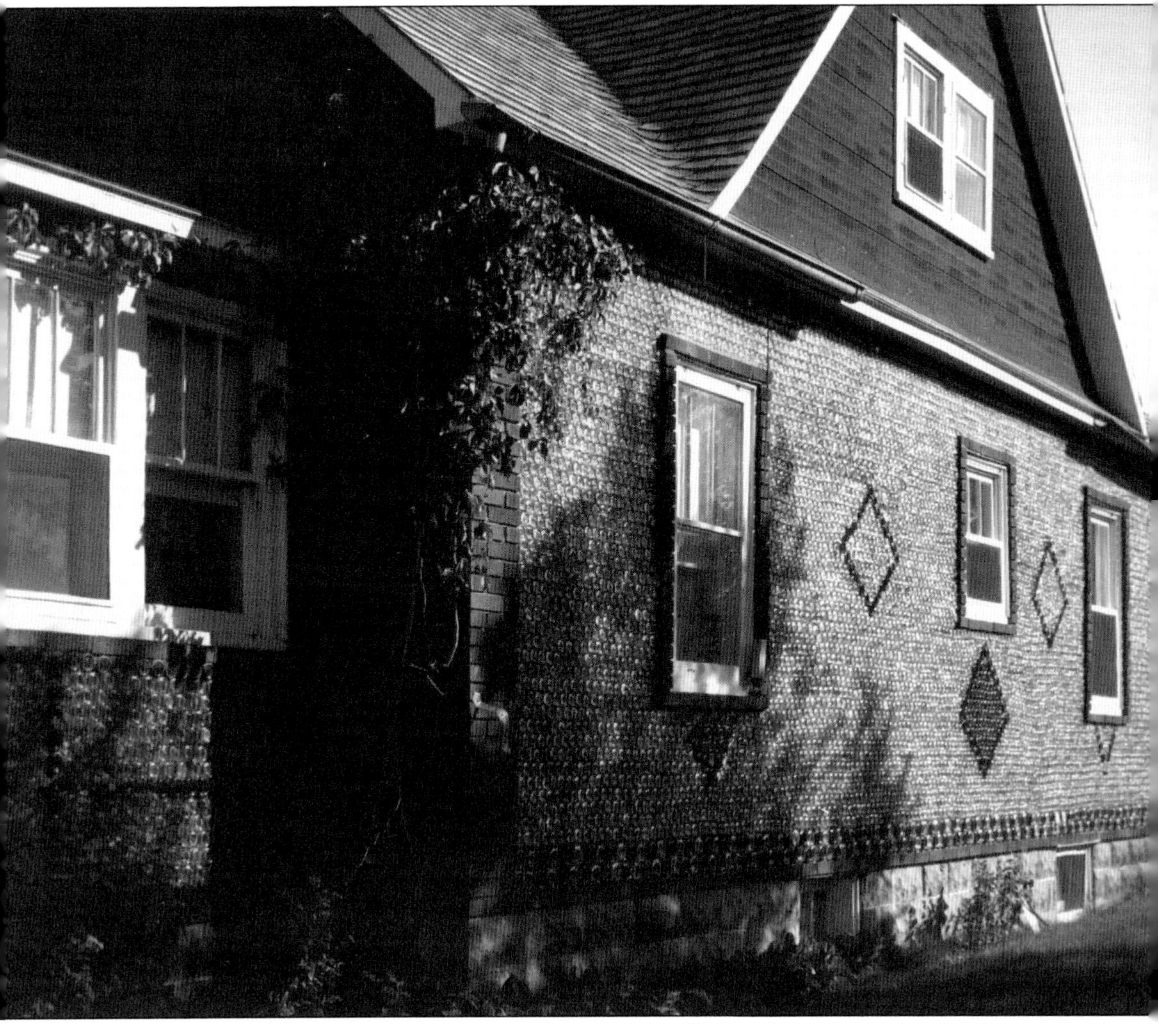

Unusual roadside attractions were common features of small-town America during the Depression: colossal statues, dairy stores shaped like milk bottles, giant balls of string, and the like. Sometimes they were designed solely to entice automobile tourists, but some of these fanciful constructions simply represented monuments to local industries, or else practical uses for abundant local materials. John Makinen, for instance, originally intended his famous Kaleva Bottle House as a family residence. He built it in 1941 on 14551 Wuosi Avenue, with over 60,000 bottles from his bottling works, but unfortunately died before the family moved in. Although the Kaleva bottle house is unique to the midwest, house construction with unusual materials has been something of an American phenomenon since the early twentieth century. The building currently houses the Kaleva Historic Bottle House Museum. (Courtesy of the Kaleva Historical Society.)

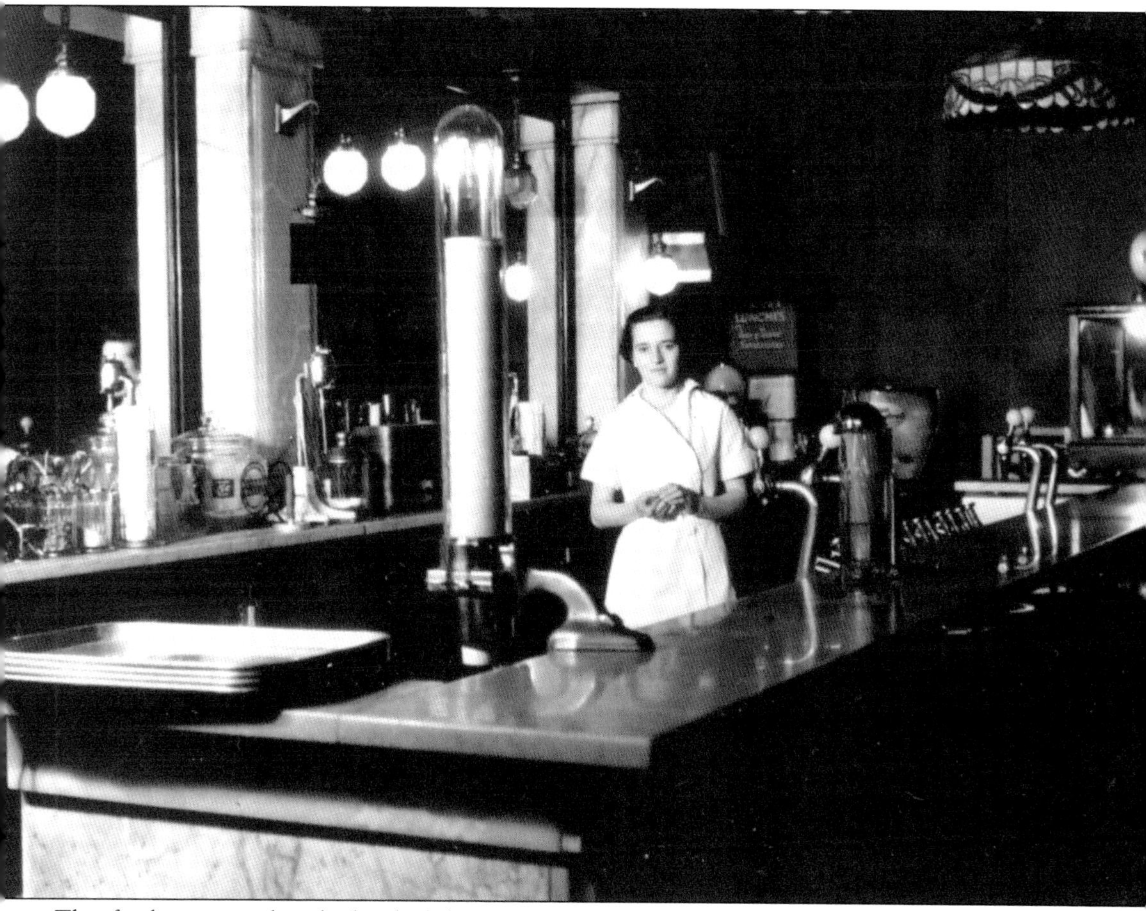

This final image evokes the kind of cheer, optimism, and welcoming hometown coziness to be found in 1930s Manistee—a perpetually resilient town that has persistently reinvented itself, yet retained its singular character. Clara Kubacki was a soda jerk at City Drugs for at least five years. Located on River and Maple Streets, the building, which is now the Ramsdell Inn, had a complex floor plan. Customers had to walk downstairs to enter the drugstore, but upstairs for the soda fountain, which was above Snyders Shoes. Directly above the drugstore was a bank. Clara did her job so well that when she left, it remained in the family. When she went to work with Campbell and Campbell attorneys, she passed the job on to her brother Eddie. (Courtesy of Janet Newman-Graham.)

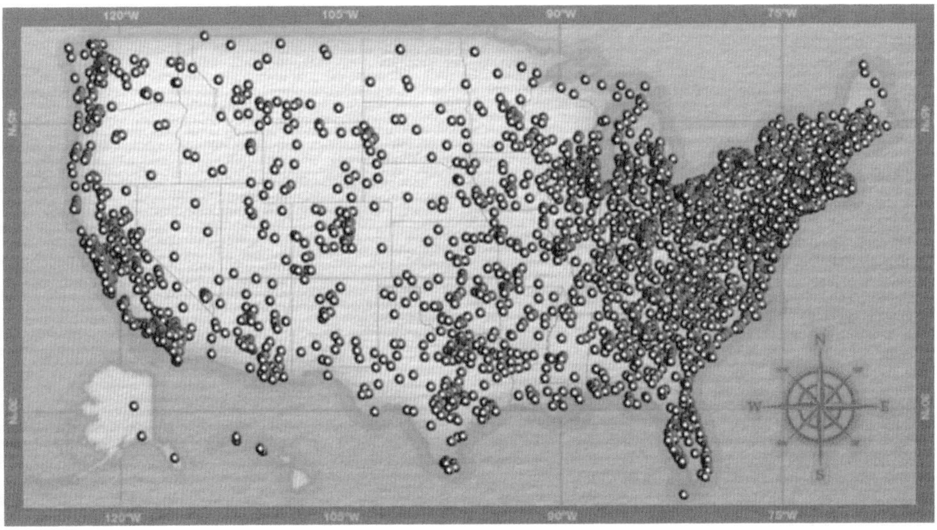